THE NATION ON THE
FLYING TRAPEZE

THE NATION ON THE FLYING TRAPEZE

*The United States as the
People of the East See Us*

by JAMES SAXON CHILDERS

DAVID McKAY COMPANY, INC.
New York

Copyright © 1960 by James Saxon Childers

All rights reserved, including the right to reproduce this book, or parts thereof, in any form, except for the inclusion of brief quotations in a review.

Library of Congress Catalogue Card Number: 60-9566

MANUFACTURED IN THE UNITED STATES OF AMERICA

VAN REES PRESS • NEW YORK

For
—AND WITH—
MAURINE

1

A red carpet led to the steps of the plane and "Song of the Islands," played on steel guitars, was being beamed from somewhere. A golden rope, made of silk and looped through polished chrome standards, formed the handrail. The setting was so flattering, with the music and the royal carpet, that we walked along as if we were entering an intimate night club instead of going toward an airplane to fly a part of the Pacific Ocean, two thousand miles of darkness and the sea below.

At the top of the stairs stood the stewardesses, pretty girls, tall and lithe, each wearing a *muumuu*, a kind of Hawaiian Mother Hubbard thing tied at the neck and hanging loose to the ankles. The girls moved along the aisles smiling and welcoming us in, showing us to our seats and putting our hats and overcoats away—"Glad to have you aboard, sir, happy to have you flying with us."

Besides the three stewardesses there was the chief steward, and he slammed the door and locked it, making sure that all the locks were fastened, and then the high flight of stairs was wheeled away, the music ended, and the lights went out. The show was over and we were on our own. The girls were quickly checking our seat belts and the pilot was jockeying his plane into position.

The time was 23:59, the scheduled time of take-off, one minute short of midnight, and the lull of the engines rose until they were loud and we were traveling down the runway, pulling at the air, pulling to climb, and the bump of the wheels became a skip, a touch, and then all was smooth, and the purr of the engines was like a contented thing.

San Francisco, a blazing circle about the dark bay, was now beneath us—now behind us—and we were out over the sea. The stewardess was busy demonstrating how to put on a life jacket, treating the demonstration as something just routine, but also making certain that we knew how to care for ourselves in case we had to come down at sea.

The demonstration was quickly over, and even the thought of danger was laid aside; then the stewardesses were coming along the aisle again, this time bringing glasses and trays—"Will you have champagne, sir?"

We were on Pan American Flight No. 803, my wife and I, for Honolulu, and I was a "Specialist" for the State Department. Some months before a letter had come from Washington: "I am writing to ask about your interest in participating as an American Specialist in the International Educational Exchange Program of the Department of State." It would mean three months in India, lecturing at universities, consulting with Indian writers, talking with Indian teachers, and meeting with Indian newspaper reporters and editors. The letter went on: "The American Specialist grant provides direct round-trip transportation, per diem, and a stipend of $700 monthly. We are not yet certain that we will have the funds for this program, but before proceeding further with it we wish to ascertain your interest."

I had never heard of the International Educational Exchange Program and had no idea what an American Specialist was. But I talked with friends in Washington and found out that our State Department has a regular program for these "Specialists."

They are ordinary American citizens, a lawyer, a businessman, an artist, who go out to supplement the information and cultural program that our government maintains in all countries. An embassy somewhere, believing that its program would be helped by the visit of a Specialist, asks the State Department in Washington to find a person who can do whatever it is that the embassy wants done. A lawyer, for example, may be wanted to come out and speak about the American courts and our legal system. An educator would meet with teachers and tell about our schools. An economist would lecture on American business.

The three-month trip that Washington was proposing to me would take time that I needed for my regular work and would mean a reduction in income that I couldn't afford; but the letter had said India, and I had been to India a number of times before, and I wanted my wife to see this most colorful country on earth. The lure of a far-off land played its part, and our plain selfish desire to go traveling influenced us; but the letter had said, too, that I could be of some use in India. Taking into account what has already happened to the United States abroad, and what is happening to us in other countries now, a man who can be of even a little use in foreign affairs these days had better go. So I wrote to Washington that I was interested in going to India as a part of their State Department program.

Sometime later a second letter came, telling me that funds were available and setting exact dates. Soon after this the State Department asked that I go to Korea and the Philippines also. I had been the editor of a big city newspaper, had written some books, had been a college teacher of literature, and had been in the intelligence service for five years during World War II, both in Europe and Asia. A man with this background, the letter said, could be useful in Korea and the Philippines as well as in India.

The State Department then requested that I come to Washington for a briefing. They asked that I come for only one day, and I was surprised. How could they tell me in one day all that I needed to know about India, about Korea and the Philippines? They would need to explain their program and tell me my duties, for I was to be an official representative of the State Department and of our government, and there was much instruction that I needed.

I did not believe that they could possibly give it all to me in one day; but I reported as I had been told. In the morning a man talked with me for perhaps twenty minutes about Korea. In the afternoon a lady talked with me for half an hour about India. The conversations were pleasant, and they told me of their travels, remembering little happenings that made entertaining stories. They recommended famous sights and suggested the better hotels. That was all—and the Philippines was not mentioned.

This was my briefing, my total preparation by the Department of State for a three-month stay in India and for visits to Korea and the Philippines. When I tried to find out more about my job and what I was supposed to do, no one seemed to be quite clear about it, and I came away from Washington with little understanding of my duties.

We rented our house, took care of the many things that one finds that he must do before leaving home for an extended time, and here we were on Flight No. 803 for Honolulu.

The champagne glasses had been collected, and again the girls were coming around with their almost-endless hospitality, and this time we were being offered fruit colorfully arranged in big baskets and little sandwiches and a taste of brandy to help us sleep. Blankets and pillows were being passed around and sleeping socks were given us, small knitted cotton socks to take the place of our shoes and make us more comfortable during the night. We slipped on the socks and now the lights beside the passengers were going out, and the lights in the cabin overhead were dim, hardly enough to make a shadow when anyone moved. We tilted back our seats and tucked our blankets around us, and outside as far as we could see was the deep, rolling tumble of the clouds.

There is always a curious feeling, almost like going home, when a person is going back to some part of the world where he has been before. Every place, every region, has its own character, and it is also different for each person who goes there. It is different, too, each time one goes back.

I had first traveled in the Orient a good many years ago, back in 1930, coming to the East as a young newspaper reporter and traveling through most of Japan and Korea and living for a while in China. I had gone on south from China through the smaller countries of Asia, coming at last to India—and I had stayed longer in India than I had planned. India is not an easy country to live in, nor is it an easy country to leave.

The next time I came to the East, a number of years later, I was in the Air Force, flying again to India and China, and always coming back to our island bases in the Pacific, working in intelligence for our attacks on Japan.

And now, in this sleeping plane, I was going to the East again. Lying there listening to the even hum of the engines, and occasionally feeling an easy tilt or sway, I was wondering what the changes would be, and wondering about the countries themselves, for so much has happened in China, in Japan, in India. But even more, I was concerned about the United States and how we are being affected by what is going on in Asia. On this trip I would be traveling in Asia once more and seeing the sights of the Orient again, going to the famous places; but more than the travel, and along with all the touring and sight-seeing, I intended to find out the position of the United States in the Orient today, what the people of the East think of us, and what is the outlook for the United States as a nation in our struggle here with Russia and China.

Our knowledge of the Orient is still vague and far off, and some of the changes in that part of the world we have not yet comprehended; certainly we have not yet grasped their significance to us. We seem to have almost no concern for the magnitude of China's accomplishment, as if it cannot possibly affect us that China in so short a time has disciplined her man power and turned her farming peasants, who for so long had worked the ground with sticks and winnowed the wheat by the wind, into makers of steel and builders of airplanes.

Less than a quarter of a century ago China was a tangled mass of starving millions, without national purpose or organization, lacking any sign of a nation. I had been in China, only three decades ago, when the land was chaos and the people were in multiple confusion. There was only the meaningless name of a government, and the war lords fought in their various regions for personal power and the license to pillage and murder as they pleased. No man who knew China then could have believed that today there would be a nation, however brutal its bondage, that could challenge the world, driving the United States back in Korea, driving France out of Asia, moving now in powerful alliance with Russia against India and on to the conquest of all Asia. China is the national miracle of our time.

And India, the new nation, the legacy of Gandhi. What is happening in India? Less powerful than China, India is a slower force; but whether she goes to communism or to the West will determine the fate of Asia, influence the power struggle in the world, and change policies of the United States, deciding our position in the Orient.

On through the night that seemed so long we flew, and the mutter and murmur of sleeping people troubled the quiet as we dreamed and half-waked, turning now and then, fumbling with the pillow, and sleeping again.

It was sometime before daybreak, but the moon gone and the dark thinning behind us, when one of the girls came around and touched us, saying that we had come into rough air and the captain had ordered that we fasten our seat belts. Still lying tilted back, still drowsy, we lay there watching the first shimmer of the light through the lessening dark, and then the white circle of the sun was showing itself. Looking down, far below, we could see the water as black and gleaming as onyx, the white crests breaking and riding fast. The stewardesses, their faces freshly made up, but sleepy now and not quite able to hide their tiredness, were coming around with coffee and promising breakfast when we wanted it.

Flying in low, with Diamond Head off to one side, and over there Pearl Harbor and its sunken ships, we came in fast to our field. The ground was wet, but the sun was out and our friends were there to meet us. They adorned us with leis and gave each of us the traditional kiss of welcome to the island.

Driving in from the air terminal to the city, I saw new buildings since the war. There were more automobiles and more trucks, more stores and more people, but there seemed no especial changes in Honolulu. Waikiki was the same, the restless surf rolling in toward us, high, blue, and white-crested, bending as it broke and hissing as it slid back into the sea. And the Pali, the tower of the island, the lookout, it was the same—the wind still pushing us back, forcing us to bend into it as we stood behind the wall high above the valley. The angle of the land, far below, still widened out and on toward the sea, green and rippling in the wind, cut here and there by the roads.

Hawaii is such a pleasant place, and there are so many friends there, and we wanted to stay; but Hawaii was not a part of my job and that night, after only a glimpse of the island and a breath of its flowers, we knew that we must go on to Tokyo.

Our departure from Honolulu was minus all the glamour and hoopla that had accompanied our leaving San Francisco. No red carpet, no music—this time only the lighted sign beside the plane—Flight No. 1, Tokyo—as if the job of flying from one place to another had become a business instead of a jubilee. The stewardesses, these wearing the customary flight uniforms of the air line, and one of them a Japanese-Hawaiian for the Japanese-speaking passengers, were just as pleasant and just as pretty as our previous ones. They went through the usual flight routine, welcoming us aboard in English and Japanese, introducing the crew, and demonstrating how to put on the life jacket, all that is customary at the beginning of every over-water flight. Then they came with newspapers and magazines, with trays of fruit and sandwiches, and whatever we might like to drink, from champagne, to whisky, to beer. They made everything very cozy and comfortable.

This flight is one of the memorable flights of the world, some four thousand miles. One leaves Honolulu at six-thirty at night, and nine hours later, at three o'clock in the morning, the plane lands at Wake Island. There is a small building not far from the landing field, and one can ride to it in a truck or walk along the coral road. We walked, enjoying the soft feel of the air, and even in the black dark the road was white and clear. There were sandwiches and doughnuts, fruits and cake, and the most wonderful coffee.

We talked with the new crew that were coming aboard, and it seemed strange to be changing crews here in the middle of the Pacific, but the girls said that they always shifted on each flight; for Wake Island is about halfway between Honolulu and Tokyo and the crew that had brought us this far, and that were leaving us, would stay on the island until the plane came back, and then they would return to Honolulu. The girls said that they usually enjoyed their stay on Wake Island. They swam and darkened their sun tan. They caught up on their letter writing and went hunting for shells along the beach.

The second leg of the flight, the nine hours from Wake Island to Tokyo, seemed long because we kept expecting daylight to catch up with us, and it kept on being night as we flew away from the sun. Then, too, there was a typhoon in our path, and our pilot told us that he would have to fly over it and around it, and this made the flight even longer.

Daybreak finally came, though, slow and grudging, the sky heavy and gray and no sign of the sun. More than once we flew through rain squalls, looking down and seeing the rain denting the sea.

Our flight over the land of Japan seemed short, for we were either shut in by the rain or the clouds were patched beneath us and only now and then could we see the mountains or glimpse a a farm. These clouds were low, and we had to come in low for our landing at Tokyo.

It was cold that morning, bleak and cold, the wind sharp, and we hurried from the plane into the air terminal. As we waited for our luggage, a radio was playing. When the music ended, the announcer said that the program had been presented by the Armed Forces of the United States, and he mentioned the date. By sheer coincidence we had arrived in Japan on December 7.

Japan, like Hawaii, was not a part of my job, and I went on that night to Korea, leaving my wife in Tokyo. The plane was to arrive in Seoul at midnight, and the night was black, not a moon, not a star to keep a man company as he walked toward the small terminal, vague and dim with its cobwebbed windows.

I had been told in Washington that I would be met, but there was no one here, and soon the baggage was delivered, and the people were leaving, and the men in the terminal were turning out the lights. I could speak no Korean or find anyone who could speak English, and there were no taxis. Standing there, cold, and wondering what to do, I heard someone call my name.

He introduced himself, and was sorry that he had been delayed and was late. "I am the CAO from USIS," he said. (Even that far from Washington, they talk in the jargon of initials—he was the Cultural Affairs Officer of the United States Information Service.)

We drove into Seoul, and along the way he told me about my schedule. At the entrance of the hotel he gave me a copy. I was to lecture at universities and have luncheons and teas with the professors. I was to visit the oldest university in Korea, meet with the president and the faculty, and discuss with them the organization of an American university and American ways of teaching. I was to speak at two of Seoul's Rotary Clubs, at a luncheon of writers, and at a meeting of International PEN Club. There was a cocktail meeting with newspapermen, a speech to editors and reporters, and visits to the newspapers of the city. There were to be meetings with American officials and with men in the Korean government.

This was my schedule for the week that I was to be in Korea, and I found out, as I traveled on in other countries, that it was about an average one. These people of the United States Information Service, who usually have a Specialist in their country for only a short time, set up a hard schedule for him and they keep him at it. I have had as many as six speaking engagements in one day, and while this is the extreme, three and four were not uncommon. Along with the speaking there is a luncheon, a tea, a cocktail party, or a dinner almost every day, and sometimes more than one of these. It sounds very tiring, and it is, but it is all so unusual that a man keeps going with steady interest.

My first lecture was at a university the next morning. The weather still was cold and the campus was bleak and the stone buildings few and scattered, the wind whipping toward them across the frozen ground. Inside these buildings there was no central heat, and the halls and corridors seemed as cold as the wind outside. Only in a room where a lecture was to be given was there a fire in a low, round-bellied stove—and briquettes, pressed blocks of coal dust, were the fuel. There is no wood for fuel in Korea, for so many of the trees were burned by the fire bombs and rockets during the fighting that many of the hills now are bare and black, and trees everywhere are so few that there is a national law against a man's cutting one. Even this coal dust is guarded, meagerly fed into the stove, and I followed the example of the professor who introduced me and kept on my overcoat while I lectured. The students who had overcoats wore them and turned up their collars, sitting low in their seats, and now and then they rubbed their hands. Those without topcoats huddled into themselves as best they could.

The subject of the lecture was "American Novelists," and it had been chosen by the professors in the Department of Literature. The students themselves seemed to know little or almost nothing about American novelists, and, what's more, they didn't seem to care about these writers whose names they hardly knew and the books that they had no intention of reading. They just sat silent and polite in their customary classroom politeness while

I tried every plan, every trick that I had ever used with American students, and nothing seemed to work.

Part of the reason, I believed, was the barrier of language, for I was talking through an interpreter, and this is never fully successful; but whatever the reason, there was no glimmer of interest from the Korean students, and I could feel their detachment as I talked. I suspected that the professors had chosen the subject more for themselves than for their students—and this was the first lesson that I learned on this trip. For an American to lecture on some subject just because it is American, or because it is his specialty, or is the hobby of some professor or program chairman, is a foolish and harmful waste when the people he is talking to have no background for what he is talking about. I learned always to find out about my audience, the background and the interest of my audience, before I agreed on any lecture subject again.

After this first lecture, even though it had fallen flat, the students came around fast, hurrying up to gang around my desk, and asking, and kept on asking, about the United States. It was easy to see that the United States was something strange to them, and they wanted to know everything. Please, where did I live? Please, where *is* Georgia? Please, how long does it take to make a Ford automobile? Please, does *every* college student in America have an automobile?

Some of them, a good number of them, wanted to know how to get to the United States. Was there any way to get a scholarship to an American university? If they managed somehow to get to the United States, could they stay?

When the time came for me to leave the classroom, the president of the university rose and all the students sat down quickly, everyone getting quiet. The president made a friendly and a generous speech, and then he accepted a potted plant that one of the deans handed him, and presented it to me. I thanked him as best I could and went out carrying the plant, its pot wrapped in a spout of shining green paper, and wondering just what I was going to do with it. But I took it to my hotel and kept it, along with the others that were presented to me at each of the Korean universities where I lectured. Every morning I watered them, in a row by the window, and they made my room a pleasant place.

At all the lectures at this university an elderly professor was the interpreter, standing on the rostrum below me and translating each sentence, or group of sentences, into Korean. Afterward, though, after the students had come around my desk, he would stand back and interpret nothing, giving us no help, not even when we asked him for a word. He insisted on the students working out their English for themselves, and he forced us to figure out our talking as best we could. Occasionally he would come to the teahouse with us, where we sat at the low tables and drank the pale, sweetened tea while we talked in our groping way, sometimes having to say it with gestures. And here, too, at the teahouse, the students asked more questions about the United States. There seemed to be no end to their interest in the United States.

The lectures at the universities and the meetings with writing groups and newspapermen were scheduled for every day in the week except Sunday. Sunday I had off, and I went to Panmunjom, where the peace negotiations were carried on, and where the line now is drawn that divides North and South Korea.

It was a bright and clear day that Sunday when we drove to Panmunjom, and I had no idea that it is so strict a place. Official papers are required to go there, and our car was stopped along the road more than once and our papers inspected. As one gets nearer to the line he is taken over by the military police of the United Nations and is driven by them, in their car, with guards mounted, to the line itself.

Along the way, as we passed the roadblocks established at each road crossing, we saw the North Korean guards and later saw other of these Communist guards in Panmunjom itself, and I was astonished by their appearance. Many of them were slovenly in their dress, and most of them wore overcoats too big for them, dirty and drooping coats that swallowed them, and caps that slid down and rode their ears, widening their ears. A uniform doesn't make a fighter, and these men had proven themselves in battle; but I had seen Chinese soldiers, back in the days of the war lords, and the Chinese weren't necessarily clean or tidy, but they were unmistakably soldiers, and I was surprised at the appearance and the manner of these North Korean guards.

At Panmunjom there is a narrow strip of land that is the neutral zone, and here an American visitor is under the constant escort of the United Nations military police. But here in this zone the North Koreans also have equal rights, and their guards stay near you. They slouch along, taking their time, eying you and looking you over, sizing you up, keeping a technical distance but always staying close, watching and seeing everything you do, seeing especially that you don't get too near to their line or dare to step over onto their side.

Standing in this neutral zone, all the ground carefully cleared except for the buildings, all possible cover cut back, one can look down into the valley, and there, not far, is the White Pagoda and there is Liberty Bridge over which the Korean prisoners marched who chose to come with the United Nations—a man could walk that distance, one way or the other, in only a few minutes, but surely he would have spent his lifetime in getting ready for the moment in which he made his decision. And there, too, down at the bottom of the valley, over a gully and into North Korea, is the Bridge of No Return, across which the American turncoats walked into the Communist camp— although they *are* returning, dribbling back, wretched and twisted, still talking big, still running.

Here on this level ground, in the center of this neutral zone, is the meeting hall, a low, commonplace building little more than a quonset hut, built precisely over the line. In the center of the hall is a table, and it exactly straddles the line, so much on one side, exactly an equal amount on the other side, with chairs on one side and chairs on the other. It is on this table that two flags stand, each about the size of a man's palm, the kind of miniature flags that any person might put on his desk for decoration.

It had been agreed at one of the early meetings that each side might have a flag on its side of the table, and on the day they were put there the Reds saw that the other flag was taller than theirs, a few inches taller by happen so, and they walked out, refusing to sit at a table with a flag that was taller than theirs. This, too, was something to talk and talk and talk about, haggling, the world standing by, until it was agreed that each flag would be exactly the same height, and the height was agreed on precisely.

But when the flags were brought in, the Reds had cheated and their flag was a fraction higher than had been agreed, and it was a petty thing, beneath the consideration of man. No one said anything about it, no one on the United Nations side pointed out that the Red flag was higher, provided one looked at it closely; a petty thing and contemptible within itself, but the Reds had carried their point again, and we had permitted them to carry their point again, and we had accepted their point again. Satisfied for that instant, and encouraged, having found us weak, they started talking all over again, the spate of words, the fog of ideas, preparing the way for their next point and maneuvering toward it.

The line there at Panmunjom is the end and there is no crossing, for besides the guards the land is mined and nothing goes over except maybe one of the small Korean deer, or maybe a pig, moving along and feeding, crosses over unknowingly; or else they step on a mine and are blown up. It happens occasionally, the sound of the blast, and then, if it is near, the soldiers on duty see the dead animal, or if it is farther off, they see it with their glasses. The United Nations troops always are there at the line, as close to the line as they can get, always watching, their glasses forever shifting, endlessly scanning the opposite hills, watching to the north to see that the Communists don't come down again unnoticed. At night the soldiers still patrol the line, and there are instruments that record any moving thing.

The road out of Panmunjom, so far as any American civilian or United Nations soldier is concerned, can only go back to Seoul. It is the old traveled road of the armies, the way of advance and retreat, the military seesaw. Along beside the road most of the stone walls are blown and jagged, and the mud walls are blasted and washed away. Many of the houses are unroofed, but memory and habit have drawn the people back and the villages are filled up again. New houses have been built with surprising material, roofed with flattened United States Army gasoline tins, beamed and buttressed with pieces of blasted United States Army tanks, and supplied with coffee cups, air-blown mattresses, and all kinds of United States Army equipment that was abandoned too fast, in pressed retreats, for our troops to destroy.

The people of the villages have opened their shops again and most of the farmers have come back. The winter stubble, thick and strong, testifies that the farmers worked these fields last summer and made good crops. In a battered and scarred countryside, and in a hampered way, these people of South Korea have taken up their lives again.

Now and then, close to the road or far off, one sees a smokestack—a factory, a mill—and there is a suggestion of industry in this half-country. There is also a scattering of factories inside Seoul itself, but Seoul today is a bewildered place, burned and blasted, tearing down, rebuilding, digging, covering up, squirming with a million people, an anthill of humanity.

The military barricade at Panmunjom is hardly mentioned back in Seoul, and the division of the land is accepted in bitterness but in common sense, the people adapting themseslves to their new half-nation. I noticed the acceptance especially with the students, for one might have expected otherwise with students, because young men so often in their talk build back so quickly and so easily the castles that older men have torn down or allowed to fall; but even the young men in Seoul seldom mention the division, or speak of any reuniting of their country. The Communists have taken half of the nation, and they will keep it.

The old teacher, though, the man who had translated my lectures, spoke of the division one night as we walked home after an evening at the teahouse. We were walking along a small, quiet street, narrow and curving, the night warmer and the coating of black mud soft under our feet, and for a while we walked without talking. Then—we were getting nearer to my hotel—he spoke of Korea and the United States, and he said something about my lectures and my going the next day, leaving Korea, and then he said, "Your United States is a great nation, and your national strength and your power are plain, and without you we would have been destroyed. Without you, we would still be destroyed. Your ships would hardly be out to sea, and your airplanes not below the horizon, before the Red planes would be landing and they would take us over as they have taken the North. This we know."

He stopped and stood for a moment without speaking, and I was proud of what he had said. His speech was a little high-flown perhaps, as a man might talk who has learned his English from books and literature, instead of from listening to other men, but he was telling me his thanks and it was good to hear it.

His hair was white and his mustache was white, and I could see his face in the light from a lamp in a small shop. He had been kind to me and I was indebted to him. He moved aside to let another man pass, and he glanced at me. "Please, what I am about to say... Our hearts are heavy here in the Orient as we see Russia take your country's place as the dominant nation of the world. Russia is winning the minds and the loyalties of men away from the United States. It's a pity, for your product is a good one and you hide it with your prejudices and your seemingly complete concern with material things. Russia's product is an evil one and she gilds it with her dedication to it, and her belief in it, and her offer of it as a faith, a religion, that men will die for. This your country does not seem to understand." He moved nearer to the shopwindow, and again he glanced at me. "Already the people of the Orient are turning to Russia, and looking to Russia, where they used to look to the United States. And China is so strong. Does not your country see this?"

We stood there talking for a long time, and then we moved on to the entrance of the hotel and we stood there, too. There was no particular surprise in what the old man had said because most of us probably know, or at least suspect, that the position of the United States has deteriorated in the Orient, and that our present place in the East is an unfortunate one.

My understanding of this was easier because of my having been in Korea thirty years before, when Korea was owned and ruled by Japan. Those were the years when Japan was the aggressor and was making her move in Asia. Her plan was perfectly clear, her purpose entirely plain, and for years we were warned. Then, when it happened, we cried "day of infamy."

Now it is Russia who makes her move in Asia. Her plan, too, is clear, her purpose plain, and her partner, China, grows stronger day by day.

It is the same story again. Once more we are confronted by a shrewd and aggressive enemy, this time by a union of Russia and China, infinitely stronger than was Japan, infinitely more capable and more devious than was Japan; but with exactly the same intention, the taking of Asia, and exactly the same purpose and ultimate goal, the destruction of the United States.

2

The plane was late in leaving Korea and the winter dark came early; we crossed the Sea of Japan and landed at Tokyo well after nightfall. My wife was at the airport to meet me. As we drove back to our hotel I told her about my trip, about the students and the universities, the writers I had met, and the newspapers I had visited. I told of my day at Panmunjom. But I did not mention the old man and what he had said about the United States and Russia. We were to have a holiday in Japan, and Christmas was coming up.

We traveled to all the famous places in Japan, to Nikko, this single shrine that is made up of many shrines, so bewildering in its detail but so beautiful as a whole. Here we saw the original three monkeys that will have no dealing with evil, and we saw the celebrated sleeping cat, and one can almost hear the little statue purr.

We traveled south to Kamakura and while one may not join the Japanese in bowing before the Buddha here, any man will stand very still and be silent. We drank green tea and looked across a lake at Mount Fujiyama, tipped by a cloud until it blew away, and then the tall white cone stood alone in the sky; and we were fortunate because the Japanese say that "Fuji is shy," and allows few strangers to see him.

Beyond the mountains and farther south is Kyoto, the old capital of Japan, with its art treasures, and especially Nijo Castle. Here in this memorable castle is the nightingale floor that sings as one walks, and here are the hauntingly beautiful paintings on their gold-foil screens, and a small lake with two tiny islands, "The Isle of Crane" and "The Isle of Turtle."

I noticed as we traveled, and after we came back to Tokyo, that the beauty of Japan is still here, and much of the courtesy of her people is here, but something of her charm has inevitably been lost in the destruction of the war and in the changes that have taken place since then. Japan today is a nation dedicated to the difficult task of bringing herself back to full self-support, and in accomplishing this she must depend on extending her industries, on using her many skills to their fullest, and on the tireless energy of her people. She is moving steadily toward her goal and everywhere in the country one feels how *busy* Japan is.

To one remembering prewar Japan, the most noticeable change is in the dress of the people. Japanese women now wear Western dress; the lovely kimono, one of the most attractive of garments, is almost gone. The brightly colored obi, which is the wide sash, and the flowers and the ivory ornaments in the hair— they, too, are gone. Even at the temple in Kyoto, on a day especially favored by the stars for marriage, we saw more brides wearing the white bridal gowns of the West than were wearing the black kimono and intricate hair dress of the conventional Japanese bride.

Western dress does not particularly become the Japanese women, and the Japanese themselves know this. When one of their girls walks out in a pretty kimono and a pretty obi, her charm back again, her grace her own again, they notice her and are pleased. One night at the Imperial Hotel, the dance floor filled with couples, Japanese and American, a slender Japanese girl wearing a pale gray kimono faintly touched with pink flowers walked out on the floor, and when she danced, her sandals so graceful and so sure, everyone watched and openly admired.

One also misses the children of that other Japan, racing along in their little kimonos, as brightly colored as a flush of autumn leaves, laughing and playing, their wooden sandals clattering.

But now the little Japanese girl sits and pops her bubble gum at you, and the little boy is too weighted down to run, twin gats on his hips, his blue jeans tight as plaster and a five-pint hat aslant his head—quick on the draw, and "Bang! Bang!" if you speak to him.

They have picked up so much from the American troops and American civilian personnel, men and women, and from American children. Most of what they have taken from us is the superficial and the showy, the tight-fitting dresses, Hopalong and his guns, and Elvis Presley baying at his houn' dawg. It is curious how quick the world is to take our trash, labeling this "America," and disregarding the kind of decent people that most of us are, and the kind of sensible lives that most of us live. We Americans haven't yet figured out a way of exporting ourselves, and what we believe in, and telling the story of how we really live. Instead, we go right on shipping out cargoes of bubble gum, six-shooters, and Mr. Presley.

It seems, though, for all the American influence that has permeated Japanese life, that at least one night a year the Japanese people go back to their old dress and Japan is Japan again, colorful and picturesque once more. It happens on Christmas Eve, and here too is the American influence, for Japan is Shinto and Buddhist, only a fragment Christian, and yet Christmas Eve, a Christian festival, is a riotous night in Tokyo.

For weeks before that night one notices the painted signs in many of the stores and in the shopwindows—"Merry Christmas." At night, as my wife and I walked along the main streets or even the little side streets, we often saw the signs going on and off, the colored lights saying in English—"Merry Christmas."

In many of the department stores of Tokyo—some of them as big and certainly as bright and crowded and busy as the stores of New York—there were full-size Christmas trees. They stood at the entrance of the store, or in a window, each tree decorated with tinsel and gleaming baubles, with lights and a glittering star at the top. In one store was a tree so colorful and so airy that we went closer to see what it was. It had been made of feathers, the bark and leaves and twigs all feathers.

On Christmas Eve my wife and I, planning our celebration, managed to get seats at the Kabuki Theater. This is not only a famous place but one of the most effective theaters in the world, with huge revolving stages and elaborate sets, and the acting so natural that one understands and feels the emotion of the play even though he does not understand the language. We went to the Kabuki early, for there are always three or four plays each evening, and the comedians were so funny that they kept even the foreigners laughing, and certainly we all had some sense of the tragedy in the final play. Afterward the crowd moved out slowly, and when we stepped into the street it was almost midnight. Everybody, so it seemed, had gone delightfully crazy.

Some of the people wore false faces. Some wore big noses and big ears. Many of them, both men and women, were dressed in kimonos again, and some even wore the bright and fantastic costumes of priests or dancing girls. They sounded bells and horns and clappers, and many of them swung paper lanterns, Japanese lanterns, with beautiful scenes painted on them. Some of the lanterns were decorated with Japanese writing, which itself can be so beautiful, and it stood out clear in the silhouette from the candle.

The revelers sang and held up their lanterns and swung them, inspecting us, two foreigners, as we came from the theater, and they formed a ring and danced around us, poking their masked faces at us as they danced. After the dance ended we joined in the tight parade, edging in among them and pressing along the street, and it wasn't long before we, too, were singing "White Christmas" and "Jingle Bells," and who cared if the words weren't the same?

We stayed out long past midnight, and the people still were packed on the sidewalks, easing along, all moving in whatever direction the crowd was moving, shouting, blowing their horns, rattling their bells and clappers, holding up their lanterns and swaying them. Now and then a dance started, swirling, stopping all other movement, and the people squeezed back to make room for the dancers, holding firm until the swift circle broke up as abruptly as it had started, and then the space instantly was packed and the people were moving on once more.

Out in the streets the taxicabs were cold murder. They drove like rats before a fire, racing, leaping for any opening that might dare to appear among the cars or in the mass of men and women, and whoever or whatever tried to get there first was taking his chances. Even for us, as passengers, there were moments when we closed our eyes and braced. Yet only once did we skim another car, and only once did we scrape a pedestrian, and the other driver looked back at full speed and waved, and the uncomplaining pedestrian brushed himself off. It was a wonderful and glorious bedlam in Tokyo that Christmas Eve.

But Christmas Day in Tokyo was no Christmas Day at all. Men were back in their offices, bending at their desks again, women were going about their shopping, and everyone was as formal and reserved as before, bowing in proper courtesy. All was routine again, and the day was just December 25.

The streets were quiet, noses and ears had shrunk, and one wondered where all the people of the night before had gone. There was only one touch of Christmas that we saw: there were turkey and dressing and cranberry sauce on the menu at the Imperial Hotel, and we Americans were ordering it.

Our holiday in Japan ended on this Christmas Day, and that night we left for Manila and the Philippines. Our reservation was on KLM, the Royal Dutch air line, and it is interesting to fly on the air lines of the different countries. Each air line tries, whenever it can, to serve the food of its country, and it brings along some of the magazines of its country, and they are enjoyable to look through even though one cannot read them.

Also, there is interest in the languages of the various air lines, for all announcements that come over the intercom are made first in the language of the line itself; but whether this first language is Hebrew, Greek, Italian, German, or whatever it may be, one of the several languages that follow in translation is certain to be English—another indication that English is more of a world language than any other.

Whatever the various differences of the air lines of the nations may be, they all manage to find tall and pretty girls for stewardesses, and the girls on the Royal Dutch air line were just as pretty and just as blonde as one pictures a Dutch girl.

We were to leave Tokyo at ten o'clock and the flight down to Manila was seven hours. We made ourselves as comfortable as we could, bade the pretty Dutch girls good night, and went to sleep. We had been up so late on Christmas Eve that we were sound asleep the next morning at four o'clock when the girls waked us for breakfast. The Dutch breakfast of cold foods—cold ham, cold liverwurst, cheese—was not too tempting, but the tea was wonderfully hot.

The plane flew on through the dark and we landed at Manila still before daybreak, at five fifteen. Even at that time, well before the sun, the soggy blanket of Manila's air was on the city, the heat moist from the bay and steaming in from the jungle.

One of the officials of USIS had been considerate enough to meet us and he came on to the hotel for coffee. There he told us that since this was the day after Christmas, and since there would be a rather general holiday in the Philippines, we could have the day off and do with it as we pleased. My work would not begin until the next day.

With this unexpected holiday we hired a car for a tour of Manila and the area. There really isn't much for a tourist to do in Manila, and there isn't much of particular interest for him to see; but we drove to the cathedral, and to the university, and we visited the huge market. It is spread over several squares, a tangle of people and a clutter of stalls, all jammed together where pineapples, horseshoes, and singing birds are sold. We saw the prison where the Filipinos were tortured by the Japanese, and the hospital where the Americans died. We drove out of Manila to a small town, Tagaytay, and stopped by the way and looked down from our hill onto the South China Sea with its myriad small islands that were green upon the sea, like a scattering of leaves blown over the water.

We went to a famous inn in this town and we ate papaya, fresh and sweet from the tree, a squeeze of lime to heighten it. We ate green coconuts that had been cut in half and ice cream piled into the center, skimming out the thin inner layer, so delicate in its flavor, and eating it with the ice cream, leaving the coarser and less tasty meat that one ordinarily eats.

The air was cooler here in these foothills, and going back we were lazing along, traveling slowly and enjoying it, listening to our driver tell his stories of the war. They were wild tales of the jungle, of the Filipino guerrillas fighting the Japanese. These Filipino men and women fought throughout the war with almost incredible bravery and endurance, living in the jungle off whatever they could find, harassing the Japanese, destroying their supplies, attacking and disappearing, killing far more than they lost.

We were driving along listening to this talk and looking out at the people in the rice field, seeing the long lines of men and women moving slowly over the field, their red and blue blouses bright against the amber of the grain. As the long lines advanced, the sickles were swift as they rose and fell, flashing in the slant of the afternoon sun. We were seeing the water buffalo, the carabao of the Phlippines, lazy and sunk to his nose in the mud, his huge horns spread, his eyes drowsy, wallowing in the mud and cooling his hot hide. We were seeing the banana groves and the papaya trees and coconut palms, the fields of pineapples and melons, and we were driving along slowly, at peace with ourselves and with everyone, when we came to a village and we heard a shout.

Down a side street we saw a crowd and a latticed shack, and at that moment we heard a rooster crow. The Filipinos were engaged in the serious business of their living—they were fighting their chickens. Those other men of the field, unimaginative and plodding, might live by the glint of their sickles, but these men with their tall, lean chickens—they feasted, or they went ragged and hungry, by the flick of a gaff as pointed as a pin and as sharp as a razor.

We watched them fasten the gaff, the long and curved spur, over the natural spur, which is only a blunt and soft weapon, but the gaff is steel death. We saw them put the gaffs on the legs of the chickens, fastening them with precise care, wrapping the bindings securely, and testing the strike of the point.

Then we went inside and stood close to the pit, while the owners of the cocks crouched opposite each other, holding their birds carefully, stroking them. The gamblers moved about swiftly, darting about the pit, holding up their hands, shouting their bets and calling the odds they offered.

While the betting still was going on, the gamblers still calling and turning quickly, searching for bets, the owners of the birds moved to the center of the pit. Still crouched, still stroking their birds, they eased the cocks together on the dirt floor, allowing them to peck each other, to lunge and peck, though each of them was held firmly by its owner until the signal was given, and then the men loosed their birds and they flew together, striking and stabbing with the gaffs.

Lunging upward, fluttering in the air, always the birds stab and fall back, then come together again, rising and fluttering up together, hovering for a moment, their legs lashing out until one of them, striking blindly, sinks his gaff into the brain of the other. And while the dead bird lies stretched, quivering and jerking, the victor, the long gaff still fastened to him, stalks around, stiff-legged and awkward, until he is caught and held.

Always after each fight the owner of the dead bird comes forward and picks up his chicken, peering at it in a puzzled, disconsolate way, turning it over, a skinny, dangling thing, its feathers hacked away—and a moment before it had been sleek and shiny, stretching and crowing for the fight. In that moment before, it had been a promise of a new suit, a hat, a bottle of wine, a girl perhaps; but now it is only a limp bird for the pot, a stringy and tasteless dish in place of the feast, the wine, and a girl perhaps.

All this day we drove around and enjoyed ourselves, even in the muggy air of Manila, and that night we had a pleasant dinner and went to bed early, for I was to be up early to begin my chief assignment in the Philippines. I was to travel north of Manila to Baguio City, flying to this resort town high in the mountains to attend a conference of writers and editors, the literary men and women of the Philippines. It was to be a meeting of the International PEN Club, and the American Department of State had been invited by this Filipino club to name and to send a speaker.

I had been looking forward to coming to the Philippines, for this nation had been a part of America, and it would be pleasant to hear their thanks and gratitude for the way in which the United States had granted them their independence. They had not been required to fight for their freedom, as the American colonists had fought. Nor had they been called on to stage a long and costly campaign of passive resistance, as the Indians with Gandhi had done. The people of the United States, on July 4, 1946, had simply said to the people of the Philippines: "Here is your independence. We give it to you. You are free." And the Philippine Republic was born. I was glad that we had done it this way, and I was looking forward to meeting the Filipinos.

The story of the young country and the record of the decent and friendly way in which we had treated it were in my mind as I flew on toward the mountains, seeing them rise sharp out of the low and swampy plains. Except for knowing that I was going to a literary conference I knew nothing of the details of the meetings until I arrived in Baguio, and there in the large resort hotel, at the registration booth in the lobby, I was given a program. It was an elaborate booklet, well printed, and I quickly recognized the importance of the conference when I saw that the first address was to be given by the president of the Philippines, President

Carlos P. García. At other meetings that came after there were to be addresses by the president of the University of the Philippines, by senators, university deans and teachers, historians, publishers, editors, novelists, playwrights, and poets. It was to be a top-flight meeting, and I was proud that our State Department had sent me as the official American representative.

I looked on through the program and saw that the general subject for the meeting was, "The Filipino Writer and National Growth." Then, as I turned the pages, I came across a statement that stopped me: "Like all new countries, the Philippines needs the talent, the energy, and the devotion of its citizens. Colonial domination has shaped the Philippines economy into a producer of raw materials for imperial industry, while our people continue to live on subsistence agriculture."

I didn't understand these references to "colonial domination" and "imperial industry," and I read the statement again. Spain had been in the Philippines during the nineteenth century, but the United States had administered the islands during the first half of the present century, and I wondered if they could possibly be talking about us. I didn't see how they could, particularly after the way we had given them their independence. There seemed to be something mixed up here in this statement, something contradictory, but there wasn't time now for me to ask about it. I considered that my job at the conference, as a representative of the State Department, was to move around and meet people, to let them know how friendly the United States is, and I introduced myself and was as cordial as I knew how to be.

But the next day, when the conference got under way, I heard more of the same kind of talk that I had read in the program, and this time it could not possibly be misunderstood, for it was aimed specifically and point-blank at the United States. One speaker said: "A new colonial regime was established at the turn of the nineteenth century, inaugurating the American period in our history. What could be more natural than for the Filipinos to expect the new ruling nation to follow a policy in accord with her tradition of freedom? However, the optimism of the Filipinos was soon dispelled." The speaker continued, and spoke of "the revulsion of patriotic Filipinos against the Americans."

During the next three days of the conference I heard this talk continued, and with more than one reference to "revulsion" against Americans—"slaves to the power and might of the American dollar"—"colonial domination"—"imperialism"—"the source of injustice and complaint."

On the night before the day that I was scheduled to speak, I didn't know what to talk about. I had been expecting to pick up a subject from the talks that preceded mine, fitting my speech into the general theme and tenor of the conference; but I wasn't the slightest bit interested in talking about the "imperialism" of the United States.

Puzzling about what to do, I thought of a subject that I believed was suitable, and I invited an officer of the conference aside and asked him about it. I suggested that since the conference was made up chiefly of professional writers, and since most writers want to dispose of their writings, to sell them somewhere, I believed that I could be useful if I told them about the American markets for novels, plays, and poems. I could tell about books and magazines, radio, and television in the United States, about publishers and agents, and let the Filipinos know what contracts they should ask for, and what royalties they should receive. Throughout the conference I had heard them complaining about having no outlets for their writings, the small number of publishers and magazines in the Philippines, and I believed that information about outlets in the United States would help them.

The officer of the conference sat still, listening, his face noncommittal until I had finished, and then he leaned toward the table and carefully wiped the ashes from his cigarette. "How American!" he said. "How very American. Your speech would concern money—dollars. Always with you Americans everything is money and dollars."

I did not answer and I did not make the speech that I had

suggested. Instead, I spoke about a group of people coming together and talking about nationalism when supposedly they had come to talk about the art and skill of writing, the creating of books. Their steady criticism of the United States, and their loud hurrah for the Philippines, had nothing to do with literature and was only a form of evasion by men and women who would not face the hard reality of writing, the lonely, draining job of just sitting down somewhere and writing.

They sat still for a moment after the talk was over, and then somebody stood, and somebody else stood, and they gave that speech a standing ovation—the first time, I was told, that this kind of ovation had been given by this group to an American.

And this was the second lesson that I learned on this trip—an American does not have to sit still and let them insult him and run down the United States. As a man in India was to tell me later, "It is fashionable to attack the United States." But an American doesn't have to take it. He can stand up and tell his opinions, no matter what country he is in, or what people he is talking to, and they will like him better for it and respect him for it. For some reason our government has adopted a policy of placating, of the soft answer, of just plain pussyfooting. It won't work. And the sooner we decide to tell them what we think in straight-out American language, and state our terms, the sooner there is going to be more respect for us as men and more regard for us as a nation when we sit down at the conference table to transact our international business.

After the session was over and my speech was done with, a young newspaper editor came to me. "That was the first time that an American has told us what *he* thinks." He offered me a cigarette and lighted his own. "Just why in the hell doesn't the United States Government, and the people that they send out here, realize that we can recognize the official line when we hear it, and that we know American soft soap and glad-handing, and we are sick of it?"

Things were different that night. On the night of my arrival at the conference, even though it was known that I was an official representative of the Department of State, and although I wore a conspicuous badge, "SPEAKER," no one invited me to sit by the log fire, no one offered me a drink, and in the dining room with a score of empty chairs at half-a-dozen tables no one asked me to sit down. I was an American, and that was enough. They didn't like me.

But on the night after the speech I was asked to sit at a dozen tables, and I sat up until four o'clock in the morning with a group of people by the fire, and I would have been more drunk than I should have been if I had accepted all the offers that were made to me of whisky, and brandy, and hot rum. And to tell the truth about it, the speech was not *that* good. It was just honest.

Some of the criticism of the United States during the conference had a basis in history, and it could be called justified; but to me it seemed pointless at this time because the reasons for it were so long ago and now so completely out of date. Some of the criticism even went as far back as the American Sedition Act of November 4, 1901, passed shortly after the United States had taken over the administration of the Philippines.

Filipino writers and speakers at this time were asking for independence for their country, often in the very language of Patrick Henry and Samuel Adams, and yet in the midst of this plea our government passed and enforced the following act: "Until it is officially proclaimed that a state of war or insurrection against the authority or sovereignty of the United States no longer exists in the Philippine Islands, it shall be unlawful for any person to advocate orally or by writing or printing or like methods the independence of the Philippine Islands or its separation from the United States whether by peaceable or forcible means, or to print, publish, or circulate any handbill, newspaper, or other publication, advocating such independence or separation."

This is a shameful act, in direct and total violation of the First Amendment of the Constitution and its guarantee of free speech and a free press. The act was wrong, and we were wrong, and we might as well admit it; but I still don't see why this act should have been dragged into the conference at Baguio, why it should have been read and paraded at this late and nonassociated date, except that it gave another speaker another chance to slur and discredit the United States.

Most of the criticism of the United States was not so historically justified as this attack on the Sedition Act of 1901. A good deal of the criticism was strained, an obvious play to the prejudices of the listeners, and some of it was just plain silly.

At the conference I was given two newspaper columns by Mr. I. P. Soliongco, of the Manila *Chronicle*. Mr. Soliongco had this to say:

> A number of writers will soon go up to Baguio, convene and discuss among themselves and with chosen guests the weighty matters concerned with their craft, with their responsibilities as writers, and with their role in society.
>
> All Filipinos today, particularly the writers, are the logical and rightful spiritual heirs of the men of the Propaganda Movement... and there is no reason why the writer of today, from the poet to the editorialist, should not carry on the tradition of Rizal, Del Pilar, and Lopez Jaena.
>
> But they are unable to do so because the Americans who came here in 1898 were so successful in frustrating the work of the men of the Propaganda Movement. The Americans did their work deliberately and with consummate subtlety....
>
> They erected a barrier which effectively prevented the Filipinos from going back to their natural heroes and mentors for wisdom and guidance. The barrier they erected consisted of Washington and the cherry tree, of the theology of William Cullen Bryant and the moral precepts of the older Oliver Wendell Holmes, of the letter to Mrs. Bixby and the Gettysburg Address, the tale of Hiawatha, and the coyness of Priscilla and the story of Gabriel and Evangeline.

Here, now, surely is news for Americans! We had never thought of the immaculate Mr. Longfellow and the pious Mr. Bryant as instruments of bondage. But, so it seems, they were—or maybe Mr. Soliongco doesn't know that at the same time as Filipino children were chanting the song of Hiawatha, and learning of the prim Priscilla, we American children were being handed the same stuff. We, too, suffered.

Mr. Soliongco concludes: "The realization of America's manifest destiny which, for all its benevolence, was still another form of Western domination," was subtly and effectively aided "by the optimism and progress contained in the verses of Henry Wadsworth Longfellow and the poems of Edgar A. Guest...." (One learns as he lives. Longfellow and Eddie Guest! A couple of shrewd propagandists.)

This, of course, is open nonsense, but it was published in one of the most important newspapers in the Philippines and when I asked some half-dozen writers at the conference what they thought of it, they agreed with it and said that the Americans had stifled any appreciation of Filipino literature by failing to teach it at all, or at least failing to teach it with any enthusiasm or loyalty, while they had insisted on serving the Filipino children this pap from the so-called American poets.

Now and then, amid the continual criticism of the United States, there was some of it that lacked the acid sting and some that was almost gentle. There was, for example, the comments of Mr. Alejandro R. Roces, another Manila columnist, of the Manila *Times*, whose barbs were sharp but did not go too deep.

He was at the conference and he made a speech, telling of how the American administrators, during the years that they were in the Philippines, had carried on the American practice of always trying to change the satisfactory customs and habits of other people to conform to the American way of doing things. As an example he mentioned punctuality, and he admitted that punctuality has its merit. "But we people have to make these changes slowly. For instance, let's take what we call 'Filipino time.' To people who come from the barrio it is useless to say, 'I will meet you at the river with the carabao at eight o'clock sharp.' It does not make sense. Why eight o'clock? Why not nine—ten—ten thirty?... My point is that these things must be introduced as much as possible from within."

Mr. Roces then spoke of Americans today, and how in their big-hearted but determined way they still are pressing on and trying to remake the Filipinos, trying to change them and make them like Americans, wanting them to do everything as the Americans do. "Take the case of American aid in the Philippines," he said. "The ICA now has a Chicken Exchange Program. The Americans, handing out their aid, go out to the barrios, and there they take a man's chicken and they give him a fine leghorn, but the leghorns won't fight, and we want chickens to take to the cockpit as well as to eat. That's what I mean."

In the three days at the conference, at which the president of the Philippines and scores of other prominent Filipinos spoke, men of influence in their nation, I heard continual criticism, some of it lighthearted, some of it silly, some of it bitter, against the United States. I heard no expression of friendship or any indication whatsoever of respect for the United States.

One can overlook some of this talk because the Philippines is a young nation, and these Filipinos were swaggering a bit, showing off, impressing themselves and each other with big talk. Also, as a young nation they have just been turned out to fend for themselves, and they are a little frightened and irritated because they lack the security that had been theirs when the United States was in the islands. They resented the United States while we were there, but we were mighty handy to have around, and they are just a little bit at sea now that we have gone.

Enough time has passed for the patriotic tumult and the shouting to die, but they have not yet accustomed themselves to accepting the hard obligations of independence as well as its glory. Not wanting to blame themselves, even though they still run on

"Filipino time" and fight lean chickens instead of eating fat ones, they blame the United States.

And yet however much this criticism of the Filipinos may be explained and discounted, however farfetched and petty we may consider it, the fact remains that here is a nation, in a key position in the Pacific, whose alignment with the United States at any moment of critical world decision can certainly be doubted.

3

My assignment for the State Department had specified that I represent them in three countries: Korea, the Philippines, and India. When my schedule was arranged, I had been allowed some time in between these countries to travel where I pleased as a tourist, and the State Department would then not be concerned with me in any way. At these times I went off the State Department's payroll and paid my own way. My wife's expenses, of course, for the entire trip were paid by me.

When I had finished my work in the Philippines, I was on leave and we were to be tourists all the way across to India, going first to Hong Kong. We were to make the trip to Hong Kong with the Philippine Airways and we had expected about the usual passenger list that one encounters on most airplanes in this part of the world—some American tourists, some Japanese salesmen, a few West German salesmen, an Englishman or two, now and then a Chinese, and often an Indian man or woman going back home after a time of study and travel in the United States.

But it was not to be this way on the plane out of Manila. Except for one couple from Norway and two Filipino businessmen, everybody else on the plane except ourselves was an American schoolteacher. They were all stationed in Japan, sent there to teach the children of army personnel, and this was their holiday tour. They had left Japan before Christmas and had flown down as far as Singapore. They had been to Thailand and to Vietnam and all of them had bought the big straw hats of Vietnam; when we came aboard the plane those American teachers had filled every rack and corner with the things they had collected.

The girl across the aisle from me was from Utah and there were some from a number of the other states, mostly the Far Western states, California, Washington, Idaho. The teachers were working at different installations throughout Japan but all of them were carrying out the same kind of duties and finding that teaching American children in Japan was little different from teaching them back at home—"Except when one of them springs some Japanese expression on you that he has picked up from somewhere." They were going on to Hong Kong and would fly back from there to Japan in time to begin their teaching again at the end of the holidays.

After we were in Hong Kong, settled in our hotel and going here and there about the city, we again saw these girls, and almost invariably they were busy in the shops, looking and buying, for they, like almost all tourists, were devoting their time to the shops of Hong Kong. The city is a free port, charging no duty, either import or export, and goods from everywhere can be shipped in here and sold cheaper than in the countries where they are produced. Here in Hong Kong is the market place of the world, the bazaar of everything, and here the people of the Orient come partly for vacation, but mostly to do their shopping; and many travelers, especially Americans, put off all buying until they get to Hong Kong. Here are woolens from England, linens from Brussels, Swiss cottons, and pearls from Japan at a less cost than in Tokyo. Here is gold, porcelain, silk, ivory, jade—and it induces a buying madness.

Not only are all the materials here, and at these low prices, but here are the craftsmen—the tailors, leatherworkers, goldsmiths—and they are in shop after shop, lining both sides of the streets, and they can make anything you want. If you want something copied, they can do it. If you want something created, just give them an idea. From a pair of shoes to a pearl pendant, they can make it exactly to your wish.

Furthermore, they can make it as fast as you want. They are accustomed to the big Pacific liners and the round-the-world cruise ships coming in and docking for only twenty-four hours and the people swarming off and jamming the shops. Everybody must have everything, and have it fast. Some of them examine the woolens, some reach for the bolts of silk, stretching for the pieces they want.

They no sooner make the selection of their cloths, and tell how many suits they want, than the chalk of the fitters is flying, the scissors of the cutters gleam, and the tailors upstairs are working all day and all night. The suits and dresses, pajamas and shirts, all will be handmade and all will be finished. Before sailing time the next morning a line of tailors will go up the gangplank loaded with garments, followed by other men with shoes and pocketbooks, and still others with smaller parcels, a bracelet, a ring, a necklace of gold.

Hong Kong is a heady place to go, a city of commercial quicksand, and after several days of it my wife and I forced ourselves to balance our checkbook, and then we knew that we had to pull out of these shops and stay away from them. There was nothing left for us to do but to go sight-seeing.

The chief attraction of Hong Kong is, of course, the Peak, and we rode up to it on the cable car. Sailors say that Hong Kong is one of the finest harbors in the world, and certainly from the Peak it is one of the most magnificent sights with its far spread of ships at anchor and all the other ships coming in and going out, the liners and the freighters weaving their slow way through the channel and then straightening out as they touch the sea. The big ships move carefully, always watching, for under their tall bows the blunt-nosed ferryboats are constantly crossing, busy at their shuttle, and in the harbor is the scattering of careless and irresponsible craft, the ragged flotilla of sampans and junks, slow, undecided, and drifting, their ancient sails a medley of dirty patches.

Here is the far line of the Pacific, the boundary, the end of the

West and the beginning of Asia. Here is still a remnant of Empire, one of the final traces of European rule in Asia, for Hong Kong is still a British crown colony, permitted and tolerated at Red China's door because it is convenient and useful to China. She can use it to market her goods and it is an excellent place to release her propaganda.

During the time of our sight-seeing in Hong Kong we drove about the city with American friends, a couple who have lived in the Orient for twenty years, going along Queen's Road, seeing Tiger Balm Palace, and visiting Repulse Bay. On a bright day, warm and the breeze easy, we drove to Aberdeen, a fishing village, and there had lunch on a long flat-bottomed boat, a floating restaurant. Our table was on the top deck and we could look down on innumerable small boats packed around us, packed so close together that they were like a tight platform stretching on toward the sea. Here and there was a narrow water lane, a slender passage, and down one of these lanes came a sampan with a family on board, their belongings piled on the deck and roped in place. The small craft was heavy with its load and slow moving.

Our friend glanced at them, at the man bending to the swing of the scull, and he looked at the children, and at the stolid face of the woman. "They're in from China," he said. "They left there last night."

Sometimes the Red gunboats ignore them when they try to escape, paying no attention as they ease out of the fishing line, working their way farther from the shore until they disappear into the dark. Sometimes, though, the gunboats use their searchlights and come after the fishermen and their families, taking them back to prison. Sometimes they turn their guns on them and sink them.

It is estimated that more than a million Chinese have fled from Red China to Hong Kong, coming at the rate of 100,000 a year, making their way across the narrow strip of land or coming down by fishing craft. Those who come by land can bring nothing with them, only their clothes, and often their clothes are rags. They arrive in Hong Kong without food or money and there is nothing for them to do in Hong Kong, no work, no way to make a living. They live 50 to a room and 2,500 to an acre. They live on the sides of cliffs, like animals, and there is no water on the cliffs, only at the bottom, and they empty their filth on the shacks below. Even now no one knows how the 50,000 children without homes or families stay alive in Hong Kong.

At any time the government of Hong Kong begins to overcome the crowding in the city, to clean up and better its living, then Red China looks the other way while thousands of new refugees swarm over the border or come down by sea, and once more Hong Kong is in distress, a condition in which Red China intends to keep her.

We watched the sampan go by, hunting a place big enough to turn in and stop. I was seeing the children, motionless and staring, and the swing of the man at the long scull, and the drip of the scull each time it came clear, when my friend turned to me. "You are just out from the States," he said, "and I'd like for you to tell me what our government intends to do about Red China. What plan has Washington concerning China?

"China is becoming more skillful, more determined, more powerful all the time," he said. "Of course we don't like what they stand for, what they teach, what they do—but they *are*. Six hundred million of them! You can't ignore that many people. And what is our government doing to make it possible for us to live on the same planet with them? We can't go on just pretending that they aren't there. One of these days, with our lives and our children's lives at stake, Red China will knock on our door. And so far as I can see, we are making no plans, no arrangements about what to do about it."

On former trips abroad I had heard criticism of the United States, and had learned somewhat to expect it and to discount it. American expatriates, living outside our country and separated from our immediate national problems, often are quick to tell us how to take care of things. And people of other countries can be critical, partly out of envy of us, partly from jealousy of us because we are richer as a nation and because we have more as individuals. But it seemed to me that on this trip the criticism that I was hearing was more frequent and a good deal more positive than the usual bickering and envy.

In the past the people of the Orient seemed to have had a curious feeling about the United States. We were regarded as something of a prodigy and there was a tolerance, almost a pride in this young and vigorous nation, inventive and daring. I remember how my small nurse, Miss Tsai, thirty years ago at the Rockefeller Hospital in Peking once had said to me: "Oh, we are very fond of the United States." And she had made a little gesture like a grown person patting a child on the head, a mixture of affection and pride in the young fellow.

But there is none of that feeling now, not even in the countries outside of China, neither tolerance nor regard for us. We have given billions of our dollars, digging deep into our pockets to aid the free nations of Asia, and yet the old friendship that we had with these people of the Orient is drifting away and ending, and they regard us with suspicion and distrust.

We had a letter of introduction to a Chinese businessman in Hong Kong, a representative of a firm of American shippers, and he invited us to dinner. There were three other Chinese with us that evening, and we ate in a noisy restaurant where the diners shouted as they played games and gambled for drinks. We ate such food as only the Chinese prepare, and the drink was a pale wine. After dinner, when the restaurant was quiet, I had a chance to talk with these men.

They told me that it was becoming difficult for them to sell American goods and products today. There was a time when anything that came from the United States was believed to be better. But the people of the oriental countries have improved their own skills, and are still improving them, and buyers in the East no longer are impressed by an article just because it comes from the United States. They have learned that things from other countries can be just as good, and they can get them at a lower price, and they are buying from these other countries and will continue to buy from them, and our trade in the East will lessen.

The talk of these Hong Kong businessmen did not surprise me. In Japan I had seen the Japanese challenging American business in areas that I had not expected. One often thinks of Japan as making the lesser things: dolls, toys, cheap baubles of all kinds; but Japan now is hard at work in heavy industry, she is already the biggest shipbuilder in the world, and she makes a small car, the Toyopet, and she makes jeeps and buses. The biggest watch manufacturer in the world is in Japan—Seiko—and she is making transistor radios, tape recorders, cameras, binoculars, record players. I talked to Americans in Japan about these products and was told that they are of good quality.

In the competition for world trade, the United States cannot expect to equal prices from Japan and other oriental countries, for their cheaper labor has always enabled these Eastern countries to undersell us. Our advantage has been in quality, but oriental representatives of American business are beginning to believe that we are losing that advantage, saying that we are turning out things so fast, trying to force our speed of production to balance our rising costs of production, that we are slipping in quality. Then, too, in recent years so many Americans, having lost their labor individuality in group pressures, have also lost their personal pride in workmanship.

China has not yet challenged in the industrial market, but as soon as China has built up her industries to equip and maintain her war machine, she will come into these international markets and she will flood them. Her ultimate plan, of course, is the old plan of Japan—a united Asia.

Japan fifty years ago conquered Korea as a steppingstone onto the continent, and from Korea in 1931 Japan marched on into Manchuria, carrying out her plan and going deeper into China, which at that time was chaotic and helpless. The joining of China and Japan, and the ultimate control of all Asia, was Japan's dream—the "Asian Co-prosperity Sphere." Pearl Harbor, however, became a sudden new objective, and the war interrupted and ended her continental expansion.

The plan still is perfectly plain and its economic advantages are unmistakable. A joining of Japan and China, for products and markets, will form such an economic bloc that no other industrial power can likely withstand it. Japan's industrial skill and her organizational genius combined with China's raw materials, her vast spaces for expansion, and her masses of pauper labor, will produce such goods at such costs that the American economy in the Orient inevitably will collapse.

When China moved down into Korea in 1950, she had all this in mind, and she was only reversing the Japanese plan; this time a conqueror trying to get into position to take over the island, instead of the island moving up to take over the continent. But whichever one takes the other, the normal alliance in this part of Asia is between China and Japan, and already Japanese businessmen and the Japanese Socialist party, as well as the Japanese Communists, are pressing for an economic union with Red China. Even senior advisors in the Liberal-Democratic party, which supposedly is favorable and friendly to the United States, are warning the Japanese Government that the Peiping regime will be "a mighty power within five or ten years." Mr. Kenzo Matsumura, one of the most influential leaders among the Liberal-Democratic party, the party in power in Japan, recently demanded, "Why not face up to the reality that Communist China today is an awakening nation?"

The present economic buttress of Japan by the United States, maintained across the expanse of the Pacific Ocean by our money and our military installations, cannot endure. It would seem wise for us to recognize this fact, and only common sense for us to examine our whole economic structure, at home and abroad, instead of waiting for the inevitable day of economic disruption in the Orient when some spokesman of our government will be forced to stand before the nation, and in sudden astonishment and oratorical indignation reveal to us "a day of *economic* infamy."

Unwilling to come face to face with this stern and increasing competition from the Orient, unwilling to admit that the cheap labor of the East is a basic and enduring factor in world economy, we fall back on inherited devices, unimaginative and outmoded, in our losing effort to maintain an economic superiority. But our tariffs and restrictive trading laws, no matter how we tighten them, will not save us. In the past, whenever we were annoyed economically, we passed a new law or put up a higher barrier. But our laws and barriers no longer have any weight in the world, because our economy and general national influence no longer are strong enough to enforce our will.

Now when we seek to influence international trade by tariffs and legislation, instead of by trying to hold markets by the compelling factors of quality and price, the Communist countries simply move into the affected areas and instantly flood these markets with goods under the normal price. We haven't yet caught on to the fact that these countries, China and Russia with their state-controlled prices, can move in almost overnight and sell quality goods at such prices that they can take the market and hold it completely, until we have lost it completely. This is another factor that a forty-hour week and two automobiles a man cannot compete against.

4

From Hong Kong, still traveling as tourists, we went on south to Vietnam. Vietnam is a low and hot country, tropical, a good part of it jungle. Saigon, the capital, is a city in this jungle setting, itself moist and soggy hot, a broad river almost level with its streets and flowing so slowly that one must watch the drift of a branch or a leaf to know that it moves. Outside the city, wherever the jungle has been cut back, are the rice paddies, small green-and-yellow plots like patchwork, and the plots divided by low walls of packed earth. Here the Vietnamese men follow the slow plodding of their buffaloes, plowing with wooden plows, and their women wade deep in the muddy water, bending over and setting the rice plants. The pace of the buffalo seems the pace of the country, and it is drowsy.

In Saigon itself the pace is different, for here is a scurry of automobiles and motorcycles, and the flash of bicycles that dart out from around corners, leaning, crisscrossing, and racing on. The women of Saigon are slender, pale in their coloring, and they wear trousers that are like pajama trousers, long and full, and usually they are of satin. The upper garment is a tunic of sheer silk, its collar high and tight-fitting like the Chinese, and the tunic hangs almost to the ankles, slit deep on each side. These women in their airy tunics and satin trousers often wear a wide-brimmed straw hat that sometimes they fasten with a ribbon under their chin. It is a sight to see one of these pretty girls, her tunic skirt tucked up under her, her big hat tied on securely, scooting along on her motorbike, sounding her horn now and then for passage, but occasionally one suspects, when a young man is near, for attention.

Saigon is a faster town and more brisk than it was in the days of the French. The people of Saigon were slow-moving then, quiet, looking down and seldom speaking, almost hangdog; but now they are quick in what they do, gay and eager to talk to anyone wherever he goes in the city.

We visited a street market where flowers are sold, and the place was a riot of colors and sweet as all spring. We went to the large city market, covering several blocks, and it is like so many markets and bazaars in the East, a continuous shifting and an unbroken shouting, a loud confusion. One man squatted behind a tray of rusty nails and screws, and this was his entire stock. Another man flung out his gorgeous silks, his face close to the customer, shaking the silk and shouting. There was a cubbyhole of incense, two sticks burning and the gray smoke wavering, and there were stacks of hides and kegs of dried fish.

Saigon was built by the French with wide boulevards and sidewalk cafés, and once they boasted that it was a Paris in the East. But now with the French gone, all trace of Paris is gone, and the place is sinking back into an ordinary oriental city off the main highway of travel, lacking the profit and benefit of tourist trade. The big stores that flourished in other days are closing, for now there is no one here to buy the expensive goods, the dresses from Paris, and the perfumes from France that the Frenchwomen of Saigon used to require.

More than the stores are closing, more than these symbols are passing, and today there seems to be only a remnant and a shadow of the French. Only now and then does one see a bearded man in a dirty, rumpled suit slouched at a table at some sidewalk café, staring at the ground, drinking his cognac in gulps. Occasionally, too, one may see some other trace and reminder of the French past, a priest, perhaps, also bearded, his cassock carefully washed and white, but his sun helmet often is old and faded and stained.

The decay of the French rule in Saigon will surprise no one who knew the city in other years. Long before the breakup of France's empire in the East one knew the unreality of French rule in this far-off country. Here, more than anywhere else in Asia, one felt the failure of European colonialism. The Frenchman, trapped in the heat and miasma of this country, baffled by these little people that he didn't like, found relief in absinthe, in opium and women. I have seen brothels in Saigon as elaborate as those of Paris and filled with glittering blonde women from France, with women from other countries of Europe, and with the smaller women of the Orient. Back then, thirty years ago in the homes of Frenchmen in Saigon, I have retired along with other guests to the smoking rooms where opium pipes were offered as freely as liqueurs are served elsewhere. Decadence in the tropics always is near to the white man, and the French rule in Indo-China was a shell before the Red Chinese crushed it.

Today in Saigon, with the French rule ended, one sees more Americans than Frenchmen. The Americans are there to administer our foreign aid to Vietnam and in particular to build a road.

This road starts in Saigon and it is a superhighway. It continues for thirty-two miles and it goes nowhere. It cost the American taxpayers more than $1,000,000 a mile to build it.

Its right of way is 300 feet wide. It has a 42-foot pavement in the center. It has a 42-foot graded road on either side. The Pennsylvania Turnpike is not so elaborate.

If every automobile and truck in Vietnam were strung out on this road at the same time, they would use only a fraction of it.

The Vietnamese themselves are perplexed by the road and say that they can see only one possible use for it. It will make an excellent landing strip for the planes of the Red Chinese, whenever the Red Chinese come to attack and take over Vietnam.

"But while the road is of no possible use, either commercial or industrial, since it simply goes on off into nowhere, it still has some value to us," one Vietnamese told me. "Our workmen have long made good wages off this road, and they will continue to make good wages, for of course they will never *finish* the road. They will be slow in their work and, if necessary, they will destroy what they have done, so that they can do it all over again."

This road, along with a fertilizer plant in Korea that started out to cost $11,000,000 and already has cost $60,000,000 and still is not doing what it is supposed to do, is one of the clearer examples of the kind of efficiency that the American people are getting from the administrators of our foreign-aid program, who spend three and a half billion dollars of our money each year. With these men pouring our money into a superhighway that goes nowhere into a jungle, it might seem an obligation of the American people to challenge this bureaucracy that dominates the spending of our money and to demand an accounting of it.

It isn't so much *what* we spend, as *how* we waste it, inviting dishonest men of other countries to cheat us, and providing good reason for sensible and honorable men of these countries to laugh at us and ridicule us.

Besides seeing the construction work of the Americans in Vietnam, we traveled about and saw the rest of the country, and I sensed a quiet surrender among these people that is even more plain than the hopelessness that I had felt in South Korea. The people of Vietnam, plodding behind their buffaloes out over the countryside, and gay though they may be for the moment in Saigon, seem only to be waiting. They seem to have no doubt of what will happen to them, and their only concern is how soon before the Red Chinese will come.

In South Korea, the people have no thought of getting back what the Communists have taken from them, the half of their country to the north that is gone, taken by the might of China and held by China, and the South Koreans accept the fact that they are helpless. But they feel that so long as the United States can stay in the Orient, affording the money and maintaining the military power, they in South Korea will remain free. Of course, they have the knowledge that this cost to the United States is tremendous, and that the patience of the United States, in comparison with the patience of the Orient, is short. They are fully aware of the drain on the American budget and on the American patience, and they know that China, with her limitless concept of time, need only sit behind the line and wait. But this arrangement, temporary as it may be, unrealistic as it is, affords the South Koreans some momentary sense of security.

The Vietnamese, however, do not have even a limited hope, for there is no protection for them. They know that they have no say and no answer, and that whenever the Red Chinese decide, in the decisions of world power, to come and take the country, they will come and take it. Their planes will land, along with their troops moving south, and the weaklings among the Vietnamese will raise the Communist flag and shout their welcome, and the others will be shot.

Sometimes a light and trivial thing can catch the fancy of a people and cause one nation to become suddenly and delightfully aware of another.

One night in New York, with the orchestra playing the music of Rodgers and Hammerstein, a curtain went up on *The King and I,* and the United States sampled the charm of Siam. The king that Mr. Brynner brought alive that night had been a real king who had lived a hundred years ago, and today in Bangkok a resplendent statue of him stands high above the city. There is no accompanying statue of the fair Anna—the "I" of *The King and I*—but she still lives in the talk of the people, and they smile as they tell how she tamed the king, never suggesting anything, only imparting it and allowing him to think of it himself.

A descendant of Anna's king was ruling when I first visited Siam, back in the early 1930's, and I met him, King Prajadhipok. It was near the end of his reign and he was the last of the absolute monarchs in his country, a slender, shy little man with none of the swagger of his storied ancestor.

The king today is a young man who likes American jazz, and writes it, conducting his own orchestra in palace recitals, and favoring, so it is said, the saxophones. Anna's king, and even King Prajadhipok, these older rulers of Siam, could order whatever they pleased and it was carried out, even to the death of a man. Today the young ruler of the country with its new name of Thailand and its new democratic constitution is little more than a royal symbol and can only sign the papers that his ministers place in front of him; but he is a living memory of more resplendent times, and he still has the royal palaces and the royal boats, the royal crown and the golden sword. The Thais are a merry and festival-loving people and they like all this, enjoying the ceremonies and the resplendent pageants, and they like their young king, too; they think it delightful that their king should write jazz music.

The king lives in Bangkok. Bangkok is half land and half water, and it is the city on the water that one particularly enjoys. This part is built on a wide and sprawling river with innumerable canals—the *klongs*—and life here is almost the same as that Anna saw, except that now the houses have electric lights and the postman paddles up each morning to bring the mail.

Sometime during the morning, too, the housewives come out on the verandas of their homes to welcome the coffee man as he paddles up in his boat, taking time out from their household duties for a coffee break. And the school bus, looking like an excursion boat, cruises along and toots its little whistle, the children all hurrying out, their faces scrubbed and shining, their lunch baskets packed, their book satchels ready. The captain of the school boat watches as the children at this house hop over their banisters onto the boat, waiting until they are safely aboard, then he steers out into the current again, tooting his whistle to let the others know that he is coming. And standing back at the house from where the boat has just departed, miserable at being left but too young to go this year, is another child, naked as daybreak, a piece of bamboo tied to him to keep him afloat in case he falls off the porch.

These wooden houses, open-doored and open-windowed, are built along the edge of the *klongs* with their back ends on land and their porches extending out over the water. The women dip their kettles from their front steps into the river for their cooking water. They bathe their children in the warm and muddy canals, and go down into the water themselves still dressed, squatting modestly and washing their bodies under their clothes. Then they stand and wash their hair and wring it out, and as it hangs down their backs to dry, they wash the vegetables for dinner.

Here all business is transacted on water, and the merchants and peddlers bring their wares along the river or canals, paddling their short and narrow boats like canoes, gaily painted, and each peddler sounds a horn, or a bell, or a clapper, and each shouts a distinctive call to notify of his approach. Here comes a restaurant boat, a tiny stove of charcoal to keep the food hot and wide banana leaves to serve it on. Here is a cloth merchant, his bolts of bright cloth stacked high in his boat. Here a butcher boat, shoulders and haunches of meat piled for the housewife to see, standing on her porch and picking and choosing. Here is an ice-cream boat and a candy boat, and a boat of tin buckets and pans.

Behind the houses are small vegetable and flower gardens, and also behind each house is an outdoor toilet. There are banana groves stretching back from the water and many of the rivermen make their living by working on these banana plantations. Here, too, along the banks, grow the blazing jacarandas and poincianas, and in the air the orchids trail, swayed by the wind. On the water grow the lotus leaves, each a flat circle of green, and in the center of each sits a white flower. Now and then, from somewhere, a scattering of petals may drift by, thin shavings of old and yellowed ivory flecked upon the water.

There are warehouses beside the wide river, and there are rice mills where the boats unload their mounds of grain, and lumberyards where other boats bring the heavy timbers of teak. Beyond, stretching away across the land, is the skyline of Bangkok, jagged with its spires, its pagodas, and temples. In one of these temples reclines a Buddha so large that his big toe is bigger than my wife, and in another is a Buddha of solid gold weighing hundreds of pounds, an unimagined fortune in the humble worship of men. There is still another Buddha, the Emerald Buddha, and hanging from the rafters of its brilliant shrine are the temple bells, easy in the play of the wind, their eerie music seeming faint and far off, even when the bells are near.

We saw a high pagoda flashing its bright designs, and each flower, each arabesque, was made and fashioned with bits of broken teacups and fragments of shattered saucers. In the palace yard, beside a carved doorway, we saw a low platform, resplendent with red and gold hangings, and here the king mounts his horse; but across the way is a higher platform, and there he mounts his elephant.

All this is the colorful part of Bangkok, but there is another part, surprising perhaps, with its air-conditioned hotels and busy traffic, modern buildings going up and new streets laid out. The little country of Thailand today is a long way from old Siam, and the white elephants are not worshiped as holy in the sacred royal stables; instead, they munch their sugar cane and beg for peanuts in the city zoo. Airplanes land in Bangkok now, and Cadillacs are common; there are factories and offices and shops busy at their selling.

We found that the Thai silk, soft and lustrous, is as attractive as it is famous. Also, there is much fine silver and bronze in Thailand, and innumerable shops to sell it. But most of all we searched for, and kept searching until we found them, a set of temple bells. That music would go home with us and even on winter nights, the house closed and the fire low, we would hear, far away, the whispered tingling of these bells.

And then came the evening in Bangkok when we were to learn how completely delightful the Thai people can be. On this evening we attended a meeting of the University of Alabama Alumni Association—Bangkok chapter.

Some years ago a professor of dentistry from the University of Alabama came to Bangkok. He lived with the people, practiced their language, and learned their customs. He lectured, held clinics, and worked on their teeth from daylight until dark.

When he returned to Alabama, some of the young men of Thailand followed him. Others came later. Then their sons came, and some of these sons are in Alabama now, students in Birmingham and in Tuscaloosa. And today in Bangkok there is a chapter of the University of Alabama Alumni Association—membership fourteen.

This doctor from Alabama had written ahead that we were coming, and the doctors in Bangkok met us, took care of our baggage, took care of our tickets, and drove us into the city. They took us sight-seeing, by land and by *klong*. They showed me the university, and their wives showed my wife the shops.

On the final night of our stay the alumni chapter was convened and these men of Bangkok, all practicing dentists and some of them deans and professors, entertained at the home of the senior dean. There were drinks before dinner, and the doctors put away any bottle of Scotch and drank only bourbon out of loyalty to Alabama. We talked and remembered Alabama, and the night was warm and the breeze gentle, and now and then the small lizards, the Too-kays, who were clinging to the walls and to the ceilings over our heads, swelled up and sounded their names—"Too-kay! Too-kay!"

When it was time for dinner a beautiful girl came into the room. She was the dean's daughter, a student in high school. When we were introduced, she pressed her palms together at her breast in the customary salutation of the country, then she paid us the extra homage of bowing until the tip of her nose touched the tip of her fingers. She told her father in English that dinner was ready, and he told us.

They had shrimp and fish and meat and rice and yams. They had dishes that I did not know but that I ate because they smelled so good and were so tasty. For dessert they offered us fruit, and such variety of fruit I had never known—bananas, tangerines, papayas, mangoes, mangosteens, golden melons, and the sweet-flavored persimmons.

After dinner we talked again about Alabama, and they told about this man who had come to them. The teeth of the people are better, and their health is better, because he had come. "And they will be even better because now our students, those that we have trained, are practicing in the small towns and villages, and other students are getting ready. It all comes from him."

As I was going home that night I kept thinking about how they loved and honored this American. He hadn't tried to change them or change their thinking, and he hadn't meddled with their ways. He had just lived with them, and accepted them, and respected them, and filled their teeth.

Far ahead of us, as we flew above the low and marshy land of Burma, flying on toward Rangoon, we could see the gleam of the great pagoda, loftier than St. Paul's in London, and covered with pure gold. Shining there ahead of us in the west, it was like a sunset.

This high pagoda, the Shwe Dagon, is the landmark of Rangoon and it is a holy place, a shrine for pilgrims of the Buddhist faith. They come by the thousands to worship here, and Buddhist monks, their heads shaved, their yellow robes loose and flowing, are always at prayer at this pagoda. At many shrines in many countries a person of whatever faith must take off his shoes; but here at the Golden Pagoda the shrine is so holy that he must take off his socks also, and then he walks barefooted on stones that sizzle under the tropic sun.

Rangoon doesn't get many tourists, for Burma itself is off the course of ocean ships and there is little in the country to turn them in, and little in Rangoon to see except the magnificent pagoda. As for travel outside of Rangoon, going into the uplands of Burma, it is difficult. The way there is limited and one must travel almost entirely by air or by the river, for the roads of upland Burma are few and many of them are almost impossible to use.

There was a time when Rangoon was of more interest, with its lingering smell of sandalwood and teak, and this Burmese city then seemed the spirit of the East and all the lure of far-off places. Travelers of those days still remember its colorful sights, especially the girls walking along under their umbrellas, each umbrella hand-painted, bright with dancers and flowers and birds. And each girl, small, slender, almost fragile, would be smoking a cigar as big as a banana.

But Rangoon now has fallen into dull times, not having completely put aside its past or decided to take on the industry and the commerce of the present. It hangs between the two, and days for a tourist in Rangoon are slow.

We watched the young men playing cane ball, agile and swift with their feet, keeping the ball in the air. We heard the cry of the muezzin, sudden and high and shrill at sunset, calling Islam to prayer. We saw a ruby, a perfect thing, a drop of pigeon blood in a man's palm. We watched the Royal Dancers leaping and whirling, flipping the long trains of their skirts.

President Tito of Yugoslavia came while we were there, and his yacht with all its flags flying was anchored out in the river. Rangoon hung out rows of lanterns, and dressed its flower gardens, and whitewashed the buildings along the route of his reception. Tito had come on a trade mission, trying to build up the trade between his country and Burma. There is much competition for the trade of the East.

Our days that seemed so slow in Burma perhaps were unfair, for we had just come from Bangkok, and there is a youngness, a carefree quality about Thailand and the Thai people, that is infectious. When one leaves there he must become older again, and responsibility must come back again, and perhaps that was partly why we were restless in Burma.

It may have been, too, because we were at India's border and India was our goal. We had traveled halfway around the world to get to India, and now we could stand at our window in Rangoon and look toward the late sun and know that there, only across the Bay of Bengal, was this country that we had come to see.

India was my assignment. India was why I had come. The letter from Washington had said: "The importance of India in foreign affairs is great." Any man must know that, and I was impatient to get on to India, for in India the fate of Asia is in the balance. And in India, no matter how far away it may seem to us, the fate of the United States will be influenced.

5

The airport at Rangoon was crowded, for this was a main flight to Calcutta and there was a jam around the counter of the Indian Airlines. Most of the people were Indians going home, and my wife for the first time saw the Indian women in saris and Indian men in their loose white dress, like togas, and the bearded Sikhs with their colored turbans. This crowd was more Indian than Burmese and one noticed that the Indians were taller, and that they carried themselves erect and there was a dignity about them. One could believe that these men would grant a courtesy but would permit no liberty.

Here in this shifting crowd I noticed the difference in the color of the Indian people. I saw men and women from Bengal, the women as slender as reeds and their skin the color of a day-old lily. I saw men from the great central plains of India and their skin was dark brown, like cinnamon. And there were a few men from the southernmost parts of India as black as if they had come from the Congo, although their features were thin and sharply cut.

I realized that my wife stood near me, her eyes moving swiftly, for this was strange to her. And I understood her staring for a moment, then glancing on, her gaze flicking over the crowd. No matter how long one lives in India, or how many times he sees these people in their costumes, he never tires of looking at them or at their brilliant dress. Whenever he moves about in a crowd of Indians with their turbans, their togas, their saris, their own color from cream to black, he feels that he is in the midst of a pageant.

Our plane was a Viscount and I had watched the pilot before we came aboard, a slender man, almost frail, neat in his uniform, the insigne of Indian Airlines on his cap. Every seat in the big plane was taken and most of the passengers were Indians, although there was the usual scattering of Americans, Europeans, and Japanese.

There was a small boy of about twelve who was returning after the holidays to his school in India, his parents both Indians who lived in Rangoon, both doctors, his father a surgeon. There was an elderly Indian who sat throughout the flight with his naked feet folded in his lap, sitting straight and motionless, his expression serene. An Indian girl was returning from college in the United States and in talking with her we could see that although she was excited about getting home, she was a little disturbed by coming back, by all that she had seen and what she was leaving.

The stewardess, a girl from Bengal, wore a green sari, and her ebony hair was coiled at the back, and around the coil was placed a circle of tuberoses. She served us tea and there was a suggestion of incense as she passed, as if she were not long from the temple, and this is not unusual with Indian women.

The flight was two hours across the Bay of Bengal, the sea as blue as turquoise, and we flew into a sunset that flamed from the sea, landing at Calcutta at sundown.

The customs men saw my official papers and passed us immediately. "Welcome to India," they said. The room was crowded, people pressing against the customs counter, and others making their way toward the little banking cage to change their money, and we were going toward the exit and the waiting room when I heard a voice that I recognized and a speech that I had heard before. It was coming from a tall, big-shouldered American, a Texas hat shoved on the back of his head, and he was standing at the counter booming out his explanation of just why he was traveling with twenty-two watches.

We had first seen him on an elevator in the hotel in Tokyo, big as a fullback and wearing a ten-gallon hat. I was sure that his ranch must be wide, and he probably owned half the cattle in the county. We saw him again at Nikko, this time with his wife, and it turned out that he was no rancher at all and just liked big hats. He was a businessman from Cleveland who had decided that he wanted to go traveling, and now he and his wife were on a trip around the world, seeing everything and apparently he was trying to buy a good part of it. One of his purchases was twenty-two watches for the twenty-two boys in his Scout troop.

We had met this couple again after Japan, in Hong Kong, and now here in Calcutta. It so happens that people often come together when they travel in a particular region, and it is almost like a touch of home to see each other again. The lines of travel are rather fixed and often they cross no matter how far apart people may go on some side trip for a time.

More than once we had heard him tell the story of these watches, with new chapters added as he crossed new borders, for the customs men of the Orient just couldn't understand why any man had to have twenty-two watches. Now here in Calcutta we were hearing it all over again, and there was a certain satisfaction in hearing a burly American, with the heavy twang of the Midwest, argue with the customs officer and hang onto his watches so that twenty-two boys back home could have them, and brag about where they came from, and who brought them.

We had less than an hour at the airport in Calcutta before we were to fly on to New Delhi. This flight to New Delhi was to be four hours, and we climbed high enough to see the curve of the horizon and the sunset beyond it, while below us the earth was darkening. I watched this balance of day and night until all was dark beneath us and dark ahead of us, and only now and then did we see a light as we flew on, a village or a single light, a cabin or a boat perhaps, and I was thinking of the first time I had come to India.

Shortly before I came that first time I had been a student at Oxford University in England, and I had met Indian students there and we had played rugby and tennis against each other, and had tea together, and they had told me about their country. Some of what they said I hardly listened to, their references to independence, their protest against the Empire, their vows that someday they would live as free men in a free nation. This talk was almost lost on me, for I was an American and I was young. Freedom was something that a man was born with, did not have to work for, or to keep on earning.

These friends that I had made at Oxford received me in their homes when I went to India in 1930, but the ease and cordiality of our student days were gone and they were formal and distant. I was presented to their fathers and was received with a solemn courtesy but with a coolness and a reserve that was unmistakable. I was an American, and therefore was associated in the Indian mind with England, and nothing that had to do with England was wanted in India in 1930. Men were talking of Gandhi, of independence, and saying that they would break the might of England and take India for themselves. As an American, I was considered a part of the Anglo-Saxon alliance, associated not only with England but with English colonialism, and because of this reminder of their hated status, I was courteously received by the Indians but never accepted by them. (This old association of the United States with colonialism still hangs on in the East, partly because of our open alliances with England and France, and even more because our national interests throughout the years have been similar in many ways to those of this power bloc of European nations that so long dominated Asia. The continuing and unyielding identification of the United States with the colonial powers is one of the reasons, however unjustified, that the peoples of the Orient today resent us and mistrust us.)

The formal and distant courtesy of my Oxford associates was not my only surprise in India, for certainly I had not expected, as I traveled, that many of the Indian people would bow and even salaam as I approached. I soon caught on, though, that they were mistaking me for an Englishman, and I caught on, too, that while they gave the salute, it was often grudging and sometimes even sullen. The manner of these people of the villages and the countryside showed how they felt, for they had heard the talk of Gandhi and of independence, and they were hoping; but they weren't quite ready to believe it yet, or to show their open defiance by breaking the old customs, and they continued to bow when an Englishman appeared. After all, they had been bowing for two centuries.

But fourteen years later, in 1944, when I went back to India during the war, all semblance of bowing was gone and the Indian people were aggressively positive and determined. They no longer debated independence, their only concern was when. Nor was there any trace of a salaam. Even an American uniform now and then was squeezed toward the curb and out into the street, as Indians walked upright and abreast, taking all the sidewalk just to make sure that everybody knew that it belonged to them.

Today, however, some sixteen years later, all this petty nationalism and rudeness have disappeared, and the Indian people have achieved a national maturity and dignity, along with a personal friendliness, that may surprise a visitor to their country. Having accomplished their national purpose and gained their independence, they need no longer insist on their importance or try to show how big they are. They live now in personal self-respect and national confidence, hoping that somehow they can hold back the Communist threat from within their country and head off Russia and China from their borders.

I noticed the change in India almost as soon as I landed in Calcutta. The customs officer, tall and dark, not only had waved our baggage aside, refusing to open it, and had freely welcomed us to India, but his smile had been broad as he added: "We hope that you enjoy our country." There was pride in what he said, and his bow was one of politeness only, no suggestion of the old salaam, only the warm and friendly greeting of one man speaking on completely equal terms with another.

All about me I saw this change—the customs officer, the Indian stewardess, the Indian pilot, the Indian guards—and as I flew on across India, I knew that I was coming into a new nation. My responsibilities to the State Department seemed even more complex and more difficult, and I could not be certain of how I would meet them, and I was worried as we approached New Delhi.

The city lay like a giant pinwheel of colored lights under our plane as we circled for our landing, and I had not known that Delhi had grown so large. An officer from USIS was there to meet us, bringing us a folder of mail from home. It was sharp cold as we walked to our automobile, and I shivered in the cotton suit that I had been wearing in Rangoon that afternoon.

Maiden's Hotel is one of the old hotels of Delhi, and the drive from the airport was long. We passed through the new part of the city and I could see the size of the buildings and the width of the streets, and even at night I was aware of this *New* Delhi that they have built. It was strange to me, this modern city, and I wondered about these physical changes, as well as all the other changes, in India.

But then, after a while, we came into Old Delhi and I eased back and was at home again. This was the India that I had known. Huddled men were sleeping in the parks and along the sidewalks, all of them wearing thin cotton garments and most of them without any cover, and the temperature was in the forties. I saw a camel drift up out of the dark and then go back again. I saw a cow standing in the light of a small shop, and she had a garland of flowers around her neck. "Welcome to India," I told my wife, pointing at the garland; but already I was suspecting that there are two Indias now, the new one that I had glimpsed of the tall buildings, and the other one that I had known before, the bedecked cow.

The next morning my wife and I reported to the United States

Embassy Health Department, as we had been told to do, and we were warned about foods and about dysentery, and we were given pills to put in our drinking water. I reported to the finance office, where my vouchers and my pay records were checked, and to the travel officer who gave me my tickets and my schedule. I was to go first to Bombay, beginning my assignment in India in that city.

Later that same morning an officer of USIS told me of their work in India and also outlined their plans for me, letting me know what jobs they had assigned to me.

In the afternoon I visited the political officers at the embassy and they discussed political and economic conditions in India. They had a good deal to say about the United States and India, about Russia and China and India.

That evening there was a dinner at the home of an officer from USIS, and the next morning, before daybreak, we left for Bombay.

Bombay is a gay city, a cosmopolitan city, the production center of the Indian moving-picture industry, a city of theaters, of parks and playgrounds, tennis courts and cricket fields. Lying curved around a harbor and stretching back from the sea, it is a clutter of spires and domes, of Victorian government buildings and modern business houses, a mixture of West and East. The streets are a mixture, too, a bright blending of oriental costumes and colors, along with the staid attire of businessmen and officials, all severely tailored in the British tradition.

Here in this delightful city are garden plots at street crossings, or in a midstreet, or wherever the flowers might seem to be pretty. There are fountains, and one turns a corner and sees the high and sparkling play of the water under the brilliant sun. The streets are crowded and the shops are busy, and one feels the hurry of the city; yet always, so it seems, the people have full time to enjoy themselves, for a dozen cricket matches are going on each day, the teahouses usually are filled, and there are no seats left for an evening performance at the theaters.

Besides what is going on, Bombay itself is a place of endless interest and one is always looking and he never tires of seeing. Here, in the crisscross of the streets, are all the peoples of India come to this city to visit and to shop, and one who knows the costumes of the people can say, "There is a woman from the Punjab, there a man from Mysore...." It is such a show that keeps a man watching as he walks, turning his head, and later keeps him at his window.

We stayed at the Taj Mahal Hotel, a famous place in India, a meeting place of famous men where Indian history has been written, and our windows opened on the Arabian Sea. Near to us, and off to one side, was the towering arch, the Gateway to India, through which visiting kings and viceroys have entered the country; and now, symbolically, it is open to all and any man can walk through. Beneath our windows was the wide street by the sea, with the people constantly passing. Now and then some man would stop and stand by the sea wall, gazing out, and one night a man stopped and played his flute, so softly that we could hardly hear it, and perhaps he was playing to the sea, and perhaps to his own longing.

Whenever it was time for us to go somewhere and we stepped outside this hotel, we walked into turmoil, for always hovering near, waiting for someone to appear, are snake charmers, barbers, chiropodists, masseurs, readers of horoscopes, vendors of ivory and jewels, woodcarvings and Kashmir shawls. They swarm like bees, clustering close, and they flash the gleam of their jewels, fling out their shawls, snip the scissors with which they cut hair, and hold up the scissors with which they cut corns and bunions—and always in the background the snake charmer squats, squeaking his shrill flute, uncovering his basket, and punching and jabbing his cobra to make him rise and spread his hood.

They followed us close each time we came out, pressed about

us, jockeying with each other and pushing for closer positions, and our "No!" meant nothing to them. "Kashmir shawls," they droned. "Shawls, Kashmir shawls." "Ivory! Ivory!" "Feet, sahib! Fix feet."

For days at our every appearance they swarmed, until I finally managed to convince them that we were interested in neither ivory nor jewels, that our hair had been cut, our corns trimmed, and that we did not care to see a mongoose kill a snake.

But there was one that we could not pass, one who had adopted us and was the special guardian of my wife. He was a taxi driver, a Jew from Damascus who had come to Bombay some twenty-seven years ago, and he was always on hand whenever we came out. Whenever I was off lecturing at some college, or away at a meeting, Joseph David, white haired, tall in his dignity, followed my wife in and out of shops, carried her parcels, and stood near whenever she stopped to look into a window.

He was my chaperon, too, and took me to the police station where I was required to register, as all foreigners are. He also took me on another official mission, for Bombay has prohibition and it is against the law for the people of the city to buy whisky or any other liquor, or to have it in their homes. But the government will issue a permit, after a formal application, to a tourist and this permit allows him "to possess, consume, use, and buy liquor for personal consumption." It also allows him to enter the "Permit Room" at any of the large hotels where there is always a shining bar and brisk bartenders, and a police guard at the door to examine his papers and his permit before he can have a drink.

Most of the people of Bombay are Hindus, but here, too, are the Parsees. These people are descended from ancient Persians who, more than three hundred years ago, settled in Bombay.

The Parsee women are some of the most beautiful women on earth, with fair complexion and deep black hair, their graceful saris often bordered with gold. The men are successful in business and industry, and some of the most wealthy of all men are Parsees. They are followers of the Prophet Zoroaster and their religion teaches them that benevolence is the beginning of worship, and they give so freely that Bombay's standard of living and the advanced social conditions in the city are in part owing to the Parsees.

Their religion also teaches them never to bury or to burn their dead. One must be benevolent, even with his body, and must give it for food. When a Parsee dies, the body is put out in a convenient place for the vultures to come and eat it.

High on Malabar Hill, above the rest of the city of Bombay, are stone towers, tall and circular. They stand in a huge garden that covers the hilltop, and palm trees rise from the beds of brilliant flowers. All is silent here. All is still.

The towers are open at the top, and inside each tower is a sloping circle of uncovered metal gratings, each grating shaped like a basket to receive a human body. Below this top circle is another, and then another, descending like an amphitheater, and always the gratings becoming smaller in size.

Around the tops of the towers stand the vultures, the huge birds watching, picking at their feathers, and waiting. These are the Towers of Silence.

A body of a Parsee, a woman, a man, a child, is brought to one of the towers and is accompanied by the men of the family and by a few of the closest friends. These relatives and friends go as far as a certain gate, and there they turn back and the body is given over to the workmen. These workmen take the body inside the tower, close the gate, and carry their burden toward the top. They judge its length and select a grating of proper size. They place the body in the open grating, strip it, and turn away.

Then immediately there is the swoop of the wide wings and the thick swarming, and for a few moments the rims of the towers are bare. But this is soon over, and then the vultures are on their perch again, watching again, looking toward the bottom of the hill and waiting.

What goes on here no man shall see, and even the airplanes are routed in and out of Bombay in such a way that no one can look down into the Towers of Silence when the vultures are swarming.

One night in Bombay we had dinner with a young businessman and his wife, Parsees, and after dinner he drove us to the high ridge around the harbor with its anchored ships at their slow riding, and we saw the far curve of the city and the sweep of its lights. I was riding with him in front, and his wife and my wife were in the back, and he told us that many of the younger men and women want to stop this practice of giving their bodies to the vultures. There is a growing protest against the practice and one Parsee of great wealth has offered to build a crematory and pay for it entirely himself.

"But it is the old men and the priests who shake their heads," our friend told us. "They want no change. The priests are shrewd and the old men are afraid." He said that his children might be freed from the custom, but that he and his wife probably would be taken to the towers. His wife shuddered as he spoke.

We were driving along the ridge, looking out across the harbor and at the lighted city beyond, when we came to a crossroads and he hesitated for an instant, then turned away, going in a new direction.

His wife leaned over quickly and touched him. "You aren't going there? Not tonight?"

He didn't answer. He drove swiftly along the ridge, and then curved on up Malabar Hill to the top, turning through a gateway. It was black and I could see only the shape of the trees, and then the outline of the towers, tall and circular. He drove past them slowly, and none of us spoke.

He made the circle of the hill, then came out of the gateway and turned down toward the city and toward our hotel, and we had little to say. We told them good-by, and we thanked them for the evening, and I didn't know then, and I don't know now, why he took us to the hill and the towers.

The Indian universities are fashioned, as one would expect, after the universities of England, and just as the colleges of Oxford University are scattered over that city, so the colleges of Bombay University are scattered over Bombay, some of them miles apart. During the two weeks that I was in Bombay I taught and lectured at eight of these colleges, usually talking to students on literary subjects, and to college officials and faculties on the organization and operation of an American university. Occasionally, though, students asked for special subjects, and one of the most popular was "The Relationship Between Professors and Students at American Universities." Here again, as in Korea, students at these Indian universities wanted to know all that they could find out about the United States. Our country is the mecca of the dreams of students all over the world, and it is a perplexing thing that the United States does not make better use of this.

In Bombay there were meetings with editors and with reporters of the newspapers of the city and of the area. There was a talk to the Bombay Rotary Club, a very large club, filling one of the dining halls at the Taj Mahal Hotel. There were talks to literary groups and societies, and meetings with authors and moving-picture producers. There were speeches to industrialists and public-relations men, to the Indo-Pan American Association and to the Asiatic Society. There was a daily program of luncheons, teas, or dinners, and sometimes all three in one day. Bombay is one of those places where the United States Information Service keeps its visitors busy, and I believe that most Specialists prefer it so, for there is so much to learn from meeting with these men of other countries, businessmen, government officials, editors, authors, college presidents, teachers, and students.

All of my time was not spent in Bombay itself. I was sent out to cities and towns within the area of the Bombay USIS office, and one of the more interesting of these places was Aurangabad, to which I traveled by automobile, stopping at various cities along the way.

Aurangabad is scarcely more than a large village northeast of Bombay, but near here are the famous caves of Ellora and Ajanta, and people come here from over the world to see these caves with their carvings and paintings. In Aurangabad is a hotel as comfortable and pleasant as one could imagine, and at the end of the day a guest can sit on the veranda in the cool air of the coming evening and look at the flower garden that is spread before him, and see the mountains dimming far away, the massive blue outlines of the Western Ghats of India, and wonder if he ever wants to leave.

The Duke of Edinburgh was there when I was there, and a lady whom I shall remember. She was pretty and so neat and attractive in her simple dress. She was an American, and I knew this at a glance. She was having her luncheon alone and that night she dined alone, and the next noon again. That evening I came in with a garland of flowers and a bouquet, given to me at my lecture, and she was sitting in the lobby. When I came downstairs again, she spoke to me. I must have been making a lecture. Where? At which of the colleges? How long had I been in India?

It seemed to me that I had seldom met a lady so completely charming, so considerate. We talked on, and I told her of many of the things that I was doing. I told her that it was difficult to face Indian audiences, for one felt especial obligations before them, and he often came away with a sense of failure, a belief that he had not talked well about his subject, or managed to bring in clarifying references or comments about the United States. Again, but more rarely, there might be a feeling almost of triumph, the idea that he had said something and they had heard it, and that maybe now they knew more about the United States and understood us better, and the distrust was less.

I was telling this lady, who had a way of starting talk and winning confidences, practically everything about myself and then I realized that the talk had been all about me, about what I was doing in India, where I worked back in the United States, and what my job was. I had been thoughtless, almost rude, and trying to make amends I said: "And your husband? What does he do for a living?"

The lady seemed almost to blush. "My husband," she said, "is John D. Rockefeller III. He is upstairs with a head cold."

I learned later that Mr. Rockefeller was in India to confer with his associates, Americans who are stationed in India, kept there by the Rockefeller Foundation, and he was to decide with them how best to use the millions of dollars that the Rockefellers are giving to help the people of India.

At this hotel in Aurangabad the upper walls of the dining room are open and the doors are open, and the sparrows and all the little birds fly in. Sometimes one of them will perch on the electric fan in the ceiling, and the people at the table below will look up and cringe. Then one of the bearers will go to a corner and turn on the fan and make the bird fly. But he holds on and rides as long as he can, his wings beating and fluttering before the whirl of the fan becomes too fast for him and he slides off.

Sometimes the birds come flying in and dip suddenly to the edge of the table, standing there and looking around, waiting for crumbs. One morning at breakfast I was called to the telephone and when I came back into the dining room my plate was a flurry of scrambled eggs. As I got nearer, the flurry increased, and then they all flew away, each beak dripping scrambled eggs. There was one bird, however, perched on the edge of my water glass who was in less of a hurry than the others, and he finished his drink, tilting over low to get it.

Besides this trip to Aurangabad by automobile, some of my trips in the Bombay area were made by train, and one night I was to go to Ahmedabad, a city in the north. Shortly before the train was to leave, an Indian gentleman came into the compartment, my companion for the night, and we introduced ourselves and spoke sparingly for a while, making merely polite and incidental comments; but as the train traveled on, fast and smooth on its good roadbed, we drifted into more serious talk. The train left Bombay at nine o'clock, and we talked until past two, trading information about our countries.

He told me that the caste system, now taboo and frowned on in India, had not been completely broken but that changes had come about which could not have been imagined ten years ago. He said that he himself was a Brahmin, but that now he would sit down and eat with a man of a lower caste. His mother would drink coffee brought to her by a person of lower caste, even though that person had actually touched the cup. His grandfather would eat food over which the shadow of an Untouchable had passed. And his cousin, who long has been married to a woman of a lower caste, and of course had always slept with her, has now begun to eat with her, sitting at the same table with her and even using the same dishes.

He told me, though, that caste still plays its part in weddings and is a requirement for many marriages. He called my attention to the "Matrimonial" column in the want-ad section of that day's newspaper.

WANTED: Parents seek gentleman to marry fair, pretty, and accomplished virgin. Age 20. Sound health. Cash Rs. 2,000. Jewels Rs. 2,000. Only Madhva Brahmins need reply. Give particulars and horoscope. Box 673.

WANTED: Non Srivastava girl for handsome Vadama Brahmin man, age 30. Income, Rs. 1,000 month. Prospects excellent. Virgin or virgin-widow preferred. Give particulars and horoscope. (Also suitable match for his sister, age 24.) Box 521.

My companion on the train was a businessman, and he told me that he was less concerned with caste in its religious and social implications than in its persistent effect on labor. He told me of a

Brahmin who was starving. He had no work, was untrained for any work, and his inherited income had disappeared. A friend offered him a job at a living pay, but a part of his job would be to sweep a room. He said no. To sweep was the birth stigma of a lower caste. His father had never swept, nor would he. So he sat in his dignity and his rags and he died. The other old Brahmins followed him to the funeral pyre and they spoke of him as a tragic hero.

"I don't think that he was a hero. I think that he was a damn fool," the younger Brahmin said. "But he is a part of one of the industrial burdens of India. What a man is born to, he must do. What is beneath his birth is degrading and shameful. If I, for instance, were to pick up a broom at my house and my wife saw me, she would snatch it from my hands. Our servants would be horrified."

He suggested that this caste handicap would increase India's difficulty in meeting one of the country's major needs, which is the creating of small industries and small businesses where everyone, including the owner, works with his hands. When I suggested preparation for this work through schools of vocational training, such as turn out so many skilled workmen in the United States, he said that such schools would be long and slow in India, and at present would be impossible.

I asked the same question of a young man in his second year in college. His father will soon be fifty-five, required retirement age for government employees in India, and his income would then be so reduced that he could not go on sending his son to college. I mentioned to the young man that he lived in a town where many tourists visit. Why didn't he make Indian toys and sell them? Why didn't he make the kind of furniture that tourists buy? He drew back from me, red faced and indignant. "How could I? I am a Brahmin." Instead, he would quit college. "What will you do?" I asked. He didn't know.

This matter of high-caste men refusing to work with their hands seems to be an enduring part of India's labor problem, and another enduring difficulty is getting men to change any of the work methods that were used by their fathers and their grandfathers. At the Taj Mahal Hotel in Bombay, a large and almost luxurious hotel, the corridors are of marble and they are wide. Each morning one man comes along, sloshing water out of a bucket. Behind him comes another man, a rag on the floor stretched between his spraddled feet, and, balanced on it, he waddles along—sliding one foot forward, then the other, zigzagging the rag over the floor and drying a part of the water. Behind him comes another waddler. Then another. And all it needed in the first place was one man and a mop. At this same hotel it took five men to clean our bedroom and bath each morning, and my fuming wife vowed that she could do it in an hour.

My companion and I kept talking as the train headed on through the night toward Ahmedabad. He was concerned about all factors in the commercial and industrial future of India, but above all else he was worried about this lack of small businesses, the gap between a textile mill and a spinning wheel, between a steel mill and a grindstone.

We talked on until it was late, and then he was asking me about industry and business in my country. How could we in America build and maintain such a massive economy? He wanted to know about the big companies and the small businesses, and he hoped someday to come to the United States to see them.

I was in Bombay on January 20, and everybody was busy getting ready for something. Men were climbing over the big government buildings and other men were working on private buildings. They were lashing bamboo poles together, making scaffolds that rose up the face of the buildings, and then they were climbing around on these scaffolds, stringing wires and putting up lights.

People stopped on the street corners and looked up, and I asked some of them what was going on. They stared at me. Didn't

I know? January 26 was Republic Day! January 26, 1950, was the day when the Indian nation became a sovereign democratic republic.

As I heard these people speak, their heads high, their pride plain to see, all the talk at Oxford came back again, the young men boasting that someday their nation would be independent. The memory of Gandhi came clear, too, the slight little man sitting down in the path of Empire and remaking a world. January 26. A Republic! A free India. And now they were getting ready to acclaim that freedom.

It came to me, as I watched these men at work, and saw these people on the street corners, that a strange thing has happened in India. When I first was here, they were bitter against England. Later I saw the country when it was determined to shove England out. But today there is a feeling almost of warmth, certainly of honor, for these Englishmen who had come to India and ruled with a hard hand, but had laid the foundation on which the Indians themselves now are building.

The law and the courts are English. The universities and the schools are English. The cricket fields are English. The tradition of fair play and decency in the dealings between men, they are English. A stern parent has left the house but his training continues, and he is respected and copied by those he has left. (In the time that I was in India I was to hear only one Indian speak of England with resentment, and even he indicated respect. England's rule in the East is ended, her authority and military power gone, but her word is remembered as firm, her position fixed, and by sheer character she still holds the esteem of men and retains influence in the Orient. There is a curious conflict between the difference in this continuing regard for England, who took so much for herself but whose policies were made clear and held steadfast, with the present disregard and even disrespect for the United States who has given so liberally, has frequently been willing to adapt her position, and has been lenient almost to the point of softness.)

The preparations in Bombay continued, the scaffolds rising, and the wires were strung so that the lights traced each building; every window, every door, every gable was outlined in lights—saffron and white and green. At early dark, two nights before the official night, all these lights were turned on and each building became a giant jeweled charm and the city itself was a fairy place. Late that afternoon the people had begun pouring into the city; by the thousands and the hundreds of thousands they came from the small towns, from the villages, the mud huts and straw shacks of the countryside, to see the lights and celebrate their Republic, and they packed the streets and moved slowly before the buildings lighted in the colors of their flag.

The first night my wife and I sat at our window and looked down at the street by the sea, and at the lighted Gateway of India, and there was a solid mass of people wherever we looked; there was no man, no woman, no child, only this mass of people. Packed in among them, locked in, were automobiles, bullock carts, and double-decker buses, all moving like the slowest river, and sometimes the mass was still, halted by something, standing solid and fixed.

Almost everyone had a horn, but there was no distinguishing of sounds, either of the horns or of the shouting, and the roar rose complete and unbroken. It began before dark and there was no faltering or lessening until past three o'clock the next morning. To sleep in the hotel, to sleep anywhere in downtown Bombay, was impossible. But none of us wanted to sleep, we wanted to stand at the window and look down and see these people and hear them cry their freedom. Patriotism can be a shoddy thing on the lips of some men, but here was a nation shouting in its own dedication.

This unwavering celebration continued for four nights. Buses brought the children in from the countryside to see the lighted buildings and to hear of something that now was theirs. Men and women came into the city, walking, riding their horses, driving bullock carts, moving in the flow of the people, raising their hands and joining in the multitude of sound.

"This is wonderful," an Indian lady told us as she stood in our room looking down. "But you should have been here on the first day of our independence, when their flag came down and our flag went up and the bugles were sounding, and we yelled and shouted until we all were sobbing."

Our time was coming toward a close in Bombay, and we were unhappy about leaving. Whatever else might be ahead for us in India, we knew Bombay now, and we liked this pretty city and its people. We had been entertained in their homes, and they had taken us on interesting trips. One Sunday some of our Indian friends had taken us out on a boat through the long waterway that curves through the harbor, winding among the many islands that are heavy with palms, and we had gone on out to the island of Elephanta and the celebrated Temple Caves.

Here are carved, cut from solid rock, whole rooms and high passageways, all filled with giant statues of Brahma and Siva and Vishnu, the Trinity of the Hindu gods, carved in this rock more than a thousand years ago. Here at times the gods are fierce with swords upraised and skulls at their feet. Again they are meditating, seated with folded legs upon lotus leaves. In one room Lord Siva is dancing with his wife, Parvati, and Siva, even in stone, has a look upon his face that is a good deal less than divine as he cuts his eyes and gazes on this pretty woman. In all the books about India no one has fully told about India's sly sense of humor, even in matters concerning the gods.

Up in the north of India there is another statue of Siva and Parvati, this one on their wedding day, Parvati standing with head slightly bowed in proper modesty during the ceremony. Then one notices that she has one big toe lapped over the toe next to it, as any barefooted girl, so pleased with herself, might stand at the moment that she is marrying so great a god and so wonderful a man.

Another reason for our wanting to stay in Bombay was that our room at the Taj Mahal Hotel had become a meeting place for so many enjoyable people. There were students from the colleges, professors, businessmen, an official now and then, and mostly newspapermen. We gave up trying to get much sleep, even after Republic Day, and we just sat and talked.

One afternoon we were talking with three young newspapermen, each of whom had been to the United States, and I asked them what had impressesd them most about the United States.

One spoke of television, not because he had become interested in the shows themselves, for he thought they were often cruel and often pointless; but he couldn't get over the American people living at such a standard that almost every American home has a television, and sometimes a home has more than one.

Another of these young men was most impressed by the kitchens in our American homes. He had never imagined so many mechanical devices, and while he could not bring home electric ovens and dishwashers, he did bring his mother a carrot and potato peeler, a swinging can opener that fastened to the wall, a whirling egg beater, and a frame of wires for cutting French-fried potatoes. He said that he showed his mother how to use all these things and that she practiced until she was good at it, and then she gave a party for her friends and demonstrated.

The third young man said that his greatest interest in the United States was in learning that the American people went to church. He had believed that Americans were always so busy at work, building up their business, that they didn't have time to go to church. He knew that Americans gave money to build churches, but he didn't think that they went to them.

On our last evening in Bombay I was to make a talk at the American consulate, and we left the hotel early so that we could go leisurely on our last trip through the city. It would not be easy to leave all that we had come to like so much; even the crowd in front of the hotel had become companions, and we were lonely as we saw the man with the Kashmir shawls and the little man with his black satchel, ready to trim a corn or ease a bunion. There was almost melody in the squeak of the snake charmer's reed, and the tired old cobra, slowly waving, seemed to be telling us good-by.

We took the long way round and followed the drive by the sea where it bends so close that sometimes the waves, smashing against the rocks, shower a passing car. We drove slowly through the shifting traffic of barefooted people and bullock carts until we came to the gateway of the consulate, and there we turned in and drove on through the garden to the house that once had been a maharajah's palace. Behind the house is the sweep of a wide lawn down to the beach and the sea. It is called "Lincoln House."

We were to have tea, and we stood on the terrace, the breeze easy, ruffling the water, and cool off the sea. We chatted with our friends, Hindus, Parsees, a few Americans, and we were introduced to people that we had not met before. I had not expected such a group, men in government, members of state councils, two former Indian ambassadors to the United States. It would be difficult to talk to so cosmopolitan a group.

But they were gracious and attentive as we sat in the large lecture room, the garden at one side and the sea at the other, and I talked about "American Politics and the Political Outlook in the United States." I sensed that this audience knew the history of the United States, the plan of our government, and that they had considerable understanding of us as a nation. So I talked quite incidentally about the form of our government, its plan and rules, and tried, instead, to say what I believe are the principles that we Americans would like to live by, and the extent of our success in doing so.

When I had finished talking, a general discussion began quickly, with questions and comments about our government. Finally, though, the talk turned away from the United States alone, and we began to discuss the position of the United States and its associations in Asia. Someone asked about the American people and their knowledge of conditions in the East. Do the *people* of the United States know what is going on in Asia, and know its significance to them? Do they know of Russia's plans in Asia, in Africa, in South America? Do they know of China's plans? Have the American people been informed, by their government, of their dangers?

The questions were asked carefully, with full respect for the privacy and the dignity of another nation; but these men, experienced in international dealings, were asking just how much the American government is letting the American people know that the United States is disliked and distrusted, that our position is deteriorating in the world, and that we are now looked on as a declining power.

After the meeting, several of us were standing in a group talking, and some of the men near me led the conversation back to Russia and China. They had visited Russia and China recently and they had seen the giant mills and factories, the huge dams and laboratories where Russian scientists are engaged in research and development of missiles, in the use of hydroelectric power, of aviation, medicine. They kept talking about these factories and dams and laboratories, their bigness and power, as if they were trying to tell me what is happening in Russia and China.

One of these men and I walked off toward the sea, and he kept on talking about Russia and China, and then he stopped and abruptly said that his regard for the United States was second only to his regard for India, his esteem of the American people and their success was unlimited, but that the world was being lost because the American people refused to recognize the possibility of their defeat. "You think of defeat only in war, and you have always won your wars, and therefore you think that you can win again. But Russia does not plan to go to war," he said. "Russia will defeat you in other ways and already, slowly and shrewdly, she is taking the world away from you. It is such a tragedy that you will not admit what is happening to you."

I looked at him. "Do you actually believe that Russia can defeat the United States?"

"Russia *is* defeating the United States." He held out his hand toward me. "And yet you ask if you *can* be defeated. This is the tragedy of your country. You cannot conceive of yourself as a conquered people."

I was watching him closely. "Do you really believe that Russia can take over the United States? Do you believe that the United States one day might be a satellite of Russia?"

"I have no doubt of it," he said.

We talked for as long as we could politely stay outside, and then we walked back to the house slowly, and went in and joined the others.

6

The airport at Belgaum, a small town some three hundred miles south of Bombay, is only a landing field of red clay, and as the plane taxies it blows back a fog of red dust and leaves it hanging. There is nothing there except one tree off to one side, and the day that we landed a group of Indians were huddled under the tree, and they gaped at the plane and watched us as we came off it.

An old lady got off with us and she spoke in Dutch to the man who greeted her, embracing him and patting his arm, smiling up at him. My wife was to go on to a larger city to wait for me, but she looked around at this lonely place and there was no one there to meet me, and she suggested that I come on with her. We were standing there, obviously worried, when the Dutchman came to us and asked, speaking in good English, if there was anything that he could do for us. I told him that I had stopped here on my way to another town where there is a university, and they were supposed to have sent someone to meet me. He said that he would take me from the airfield into the town of Belgaum, where there was a telephone, and I could call and find out what had happened.

The Dutchman waited with me while we watched the plane take off, my wife on it, and we waited for a while longer, thinking that perhaps a car would come for me; but finally we gave up and decided to drive on into Belgaum. He told me that he was the manager of a small furnace nearby, and that his mother-in-law had come back from a holiday in Holland. We put my baggage in his station wagon and he let me ride up in front with him while his mother-in-law, a gracious old lady who understood no English at all, sat behind us, smiling and gently nodding approval of all that we said.

The road was as dusty as only a road in India can be, and the high-wheeled bullock carts were coming on toward us, the big horns of the bullocks swaying and their slow, soggy hoofs puffing the white dust. Monkeys sat in the road, scratching their red-lacquered posteriors and nibbling fleas until the last moment before our car was on them; then they leaped for the branches, swarming up until they darted out on a limb and squatted, screeching and gibbering, their long tails hanging down.

The Dutchman was telling me about the furnace that he managed. It was low-grade ore, he said, but he made it pay and he had been here, in this southern part of India, for seven years and he planned to stay in India for the rest of his life. He liked India and he liked the Indian people, although he had had some trouble at first in teaching the workmen the technical processes at the furnace, and a little difficulty because some of them had not been given the right jobs for their caste. But he had taken care of all that and, once they had caught on, they were good workmen and he paid good wages and he had no labor troubles of any kind.

They were careful and steady workers, he said, and it was a mistake to think that Indians, who for so many centuries had been farmers and petty craftsmen, or artisans working with precious metals, could not learn the rougher work in a factory or a furnace. They didn't have the flair for mechanical work that some Europeans and most Americans have; but then they hadn't lived with mechanical toys from childhood, or been brought up with mechanical devices in their homes, their schools, everywhere they went. Some of them were grown men before they even saw some of the machines that are commonplace to a European or an American boy, and that he tinkers with, and pulls apart and repairs. Some Indians even die without knowing that such machines exist.

The Dutchman's furnace was a small one, but a small furnace is like a big one, except in degree, and since the Indians could learn to work with him, and turn out a good and profitable product, they could learn on a bigger scale in the bigger furnaces that are being built and planned in various parts of India. He believed that they can develop mechanical abilities that will enable India to take her place among the industrial nations, a place that she is trying so hard to win. The change will be slow, but India already has accomplished wonders since independence, and she may be able to bring about an even greater result and shift from an almost entirely agricultural people into a nation of balanced agriculture and industry.

Time, however, is India's problem, and whether there will be time for her to develop her industries and stabilize her economy is the worry of the Indian people. There are pressures from within the country, food, health, the terrible pressure of the population, and the destructive pressure of the Communists. And from outside there is the pressure of Russia and China at the borders. Whether there will be time for India to save herself no man can say.

We drove on into Belgaum, and the Dutchman—he never told me his name—took me to the post office and we booked a call to the university, telling the operator that we wanted it "express," so that it would go through ahead of ordinary calls. But he told us that we need not pay the extra fee, for he had no calls of any kind, and we booked it at the ordinary rate and it came through quicker than we had expected, only ten minutes from this town forty miles away. The registrar said that he had sent the university car hours ago, but that I should go to the hotel and wait, and he would arrange for another.

My Dutch friend would not stop off at the hotel, either for a rest or a drink, saying that his mother-in-law was tired and that he had better take her on home. He was slow in saying good-by, finding excuses and lingering, and I guessed that, for all his wanting to stay in India, this man so far from home may have been lonely in the little Indian town.

There was a small porch at the hotel and I waited there. Some of the trees were covered with flame-colored flowers and the flower plots in the yard were a blending of bright colors. Everywhere in India there is color, and the flowers are a part of it, especially the beds of marigolds that bloom everywhere, and the mustard plants that yellow the whole countryside—this color, sometimes yellow, sometimes orange in the light, is more the color of India than any other. And the smell of flowers is a part of the smell of India as much as the smell of incense, and more than the dry smell of dust and the low, hovering smell of old cow dung.

Flowers are a constant part of all life in India. They decorate the ear of a pony, or drape the statue of a god, or circle the hair of a girl. There is a custom here in India that after a speaker has been introduced and has stood, the chairman hangs a garland of flowers about his neck and hands him a bouquet. One bows and then puts the bouquet on the table, takes off the garland and lays it down by the bouquet. Afterward he carries his flowers home with him, and sometimes, as I would be walking along the street of some big Indian city, or entering the lobby of a large hotel, I would wonder just how an American with a garland over his arm and a bouquet in his hand might feel if he walked along the streets of New York or Chicago, for instance. The first time I received the flowers we put the bouquet in water and hung the garland on the bedpost; but the smell was too sweet, the tuberoses drenching the air, and in the middle of the night I had to get up and put them outside.

Along some main street, or on some side street, but always in every Indian town, in front of a home perhaps, or beside a temple, one can see the garland makers, threading the many-colored flowers and interlacing them with leaves and bits of tinsel, making them ready for offerings of love, or esteem, or worship. Each garland and each bouquet always is wrapped in lotus leaves, the leaves kept wet and tied with sewing thread, their moisture keeping the flowers fresh.

There were more than flowers for company that morning as I sat on the porch of the hotel and waited. There were birds and there was a squirrel, striped like a chipmunk, who would hang on a tree, head down, and call in tones as soft and sweet as a flute far off, or he could blast as loud as a trumpet in the still Indian countryside.

Sometime past noon a car came for me and we left the hotel and traveled out through farming country. Some fifteen miles out we passed the university car, standing at the side of the road, jacked up and one wheel gone. The heat was dry and baking and the light, even through my dark glasses, burned my eyes.

My coming down south here to Belgaum, and now going on to Karnatak University, was my entry into a new USIS division in India. There are four of these divisions, with headquarters in Bombay, Madras, Calcutta, and New Delhi. I had now left the Bombay area and was coming under the direction of Madras.

In case someone might imagine that four divisions in one country is a possible waste, it should be mentioned that there are 400,000,000 people in India and we are trying to get in touch with them. The budget of the United States Information Service in India is $2,500,000.

Russia spends more than $2,500,000 for books alone in India. Russia sends books by the unknown thousands into the country, and some of the most beautiful books for children that I have ever seen are books from Russia for the children of India, only a touch of Communist teaching here and there, sly, almost hidden, but always there. And they sell these books for one cent, two cents, although each of them costs a good deal more than that to print. The Russians would be willing to give the books away, but they are too shrewd for that and they always charge just a little.

They are wiser than we are in this, for they never *give* anything; they always let a man pay something and keep his pride.

These books that the Russians send in are only an incidental part of what they are doing to win the minds and the support of the Indian people. Russian men and women, perfect in the Indian languages, perfect in Indian history, customs, traditions, religions, taboos, come to India and live among the Indian people. These are the elite of the Communist corps, the dedicated, the devout, the determined, and they whisper to a few or they speak aloud to a group, but always they teach the Communist faith and they lead the people to it. Here is the strength of Communism far more than its missiles. Here is the taking of the world, slowly at its massed base of mankind, through this new religion and the devotion of its followers, the force that is not yet recognized and certainly not yet admitted by the West.

Besides the many individual Communists living and endlessly working in India, Russia is continually sending group missions into the country. Almost any day one can pick up an Indian newspaper and see that another Russian trade commission, another Russian cultural committee, another Russian good-will mission, has arrived in the country and will tour India, meeting the Indian people and bringing the respect and friendship, the loyalty and good will, of the people of Russia. They have come to offer peace and prosperity, and the hope of the joining of the Indian and the Russian people for their mutual good, and for the good of all men.

I was to stay for four days at Karnatak University, and this was my first visit to an Indian university where I lived on the campus and was a part of the university. These visits were among my most enjoyable times in India, and I lectured to the student body and to the faculty, taught in the departments of literature and of journalism, and spent so much time in just ordinary talk with the students.

At Indian universities I was always put up at a guesthouse and always there was the most genuine hospitality, the warmest reception for a visiting American. Some members of the faculty at each of these institutions would have taken degrees at American universities, usually a doctor of philosophy, and I was surprised at the number of Indian professors who have studied in the United States. At one university in India I was the guest of the local "American Club," all its members graduates of American universities, and the talk that day was of Harvard and Princeton, Columbia and Chicago.

In dealing with Indian students I had no need for an interpreter, and I found a great advantage in a common language. There are 845 languages and dialects in India, but the one language that is spoken almost everywhere is English. During the centuries that the English controlled India they taught the English language in every school, a compulsory study. They made a command of English a necessity for getting a government job, they carried on official business in English, and a man to better himself or gain prestige had to learn the language. Today many an Indian speaks such English that he might have lived and gone to school in England. This common language with the peoples of India gives the United States one clear advantage over the Russians and the Chinese, if we would exploit it.

The Indian students, like students everywhere, have an endless desire to learn about the United States, our customs, our beliefs, our business, our literature, our sports—they want to know it all. They come early before lectures and they stay afterward. I have had students on my veranda before I was out of bed, and they have sat with me through breakfast. I have spent whole days at Indian universities and never been alone except when I went to the bathroom. They want to know *everything* about the United States.

Karnatak University, one of the really great universities of southern India, with an extensive curriculum and a staff of distinguished professors, is in the town of Dharwar. Besides my inevitable interest in the university, in the students and in my association with the professors, I came to enjoy the little town itself.

Dharwar is like most of the small towns of India, a single road running through the center of it, a crossing of smaller streets, most of them unpaved, and then, at the back, a twisting of narrow lanes and alleys with a constant shifting of people, of carts and meandering cows, the heat and the rising dust. Along the central road are the shops, standing on both sides and built close together, filled with carpets and cloth, with sandals and brass, with anklets and bangles and beads. The shopkeepers sit in front, their legs folded, sometimes drowsy, sometimes talking with each other, but always with an eye on the people who pass, watching for anyone who might hesitate.

At the edge of the town is the roadside market spread out in the open, and here the women come with their baskets of melons and bundles of sugar cane balanced on their heads, their slim bodies straight as poles, their hips at an even swing. Other women bring trays of steaming rice and vegetables, and they lay out palm leaves on the ground as service tables, and they uncover trays of candies and sweetmeats.

Each early evening I would go for a walk in this town of Dharwar, and the shopkeepers came to know me and would nod as I went by, and one evening a lady whose sales had been slow that day and her stock was still piled beside her gave me a stalk of sugar cane. When I offered to pay for it, she told me in a language that I did not know but that I could understand that I was their guest in Dharwar.

At one of the woodcarvers' stalls I watched a boy of about fourteen work beside his father, and when the boy had finished the teakwood figure of a girl dancing, her arms upraised and her skirt aswirl, I bought it, and it was worth more than the money to see the boy's pride in his success, and see the old father's pride, too.

It was on a Sunday that I went for a special walk, about seven o'clock, and I passed the shops and spoke to my friends and went on to the small hotel for a meeting of the Dharwar Rotary Club. I was to be the speaker that evening. This speaking at Rotary Clubs was becoming a pleasant habit, for by now I had spoken at a number of them, and I was beginning fully to appreciate the meaning of Rotary *International* as I had been introduced to Rotarian Wong, Rotarian Nu, and Rotarian Ganjigatti.

The members of the club in Dharwar were professors from the university, doctors, lawyers, businessmen, bankers, and merchants. The membership was twenty-eight. We stood in the little lobby of the hotel, standing under the ceiling fan, and talked until it was time to go in and sit at the tables. They were arranged so that they formed a **U**, and the president banged a bell.

We were to have tea, which is the custom instead of luncheon in Dharwar, and we ate the little spiced dishes that were unknown to me and the sweet cakes coated with sugar and nuts. The men at the table where I sat would tell me what I was eating, and now and then some other man farther away would hold up his sugared cake or his teacup and nod and smile.

The club bulletin was distributed; in it were notices and dates of birthdays of members. There were also some old bulletins lying around, one from back in October, and in it was this announcement: "Deepavali, that Indian festival of festivals, the Festival of Lights, knocks hard at our door, and we take this opportunity to wish all our brethren a merry Deepavali and a Prosperous New Year. May the millions and millions of lamps which will be lit over the land on this festive occasion illumine our hearts and minds."

We finished our tea and pushed our cups aside and the bearers came and took them away. The business of the club was completed and a professor from the university introduced me. This was in February, near to Lincoln's Birthday, and USIS all over the world was calling attention to Lincoln. I was to speak on "Abraham Lincoln and His Place in the American Democracy," and I told them about him as best I could. I told not only about Springfield and the lanky, plodding lawyer, and the man with the big hands and the ax, but I tried to tell them what he had said and what it meant—"Of the people, by the people...." I wanted to tell not only what it had meant then, but what it means now.

They listened, now and then nodding in agreement, and occasionally someone openly spoke his approval. They were easy to talk to and when I finished and sat down, they all began talking quickly. They were having their say about Lincoln, praising him, for he is better known to the Indians than any other American. George Washington is little more than a name to them, Thomas Jefferson is in the thinking of the Indian historians and political philosophers, but Abraham Lincoln is a part of their humanity.

In the midst of this friendly talk a man asked about the United States having any dealings with Pakistan, and there was a sudden tension in the room, for Pakistan is looked on by the Indians as their enemy and they resent our having an alliance with Pakistan. There were quick and almost angry questions about it, but quieter men soon prevailed and the tension eased.

Once more we were talking in a general way, back and forth across the table, discussing India and the United States, and the relationship of the two countries, when a tall man at one side of the room rose and pushed his ash tray from in front of him and said that there was a question that he would like to ask. "We cannot understand," he said. "You come to us and you are open in your manner, without pretense or guile, and you talk about Abraham Lincoln and the democracy in your country. But all the world knows that there is no democracy in your country."

He held up his hand, halting me quickly as I stood to reply. "We know that there is no equality among men in the United States. And there can be no equality so long as one man is barred from one privilege that is open to another. The United States says that it offers friendship to India, to Burma, to Japan, to all Asia. But we are men of color, and in your country there is no friendship for men of color, for Negroes. No matter what you say, the truth is that you segregate your men of color. How can there be friendship between your country and mine? How can there be trust between the men of Asia and your United States?"

We in the United States look on segregation as a domestic issue, as something that belongs to us and does not concern the rest of the world, but the question that I was asked that night in Dharwar, I was asked again and again throughout the time I was in the East. Wherever I was speaking, at a university, to a meeting of newspaper editors, to businessmen, wherever it might be, somebody was certain to raise the question of segregation. What kind of relationship was this between white men and men of color in the United States? Why was a man's color a bar to a full place in the American democracy? How could the United States call itself a democracy?

These questions were asked not only at lectures and formal gatherings, but they came up at dinner parties, on trains, in the waiting rooms of airports. I had no idea where they would be asked next, but I could be certain that they would come. How can the United States call itself a democracy?

I was in a small town in northern India, and after a late-afternoon meeting I had gone wandering about the curving streets, stopping to watch an old man sew a satin slipper, watching the hands of a potter shape the rising clay on his wheel, or standing near the coppersmiths and the din of their hammers, and sometime after dark I realized that I was lost. I did not know how to get to my hotel and of course there were no street signs. People were going and coming, walking on the sidewalks and in the streets, and I stood on the corner and called out, asking if anybody spoke English. Three men came to me, and I explained my predicament.

One of them hesitated, looking at me, and then he said, "You're an American, aren't you?"

And when I told him that I was, he asked quickly: "What about segregation?"

I started answering his question, and soon there was a crowd, people standing on the corner and in the street of the little town, listening and asking questions about segregation.

One morning I was on an elevator, on my way to visit a representative of a textile mill, and a stranger in the elevator asked if I wasn't an American. He got off ahead of his stop, and on my floor he drew me to one side in the hall, and he said: "Tell me about Little Rock. Do they really treat those Negro children like that? Do they shout at them and embarrass them and humiliate them?"

My wife and I were having dinner in a home in Bombay. The living room was large, the library filled with books, and the curved veranda faced the sea. Our hosts were Hindus and there were a number of Parsees among the guests. Our hostess wore a green sari and a flower in her hair, and after dinner she managed to talk to my wife alone. "I have always wanted to go to the United States," she said. "I would like to go now, but I am afraid to go. Would I be treated like a Negro?"

The Indian newspapers constantly report anything concerning segregation in the United States. A lawsuit having to do with schools is started in Georgia one day, and it is reported on the front page of the Indian newspapers the next. The Supreme Court hands down a decision concerning the relationship between white men and men of color, any decision whatsoever concerning this relationship, and it is immediately reported in the Indian press. The story of Little Rock was told day by day in the Indian newspapers, with pictures and all the details, and Indians today know more about Little Rock, and are more interested in Little Rock than in New York, Chicago, or anywhere else in the United States.

We can depend on it that Russia knows this, too, and that she will use it to her steady advantage. In Indian cities Russia has large display centers, always in the heart of the city and on the main street. On the plate-glass windows of these centers there are pasted posters of laughing Russian girls driving tractors over fields of rich earth. They show Russian boys and girls, healthy and strong, running and playing games at Youth Day demonstrations. There are pictures of Russian students entering the huge buildings at Russian universities, at work inside the classrooms, at work in the laboratories that are filled with the very latest scientific equipment.

Alongside these posters, and sometimes mixed in with them, will be headlines from American newspapers, the type blown up so large that it can be read from across the street, telling of Negro children denied admittance to a school in Alabama, telling of Negro men denied admittance to a restaurant in Delaware. And always at these Russian display centers there are life-sized photographs of Little Rock. They show men with bloody heads, and Negro children surrounded by police guards, and white girls moving along before the lowered bayonets of United States troops. The Russians make no comment except for the one label—"Little Rock." They don't have to comment. The Indians stand on the sidewalk, filling the sidewalk, and they stare at the pictures.

I was in Bombay when one of the clubs, an old club that had been founded long ago by the English, was mentioned in a newspaper as still maintaining its color bar, holding its membership to Europeans and Americans and permitting no Indians to join. This fact was mentioned in the paper one day. The next morning every Russian in Bombay who was a member of this club was waiting at the door to resign. *Russians* would tolerate no distinction of color. *Russians* have respect for all men. There is no segregation in *Russia*.

This is what the Russians said, and this is what the Indian newspapers reported, and the Russians pasted the stories on the windows of their display centers. They also started the whisper that no Americans had resigned from the club. Americans, they said, are accustomed to a color bar, and at many places in the United States men of color are kept outside. But Russia, they said, is a friend to men of all colors. Russia wants only to live in peace and good will with all men.

No matter how it may sound to us, no matter how much deceit and how many lies are packed into it, we might try taking a look at it from the point of view of an Indian, himself a man of color, standing on the sidewalk and reading about how the Russians had supported him at the club, how the Russians are friends of all men. Sometimes what men are led to believe can be more powerful than all the facts that are unknown to them.

Dr. Alonzo G. Moron is president of Hampton Institute, at Hampton, Virginia, and we were in India at the same time. It happened one night that we were asked to be on the same program, and the astonishment of the Indian audience was something to watch as they beheld a white American and a Negro American forget about it and act like two Americans. They were even more surprised, after the inevitable question of segregation had come up, when he and I had about the same answers.

This wasn't the way most of the Indian people believed it was supposed to be, that a white man and a man of color from the United States could meet with respect and regard and get along in friendship and agreement. This surprise of the Indians may be difficult for many Americans to understand. It will be equally difficult for these same Americans to understand just how much, in some parts of the world, Little Rock has blotted out the United States.

A few decades ago Little Rock and all that it stands for might hardly have been noticed in the Orient, but the racial changes in the East have been swift and emphatic since the reigning days of Victoria and the rule of the British swagger stick. The inevitable weight of justice has borne heavily on the back of Empire and has broken it, and the old colonial powers have been sent home.

Then, too, the Japanese added a refinement that has not yet been accorded its full significance by our spokesmen in Washington. The Japanese failed when they shifted from their slow plan of taking Asia to their impatient attempt at destroying us at Pearl Harbor, but they managed to accomplish one of their purposes. They were sick to death of being called "little yellow men," and they intended to end the tradition of white superiority in the Orient.

This they fully accomplished. The white man laid down his burden in Asia when he picked up a shovelful of dirt, a prisoner of war, while Japanese sergeants and corporals gave him commands, and staring crowds of Asiatics from Singapore to Corregidor looked on with a strange stirring within them, and with the one certainty that they would never forget what they had seen.

The total change in Eastern thinking is indicated by a remark of Vice-Chancellor D. C. Pavate of Karnatak University, himself a graduate of Cambridge University in England, who said: "Colonialism is discredited if not yet fully disintegrated; and the White Man's Burden is fast slipping from once superior shoulders."

Reciprocal respect among nations and basic equality among men have now become so prominent in oriental thinking that the frictions of segregation in the United States leave these men of the East puzzled and distrustful. The United States, they say, is the acknowledged leader of the free nations, and also of those nations that are struggling to become free. What, then, are these things that we read in the newspapers? Explain these lawsuits, these troops, these policemen, these bloody heads.

These questions were asked me in India, in Afghanistan, in Pakistan, throughout the East. Whether I was lecturing on American poetry or American politics, segregation was brought into the meeting. I answered the questions as fully and as honestly as I could, dodging nothing, but nothing that I said seemed to satisfy them, and they kept on asking why some men in the United States have privileges that are denied other men.

I admitted that segregation is a flaw in our country, but I showed that changes are coming about, and I reminded them that perfection is not man's quality, and that improvement is his peak. But they weren't interested in improvement, and they kept on talking about what is now.

Sometimes in exasperation I would bring up their caste system. I know that it is foolish and a sign of weakness to defend by accusing, and the man who accuses, often in fluster and anger, obviously admits that he has no defense and is only on the run. Nor does a man ever cure his own illness by pointing out a sickness in another, and nobody ever got to heaven on the sins of somebody else; but these Indians can be so lofty and so self-righteous, when it suits them, and they can be so downright irritating when they are, that occasionally I turned on them and asked them about their own treatment of the Untouchables. I pointed out that no matter what they claim about things clearing up for the Untouchables, the upper-caste Indians still keep men in social and economic compartments, shut off as born inferiors.

But my questions did not affect them in the slightest, or seem even to concern them. The Indian, when he wants to, can simply retire into another world, which to us is one of complete unreality, but where he is at ease, untroubled by logic. In this mystical and convenient nirvana they merely brushed off my references to their caste system, and with surprise that I had even mentioned it. *They* are not the leader. *They* are not the symbol and the standard of democracy. India is an old country, but a young republic, and nobody looks to *India* as an example of democracy.

The world looks to the United States, and it is the United States and the democracy of America that are being compared with Russia and World Communism.

The colored peoples of the world hear reports of lawsuits and contention between white men and men of color in the United States.

But they hear reports that in Russia there is equal treatment for all men, and equal respect.

Many Indians, and other men of the East, know that these reports out of Russia are untrue and that there is no equality between the people and the rulers of Russia, but the basis of the Russian inequality is not color.

What, then, these men of color in the Orient ask, do you expect us to do? Which side do you expect us to prefer? Where will our loyalties be?

We are going where there is the possibility that we may be respected as men, and where there is a chance of equal treatment. Nothing that the United States can say, nothing that she can give us, or offer to buy from us, can make us forget that men of color in the United States are treated as inferior men.

Expressions of good will by the United States are only words, but more than these words is a fact that is clear to us, and clear to all Asia, and this fact is that a man's color is a bar to a full place in the American democracy.

7

Saying good-by at Dharwar and leaving friends at the university was not easy. I had been there only a few days but on the final day, when I spoke to the student body, I had that same feeling of parting that makes a university commencement almost a solemn thing. Some of these young men and women had told me their dreams, the books that they would write, the poems that they had already written, their hopes of coming to the United States, and we were slow as we walked away from the auditorium that final day. But I had to go on, for there was a tea at the dean's house, and the faculty were there. It was a large gathering, and we talked about their university, about books and authors; but mostly we talked about India and the United States, and now and then Russia and China were mentioned.

I spent that evening with some professors and students, and then early the next morning I was driven back across country to Belgaum again and to the red-clay landing field with its one tree off to one side. USIS was sending me on to the city of Bangalore, still another three hundred miles farther south, and my wife was waiting for me there.

Bangalore has a pleasant climate and people go there on holidays, and I found it a gay and delightful place. Its parks and driveways are beautiful, its streets wide and clean, and one goes to sleep each night and wakes again each morning to the same merry sound.

In most Indian cities there are small horse carts—called *tongas* and various other names—but in Bangalore there are carts such as one never saw before. They are two-wheeled and the body looks like Grandmother's old turtleback trunk with both ends knocked out. The open-end trunk sits on the bed of a cart, tilted slightly backward. There are no seats inside, only the floor, and the driver sits up in front, his legs tucked under him or dangling over, and his passengers, or the merchandise, or whatever it is that he is carrying, is packed in behind. It is still a wonder how so many people can get into one of these little carts, and sometimes when the driver has made his delivery and the cart is unloading, a person remembers the midgets spouting out of the fire engine at the circus.

The hood that covers each cart is wondrously decorated—green with pink birds, blue with yellow birds, painted any color at all so long as it is bright with birds and flowers, animals and jungle scenes, or whatever happened to be in the mind and the fancy of the artist on the morning he decorated that particular cart. But more fascinating than the carts themselves are the little horses that draw them. They are no larger than ponies and sometimes, as the cart fills, as more and more people crawl in, the shafts lift and teeter so high that one believes that they will lift the little horse off the ground.

But when all are in, and the last person is settled and packed into place, the driver cracks his whip and sounds the cry that one hears constantly in Bangalore—"Hup! Hup!" And away goes the horse, running fast, his colored pompons bobbing and the flowers wreathed about his neck floating back. But no matter how swift the pat of his feet, how rapid the tap on the pavement, the driver forever whirls his whip in its sharp and harmless crack and shouts, "Hup! Hup!" It was an infectious call, and my wife and I soon were using it whenever one of us was slow or was getting on late for an appointment—"Hup! Hup!"

The cry of the drivers and the quick tattoo of the horse's feet are the sounds that one goes to sleep by and that he wakes up to each morning, getting up and going to the window to look out, and there are the beds of flowers plotted bright among the grass, and everywhere the loose scattering of leaves over the lawn. Beyond, past the garden, is the street, and there the gay little carts are going by. Now and then a grumbling bullock cart strains past, the high-curved horns of the bullock painted red and blue and striped with yellow, a cluster of flowers at his ear. And over there, near the hedge, an old and withered cow noses at the garbage.

Even this early in the morning, shut off in a room that is like a Western room, with chairs and beds and bathroom like the West, one can still feel the ancient flow of this land and the endless surge of its people. It is difficult for one to comprehend this country, for here is the jumble of little things like the hurrying carts and the slow, swaying horns that are painted, and the worshiped cow at the garbage. And more than this, above all this, is the steady puzzle of these men and their ideas. In India mysticism is commonplace and wonder is usual.

In Bangalore I was to give another talk about Abraham Lincoln, this time to a learned society, and it was to be on Lincoln's Birthday. There were only a few chairs in the hall and most of the members of the society sat on the floor; the others, with their wives, sat on benches outside, listening over the loudspeaker. This society was a group of older men, noted scholars, and through the years they have chosen those leaders whose lives they respect and whose philosophies they believe in, and the pictures of these men hang about the walls—Mahatma Gandhi, Rabindranath Tagore. On this night their picture of Abraham Lincoln had been taken down from its usual place on the wall, and now it stood at the front of the room on an easel, facing the audience, and about the picture hung a garland of flowers.

The president of the society, white-haired and in the white dress of India, introduced me and talked for a while about Lincoln. The odor of tuberoses was in the air, and women in silken saris were listening to him, and long before he had finished telling of Lincoln and the eternal truths of men, I knew that there was nothing that I could say and I wished that we could all go home.

Bangalore is the capital of the state of Mysore and the state buildings are large and impressive, with extensive lawns and gardens about them. The buildings inside are wide in their corridors and high in their ceilings, and one gets the feeling that Mysore retains a trace of the old resplendent India, when the maharajas ruled in all their fabulous wealth.

There is another suggestion of this glittering past—the distinctive headdress of the men of Mysore. It is a turban, high, white, with golden bands woven in and out. I saw this headdress in a most impressive setting on the day that I made another speech in Bangalore, this one to the Bangalore Bar Association.

The meeting was to be held in a brick building in the compound of the district court, and the lawyers received me at the door. I have seldom seen a group of such distinguished-looking men, most of them wearing the high white-and-gold turban, some of them dressed in long, tight-fitting black coats that hung to their knees, and some in short morning coats and striped trousers. Most of them wore the white neckpiece, stiffly starched, of the English barrister.

The president introduced me to the members of the committee, and they welcomed me, then showed me along a corridor to the library. It was a large room with a high ceiling and shelves of old books bound in calfskin rose from the floor and up toward the ceiling. At the back of the room several lawyers were consulting the books as we came in; but they glanced up, and quickly returned the volumes to their places. The chairs, in rows across the room, were filled, and other men were standing in the passageways. As the president and I entered the room, some of the men bowed and several of them came forward and shook hands, bidding me welcome. I was quickly aware of their courtesy and of their poise. I followed the president to the front of the room, the men in the passage making way for us and nodding to me as we went by.

The air was still and hot, and the lawyers sat almost motionless as I spoke, some of them leaning forward, and only now and then did a man shift in his chair or finger his neckpiece, smoothing it. Occasionally in a moment of quiet there sounded the quick pat of the running horses, or the slow bang and sway of a bullock's bell. Two shafts of light, as sharply lined as ingots, slanted into the room, and where they touched the turbans, the golden bands seemed to blaze. I did my best in telling them about my country, its government, its economy, its faith in itself—and I made it plain that *itself* is its people—and when I had finished, the applause was quick. I had not known how hot the room was or how I was sweating.

They asked about the authority of the President and where and how his authority is limited. They wanted to know about the political parties and what issues divide them. Some were interested in the powers of the national government and of the states, and how that difference is delineated. They inquired about the esteem of the American people for the Supreme Court. They were poised, urbane, and I felt the pressure of their dignity and formality. I had visited English courts in England where this reserve and insistent courtesy were the manner of the courts, and I felt almost as if I were again in some high tribunal where all was precisely correct but distant and rigid. They were showing me every courtesy that a group of gentlemen could accord another, but there was no slight letting down of the strictly impersonal and formal relationship between us.

There was a pause—and I heard the cry of a driver—and then a man rose. He wanted permission to ask a question that had been troubling him and troubling all of them. He stepped slightly into the passageway and the others turned toward him, as if they knew what the question was to be, and this question was what they had come for and had been waiting for. There was a complete stillness in the room, and then he said: "I would like to ask about the United States and world peace." He waited, and there was no sound and no one moved, except that the man himself touched his neckpiece, his fingers sliding over it, and he looked steadily at me. "You have said that the United States wants peace in the world, but we find this hard to believe. The United States wants war in Asia. You are trying to start a war between India and Pakistan. Why do you want war? Why does your country send arms to Pakistan?"

The silence hung poised for an instant, as tense as a quivering blade, and then it shattered and a dozen men leaped to their feet and were shouting, red faced, shaking their fists, lashing their fingers. Some of them stood for a minute, shouted, and sat down, then leaped up and shouted again. Some cupped their hands and yelled. I moved back, drawing away from them, completely startled by this change in their manner. They paid no attention to me, except to shake their fists and shout that the United States was trying to start a war between India and Pakistan. Why did we want war in Asia? War! Warmongers!

I had been warned that I would be asked the question about the United States sending arms to Pakistan, and that I was to expect it at any time; but I had not expected it in such violence, and I stood looking at these men in almost disbelief of what I heard and saw. I had been told that the emotions in the issue were deep, and I had seen a touch of this at the Rotary Club in Dharwar, but certainly I was unprepared for the display by the lawyers in Bangalore.

The tension between India and Pakistan and the flare of anger in this room were a part of an old and continuing hatred between old and persistent enemies. For hundreds of years in India, Hindus and Mohammedans have hated each other and fought each other. England made her customary use of this and balanced it, faction against faction. During the two centuries that the Englishman ruled India he played the Hindu against the Moslem, the Moslem against the Hindu, and he kept himself as the third man and the deciding vote.

But in 1947, and with the Englishman getting out, the Moslems refused to remain in a country that would be overwhelmingly Hindu. They demanded a country of their own.

How wise the whole plan was, and what part was played by old hatreds and new ambitions, by arrogance and tempers, no one should say; although some men now feel that the demands on both sides were too fast and too defiant, and that the spokesmen became entrapped in their own schemes. Some men believe that if time had been given a chance for its cooling, the split of the country would never have come about and India today would still be united.

Whatever may have been, however, is behind us, and the fact is that, in 1947, India was partitioned. A part of the land remained India, and that part today is Hindu. A part of the land was cut off, sliced off at each of the upper corners, and that now is Pakistan and Moslem. The partition of the country was made solely on religious differences.

At the time of this division, when Hindus and Moslems were traveling from one country to another, each trying to get to the country of his religion, they murdered each other by the unknown thousands. They killed whole trainloads, for a train filled with Hindus would be stopped just before it could get out of Pakistan, and Moslems would go aboard and kill every man, every woman, every child, and then they would send the train on across the border loaded with dead Hindus, only the engineer left alive.

That night, or the next day, another train, this one filled with Moslems, would be trying to get across the Indian border; but it would be stopped, and Hindus would swarm through the train killing every man, woman, and child, and then they would send it on into Pakistan, balancing the debt with a load of dead Moslems.

During this time, when India and Pakistan were rioting, a man's religion could be his death warrant, when all that the mob wanted to find out was how he worshiped. Moslems circumcise.

Hindus don't. A man pleading for his life would show his uncircumcised penis to the Hindus and go free. If he held back, his pants would be snatched open, the circumcision bared, and the Hindus would cut his throat. The Mohammedans likewise exposed a man, and let him live if he had been circumcised and killed him if he hadn't.

The full extent of this hate between Hindus and Moslems was shown in 1948 when a *Hindu* shot and killed Mahatma Gandhi. Gandhi was a Hindu, but he had spoken out for tolerance and a sensible relationship between the people of the two religions.

The old bitterness still exists, still is nursed by the Hindus of India and the Moslems of Pakistan, and they live today in suspicion and steady hatred of each other.

This is the background for the question that was asked me that day by the lawyers of Bangalore. The same question is asked repeatedly throughout India, and always with anger against the United States. Why does the United States send arms to Pakistan?

The answer, of course, is that Pakistan is a military ally of the United States and we send arms to Pakistan because our government believes that these arms will strengthen our position in the world. Whether or not this is true is open to debate; but there is no debate about our right to send these arms, if it is our decision to do so.

But India will not accept this answer. Pakistan is their enemy, they say, and any strengthening of Pakistan is a threat to India. The United States, by sending arms to Pakistan, for whatever purpose or whatever reason, infuriates the Indian people.

The Indian accusation that we want war between Pakistan and India, that we are trying to start a war in Asia, is of course total nonsense. But these people are not interested in reason, for the ancient hatreds of religions are concerned, and they argue from their emotions and not from facts.

Also, their demagogues have found an issue that is profitable to them, and following the pattern of demagogues everywhere, doing anything to get notice for themselves, and sacrificing anything to get votes, they continually wave the bloody shirt of Pakistan. Finding it popular to attack the United States, and to play on the Indian distrust of the United States, they have taken up the cry and accuse us of aiding and abetting India's enemy.

Knowing so well that I would encounter this antagonistic question about Pakistan, I was ready to answer it; but the men in Bangalore who asked the question were not waiting for an answer, and they went on with their shouting, loud and angry. I listened for as long as I thought that I should; then I held up my hand and quieted them until I could tell them that I was surprised at such discourtesy in India. I told them that I would answer any question from any one of them, one at a time, but I would not accept disrespect for myself or disregard for my country.

They quieted, but they were muttering and were still red faced, and they wiped their faces. Some of them put their heads together and talked, and these talked with others, and then they called the name of one of their members, an older man.

He stood and he spoke for twenty-two minutes. He spoke patiently, and a part of his talk concerned Pakistan, and a part concerned Kashmir. He was interested, too, in the treatment of men of color in the United States. Then again he came back to Pakistan, but again he turned away from this, and he considered the United States and her relationship with Russia and China, and how well she was understanding and fulfilling her responsibilities in the world.

He told of how the United States has become the leader of the democracies. Since the end of England's power we have been left as the paramount nation among the Western nations, and the fate of the West lies with us, and he questioned the quality of the leadership by the United States. He could not determine what our plan of today was or what was our policy for tomorrow. It seemed to him that the United States was living for the solution of each moment's problem, hurrying from crisis to crisis, seemingly bewildered by Russia and strangely unaware of China's might. He said: "Free men and the free world want to believe that they can stay free. And I ask you, what faith, what confidence can we have in the world leadership of the United States?"

8

My assignment for USIS had become familiar to me, for it was pretty much the same in every city, and by now I knew the groups that I would be expected to speak to and the subjects that I was most likely to speak on. But when the Cultural Affairs Officer in Madras gave me my schedule for that city, I saw listed a group that I had never seen before. It was the Tamil Society, and I was to attend a meeting of this society.

There are many languages and dialects in India, usually centered in some city or region, and the Tamil Society is for the perpetuation of the Tamil language, which is the language of the city of Madras—and let not anyone, in any way whatsoever, take this language business lightly in the city of Madras!

The meeting of the Tamil Society that I was to attend was to be held late one afternoon, and I climbed the stairs to the small veranda, uncovered but shaded by the trees, and at one side of the veranda the reception committee stood in formal line to receive its guests and offer them the usual courtesies of the society.

First, scented oil was poured into the palms of my hands, to rub on my hands and make them soft and sweet-smelling. Then I held out my palms again, cupped together, and rose petals taken from a silver bowl were sprinkled into them. I was given a cluster of clear sugar candy, rock candy, and I put it in my mouth and sucked it until it was soft enough to crunch it.

These little customs are the treasured things of the Orient—a potted plant, a garland, a girl with palms together, her head bowed, and now rose petals and sweet-smelling oil.

Beyond the veranda and the receiving line the doorway was open wide and it led to a meeting room that was large and airy. Around the walls were only a few chairs, and in the center of the room were no chairs at all, only a scattering of rugs on the floor. At one end of the room the chairman and the seven speakers sat on a platform behind a long table, and in the warm air of the room the odor of the garlands waiting on the table was sweet. I sat between the president of the society and the mayor of Madras, and I told the mayor how much I was enjoying this beautiful city and my visit here.

Madras is not only busy in its trade, a center of commerce in South India, but it is a center of learning, of art and Indian culture. As my wife and I had gone about India, people had told us to wait until we got to Madras. There, they would say, is one of the prettiest cities of all India. It is a long and narrow city, stretching eight miles by the sea, built back from the water and housed under the shade of its palm trees. The people who live in Madras are smaller and darker than the people of northern India, and they are gentle in their manner and gracious in receiving their visitors. The sand of the beach is white and clean, wide and slow-curving for the full stretch of the eight miles, and there is a drive, the Marina, that follows the bend of the sea. On the land side bougainvillaea is piled on the garden walls, spilling over, hanging low and purple and crimson.

In Madras are automobiles, a few trucks, swarms of bicycles, and long, flat carts that are moved by men. These carts are seen everywhere on the streets of Madras, loaded past any belief that men could budge them, piled with timbers, sacks of rice, iron pipes. In front, bending under the heavy pulling ropes, are men; and behind are men who push, sometimes lowering themselves almost level with the ground as they strain. These men are as black as ebony and they wear only a white turban wrapped high on their heads and a small white sack in front, no larger than a man's hand, and tied with a single string. Their bodies gleam as they strain and sweat, their back muscles rippling, and when they stand and walk, tall and slender, they move with the grace of panthers.

The mayor and I talked about his city and now and then he mentioned its beauty, and occasionally he boasted of the accomplishments of his people, telling me especially of the fine cloth, the cottons and silks woven in Madras that for so long have been known by the name of the city. We kept on talking as we looked down at the members of the society seated on the floor, waiting for the program to begin.

They sat with their naked feet folded in their laps, and as is the habit of many Indians, they rubbed their feet and pushed and played with their toes. On the floor beside most of these gentlemen sat a small betel box, of polished silver or bright brass, and placed within easy reach. From time to time, throughout the meeting, each man would open his box and mix the lime and the betel nut, then fold this mixture into a fresh and crisp betel leaf, and place the little package in his mouth. Sucking and chewing, he would sit there looking up and listening, sometimes becoming so interested that the blood-red juice would ooze from the corners of his mouth and slide down unnoticed until it beaded crimson on his chin. Then he would wipe it away, first with the palm of his hand and then with the back of his hand, and afterward he would dry his hand on his naked feet, rubbing off the juice, and go on playing with his toes.

The University of Madras is one of the largest in India, its standards of scholarship severe, and it is a gathering place for older men of learning. I had heard of these scholars of Madras, and that their interests ranged so far and were so varied that one of them had just completed a translation of the poems of Walt Whitman into the Tamil language. This accomplishment merited a celebration, and a time had been set for a day that I was to be in the city, and now this was the reception being given by the Tamil Society.

We sat in the meeting room, this late afternoon, and the speakers, one after the other, told of Whitman and read from his poems. Sometimes they spoke in Tamil and sometimes in English, and after several of them had spoken in English, and I had heard their mystical interpretation of Whitman's poetry, I came to understand why he is the best known of the American poets in India.

Some time before, back in Bombay, an Indian friend had told me: "You talk with an Indian and he seems like any other man, even like you or like all men from the West, but cut his skin, not deep, barely enough to break the skin, and you will come upon a complete mystic. All Indians are mystics, and understanding between you and me can, at times, be difficult."

As they talked that afternoon, telling of their ideas of Whitman, I realized that they had scarcely any concern at all with the Whitman that we know best, neither the young man writing of the rivers and of the workmen of America nor the old poet sitting back and watching democracy busy at its tasks. Instead, the Indians see in Whitman a fellow mystic and this quality—"the far-darting beams of the spirit," "the fables eluding the known"—excites them and they find meanings that old Walt himself may, or may not, have intended. That night in Madras I heard such talk of Walt Whitman, so hinged in Indian mysticism that it was completely over my head. When time came for me to speak, and the garland was about my neck and the bouquet in my hand, I figured that I had better play it safe and stay away from his poetry, so I told them about Brooklyn where he had lived.

One of the speakers that afternoon had said that he would use English, out of consideration for me, since I was not blessed with an understanding of the Tamil language. "I regret," he said, "that I must use this other tongue, for there is nothing more pleasing than when the sweet breath of Tamil blows through the room."

This, I thought, even for a crowd of poets, philosophers, and mystics, was a little high flown; but I was to find out that this matter of language in Madras and in all the Tamil-speaking region can be a very touchy subject.

Back in 1947, at the time of India's independence from England, the country was a jigsaw puzzle of nine major provinces and six hundred princely states. Some of these states were larger than Oklahoma, and some of them literally were a few acres. Somebody had to make a nation out of them. So the government appointed a group of organizers, and after long study they decided that there was no way to deal with the old provinces and the princely states. They would just do away with them, abolishing all the old boundaries inside India and starting over, making new states and putting them on a clean map.

And now they hit their snag. What would be the basis for the division? Geography? Population? Economy? They debated and they quarreled, and finally they agreed that all these forces would be taken into account, but that the main factor in the division of the country would be language. Wherever a language was spoken by a large number of people and over a wide area, that area would be made into a state. This they did, reducing the former hodgepodge of little Indian governments into a workable union of fourteen states.

But then the real trouble started, for the people who had been left out were indignant; the language of their fathers had been slighted and they themselves insulted. There were dissatisfaction and grumbling in many parts of India, but the Tamil-speaking people of Madras were furious. The full extent of this fury I learned one day when I went to the radio station in Madras to make a broadcast.

This broadcasting was a regular thing for me, and the government-owned and government-controlled All India Radio—AIR—gave me an invitation in each city I visited to record a talk about American government, literature, newspapers, or something concerning the United States. There is a national law in India that all radio speeches must be paid for, and at each talk the Indian Government gave me a check for $10.00—and promptly took back

$4.80 in income tax. What was left I always gave to the station director for a charity.

On the day I went to the AIR station in Madras I saw a whirling crowd in the courtyard and parading out in the street in front of the building. Some of these people were marching and shouting, and some of them were carrying banners written in a language that I could not read. In the center of this jam was a cot, and on the cot lay a man not much more than a skeleton. Friends stood over him, looking down, now and then waving off a fly.

The column of marchers paused each time they approached the cot, lifting their banners, shaking them and yelling, and then again starting off on the slow plodding of their circle. I went over a little closer. The man's eyes were closed and his chest was only a bone frame that slowly rose and fell. One learns not to be too inquisitive in India, and I started away; but a man jumped in front of me, shoved his sweating face into mine, and shouted, but it was in a language that I couldn't understand and I went on.

Inside the AIR building I asked some questions and I found out that the Indian Government, when it had been making up the states, not only had ignored the Tamil language, but that at a later time it had designated another regional language, Hindi, as the national language for all India. What's more, the government was now using a Hindi word in its daily announcements, the word originating in New Delhi but piped into Madras to defile the air of this Tamil-speaking region. They were bootlegging a Hindi word into Tamil territory and these Tamil-speaking folks just weren't putting up with it. If the government wanted to use a Hindi word in New Delhi, that was their business; but that word had better be a Tamil word by the time it got to Madras.

They sent up a formal protest, and the government ignored it. They sent it up again, but the Hindi word kept coming in. So the leader of the Tamil speakers brought his cot and laid it down in front of the All India Radio building, and he laid himself down on it. He would lie there and die, starve to death, unless they quit sending in that Hindi word.

English, these Tamil speakers could endure; but Hindi was an insult too deep, and death would prove their protest. When I saw the man he looked as if he might die. His followers were shouting, shaking their banners, and demanding an end to that word, but he was just lying there, with no sign of life except the slow bellows of his chest.

He was still lying there when I left Madras, still breathing, his followers still marching, and the Hindi word still coming in.

Our time in Madras was a pleasant time, for the people had been considerate and they were hospitable. One evening at dinner my wife had casually remarked that she wondered how a sari was put on. The next morning the ladies came and drove her out to a lovely home where they all had coffee and cakes, and the ladies told her about the sari and what determines its fashion changes, for the women of India are as up to date in style and as jealous of their fashions as the women of the West. And if you wonder how a piece of cloth six yards long and forty-five inches wide can change style from one year to the next, it is in the border, the design that is woven down one side and across one end of the cloth. This year it is the narrow border that is stylish; but next year no woman of fashion would be caught, even dressed informally, in a sari with a narrow border, for now the broad border is in style. Color and pattern of the design also play a part. The ladies who entertained my wife that morning demonstrated how to put on the sari, and carefully taught her how to fold it and drape it.

On another evening in Madras my wife and I were guests in an Indian home and there, in an alcove off the living room, was the family shrine. In the shrine was an image of Ganesa, the elephant god. As we sipped our Scotch highballs before dinner, our host told us the story of Ganesa, this particular god that they had chosen for their shrine.

It seems that the Lord Siva had been off meditating, and he had sat so long on his lotus leaf that he came home tired and a little muddled. When he entered the yard of his home he saw a boy and, believing that he was an intruder, Siva cut off his head. But Parvati came running from the house and told Siva that this boy was our son, and you just didn't recognize him.

Siva, in panic, looked around for another head. An elephant was going by, so he cut off the elephant's head and stuck it on the boy's body, and Ganesa grew up that way. Siva favored him and trained him, and Ganesa developed until now he is one of the most important of all the Hindu gods, so important that his place always is at the entrance of the temple, and the Hindus worship him first, giving him garlands of flowers, and cups of water, and little pails of milk.

They like Ganesa in particular because he will understand them, for he, like men, sometimes gets into trouble since he enjoys dancing, and sometimes he tipples. Just as they worship him first at the temple, they always go to him first at the beginning of any venture, taking it to him and entrusting it to him because he is so bighearted and will help them get it started.

There is one thing about Ganesa, though, that is severe. He believes in keeping a promise, and no one must ever make him a promise unless he carries it out. A friend of mine, a Brahmin who works in the office of an American business firm, told me that once his little girl was desperately ill. He and his wife promised Ganesa that if he would make her well they would go to his temple and give the little girl's hair as an offering and a testament of what Ganesa had done for them.

She did get well but her hair was so pretty that her parents didn't want to give it, and they didn't go to the temple. And then, after a time, the hair began to coarsen and to snarl, and the mother would try to comb it but it would twist back into itself almost like wire, and then it began to mat, and the little girl began to sicken again. They took her to the temple and there they shaved her head and laid the hair at Ganesa's folded feet, and placed garlands over his elephant head, and placed cups of milk and water for him, and burned incense. "And we came away from the temple with our little girl laughing and skipping again, and she has never been sick since then."

Madras is not only a center of learning, a gathering place of scholars, but here in this southern region is an area of worship in ancient temples and shrines, some of them among the most holy places of India and with processions of pilgrims endlessly coming. One of these places is forty miles south of Madras, a group of temples built twelve hundred years ago, beside the sea. We drove there one day for a picnic as guests of an Indian couple, he a graduate of the University of Pennsylvania, an ear, nose, and throat specialist noted throughout India, and she an author and translator.

The road ran on through the tropical land; and we watched the farmers at work, many of them pumping water to their fields. On top of a pole that stood ten feet high there was a plank that would teeter, and the farmer, this high in the air, would run from one end of the plank to the other, working it like a seesaw, and this action drew up the water and pumped it out into the field.

Beside the road as we traveled we noticed two uprights of stone and a crosspiece of stone, a flat arch. About a mile farther on, we saw another arch, and we were told that they were put there by a generous man who had felt sorry for the people as he saw them carrying the heavy burdens on their heads. So he had the arches built at just the right height for a person to walk under, slide off the burden, and rest for a while.

We had our lunch at the guesthouse, sitting on the upper veranda and looking down past the palm trees to the slow swing of the waves muttering and hissing on the sand. We sipped our cool drinks and ate our sandwiches, and then we went down to see the temples.

India's temples are of infinite variety, but here south of

Madras, at Mahabalipuram, are the most unusual of all. Each of them is cut from solid rock, magnificently carved, and a few of these temples still stand on the shore, the water washing at their base. But most of them, long ago, were undermined by the water and slowly they went down into the sea. Now, on a still day, one can drift in a boat over the temples and look down and see the wonderful carvings of Lord Siva on his lotus leaf meditating, and Lord Krishna, the lord of music, playing his flute.

9

On the eastern coast of India is the seaport city of Visakhapatnam. We stopped there on our way up from Madras to Calcutta, and here again I saw the gap in the structure of India. In Visakhapatnam are the great shipbuilding yards with ocean ships under construction, freighters and tankers, and as I watched the Indian builders and technicians going about their exact and demanding jobs, I thought about those other Indians waddling on their drying rags across the marble floors of the Taj Mahal Hotel in Bombay. I recalled the man I had traveled with on the train that night, and how he had kept telling me about the gap in India's industry, a huge textile mill and a lone man at a spinning wheel, a steel mill and a grindstone.

India in the years of her independence has created industries that now build these ocean ships, build locomotives, automobiles, airplanes, and has established herself as the second largest producer in the world motion-picture industry. This is the ancient, but now impetuous nation, older than history, younger than her men, that wants so much to stride out in industrial independence, to prove her abilities and the justness of her pride.

And yet that morning I had come through villages where the working methods of the people were centuries old, a farmer high on a teeter board, running back and forth to pump water. I had recently been in a city where men are roped like draft animals to carts with almost impossible loads. This is the industrial gap of India that must be closed if her industrial system is to become interlocking and secure and her economy is to be established and kept stable.

While the gap in industry is perhaps the most obvious one, it is only one of the many gaps in India, and there is probably no other country on earth today where the difference between the high and the low is so great. This difference is everywhere and in everything—the difference in the education of men, the difference in their health, their homes, their families. The closing of these gaps, or at least the lessening of the differences, is one of the greatest of the internal problems that faces India today, and the future of her nation depends in considerable degree on her success in building her economic and social structure on a wider base.

And always there is the question of time. The Communists are digging to undermine India from inside, and Red China and Russia are at her borders. How long can India stand? Will there be time to build a nation that can offset the strength of Communism that here in Asia is so powerfully centered on India, and on the overthrow of India?

We left Visakhapatnam late in the afternoon and arrived at Calcutta at night, and the airport is a long way out. The air was cooler in Calcutta than it had been in Visakhapatnam that afternoon at the university where I had been lecturing, but when I commented on the coolness, the USIS man said that such weather would last in Calcutta only a few days longer. He had met us and was driving us along the small road that would take us into the city, and he said that now at the end of February the cool season was about over and that summer would begin early in March, hot and humid.

Even on this small road, far out from the center of the city, there was a mass of people, all stirring, endlessly shifting and moving. The road was filled and overflowing along both edges with men, women, and children, some carrying bundles in their hands, some with trays on their heads, all close together and mixed in with the bullock carts and donkeys, the weaving bicycles and slow-wandering cows that walked a few paces and stopped, blocking everything until the flow of the people could divide and move around the cow, leaving her standing there undisturbed.

At the side of the road other people sat on benches or on the ground in the pale light of the kerosene lamps, and some of them cooked their meals and ate them, and some stretched out on pallets beside the road and slept, and some turned their backs, squatted, and urinated. The squeak of the bullock carts and the bray of the donkeys sounded amid the calls of the people to each other and blended into the endless blare of the radios with their continuing thump of drums and the shrill quaver of the Indian flute. In the air, and in every breath, was the stirred dust and the stinging odor of old dung. We moved slowly, paced by the slow movement of the people about us who pressed in close at our sides.

The small road squirmed its way on toward the city, and then we came onto wider roads, and finally into downtown Calcutta, and there, in whatever direction we looked, we saw the sleeping men on the sidewalks, uncovered and hunched tight, their knees drawn up, or wrapped with a single piece of cotton cloth, like a sheet, from head to foot. We had seen men sleeping on the sidewalks in other Indian cities, but here in Calcutta the slender bodies were so close together, lying beside each other on the sidewalk, that they stretched on like rows of corpses.

But not all the people were sleeping, for that night there was a constant shifting below our window. All night they moved, and I could hear the scuff of their sandals and the pad of their naked feet. They seldom spoke and sometimes they moved slowly, as if they were tired, but always they were there and always there was this restless shifting of these people, and where they were going I have no idea.

The next morning I stepped out of my hotel, the day as bright and clear as sunshine, and lepers moved toward me and held out puffed palms dotted with the nubs of fingers, mumbling through their lipless mouths. Blind men twisted their heads into the blaze of the sun, pulling down their eyelids to show the holes in their faces. Cringing women whined as they came close, holding out sleeping babies almost into my arms—skeleton children that they hire each morning and keep sleeping all day with a touch of opium on their finger tip for the hungry child to suck.

I worked my way through these beggars, twisting from their dirt and scabs, to the taxi stand, and at the taxi a swarm of men with an eye, an arm, or a leg missing struggled among themselves to open the taxi door, salaaming as they drooled—"Sahib! Sahib!"

Hungry and dirty men have always crowded Calcutta, earning a few pennies a day, eating what food they could find, sleeping on the sidewalks, struggling to stay alive in the smothering press of the massed people in Calcutta. This crowding has always been a threat, but now that unnumbered thousands of refugees, fleeing from Mohammedan Pakistan, have swarmed into the city, they have increased the human distress and added to the restlessness and dissatisfaction in Calcutta. Some refugees roam the streets all day and sleep there at night, others sleep with their families at the edge of the city in refugee settlements that are pushed back as far as possible. I have walked through these settlements and they will turn a man's stomach and tighten his heart, for here are hungry and ragged people, idle and miserable in these centers of filth, embittered men sitting with limp hands, brooding as they watch their children starve.

Here is the stuff for Communism, and the Communists are making use of it. In Calcutta I have seen almost constant Communist demonstrations, day after day, in the large central square of the city and in the streets adjoining it. At one hour there will be a meeting and a speaker. Again, a column of men will be marching with banners, or a mob will be protesting wages, protesting lack of food. I watched one Communist parade with men, women, and children marching two abreast, perfectly organized, each company with its leader, each with its red flag in front, and I was told that the column was two and a half miles long. But these demonstrations and parades are open and less meaningful than the continuous moving of the Communist agents among the packed and hungry people, stirring them, pouring in the ferment of resentment of their poverty, of bitterness against the nation and the social system in which they live, and most of all repeating an unswerving hatred of the West, and particularly of the United States.

Before I had come to India on this trip I had read of the Communist threat in the country, how Communism was moving in to destroy India and to open the way for Russia and China. But after I had arrived in India, even after I had traveled for a time in the country, this threat had seemed far off and abstract to me, for I had gone first to New Delhi with its wide, clean streets and its massive government buildings, new and resplendent. I had seen Bombay, a gay and bright city, its flowers blooming, its fountains playing, the buildings ablaze for Republic Night. I had seen the golden-bordered saris of the Parsee women and the golden headdress of the men of Bangalore. Where was this Communism that I had heard about? Now and then there was a sign, a whisper, but not much more.

Then I had come to Calcutta, and here it is. Here are the crowded people, two and a half million, and here is the hunger, the dirt, the squalor, and here are the Communists. And here, for the first time, I came to realize the fact of Communism in India, and I learned a fear for India, and for my own country, as I saw the Russian strength.

I came to realize, too, the fact of how unprepared we are to face the reality of this strength that is Russia and China, the subtlety and persistence of World Communism, and the determination of the Communists to carry out their purpose. Our lack of preparedness is not only a military lack, as we ordinarily think, but it is also a lack of knowledge. We don't bother to know how Russia and World Communism are steadily moving toward their goal, winning in a way so quiet, so patient, that we have not yet recognized its power. Now and then it comes to the surface, as in Tibet, but Tibet seems so far off from us. How can Tibet possibly concern *us?* And Washington finds it easier not to say. It is politically more secure, both for self and party, just to let things ride, never making it plain, never dealing the cards face up, never telling the American people how Russia is moving toward us, coming the long way round, but coming. And never speaking of the day, never even mentioning it, when Red China will knock on our door.

In Calcutta today Russians and Russian-trained agents live among the people, endlessly talking, and Indian Communists sleep on the sidewalks, sleep in the refugee settlements, and they repeat the Russian slogans. But this is not all, for Russia and her gospel of Communism need more than the masses.

Russia maintains one of her display centers on the main street of Calcutta, showing posters and photographs and exhibits, welcoming anyone who will come in, from learned scholars to ragged men from the sidewalks and settlements. There are also bookstores with displays of books and magazines, and here, too, all are welcome, whether they can read or only stand around and listen.

In some of these stores the entire stock has come from Russia—beautiful children's books, books for adults showing the advantages that the Russian people live with and enjoy every day and that they are so anxious to share with their Indian friends, ending all this hunger and sickness and poverty of the Indian people. The Indians need only to take the Russian hand, so warmly and so freely extended.

The Russians constantly distribute stories to the Indian newspapers, and in the Sunday magazine section of one of the large Indian papers I saw a release from the Russian information center. It was a spread of pictures showing a Russian workman and his family, the house they live in, the well-filled table at supper, the clean clothes for the man, the simple but pretty clothes for the woman, schoolbooks for the children, and toys for the babies.

In these pictures, and in all other pictures sent out by Russia to the hungry and restless countries, there is always a show of work and achievement by farmers and laborers and never a suggestion of wealth and splendor. Russia makes sure to picture the simple things that these people can understand and want, never anything so impossibly far beyond their reach but that even the impoverished people of Calcutta may hope someday to have it for themselves. Russia shows them, and tempts them, adding to their bitterness, and leads them along the Communist way.

In this same magazine, on another Sunday, there was a story sent out by our American State Department. It, too, had a spread of pictures, and it showed the New York Stock Exchange, the buyers with their hands raised and stocks trading fast. The story told of how many stocks had been sold that day and their market value. The pictures showed Wall Street and some of the huge buildings and banks, and there was a report of all the money and wealth that are massed there.

The methods and devices that the Communists are using in Calcutta bring about such obvious results as the parades and the demonstrations; but these, although of emotional and excitement value within themselves, are of less significance than the restlessness among the people, and of less meaning than the steady undertow, the constant pull of the Communist strength in Calcutta.

The Communism that one sees on the streets, the parades of the ragged and the dirty, is but the outward show. Behind these masses in the forefront are the brains and the spiritual force of Communism; and no matter what the contradiction may seem, it is possible that the Communism that Russia is preaching, and spreading, and winning, is the most powerful spiritual force on the earth today.

As Russia defines Communism, Communism has something for everybody. For the hungry, there is food. For the power seeker, Communism promises fulfillment. For the idealist, it has a sermon on the mount. For the disgruntled and the misfit, it provides recognition. This is Communism, says Russia. For those who believe and accept, it becomes greater than truth, greater than loyalty, greater than honor. It is a faith, a religion that they fight for and that they will die for—and that they *do* die for in countries all over the world, in street fighting, in rioting, in whatever ways they are called on to prove their faith. From such followers as these Russia draws her disciples to go out among the masses and live among them and preach to them, to unsettle them and stir them. This is the organization that Russia is building over the world.

In Calcutta I was always aware of Lenin's permanent plan for Communism. It was Lenin forty years ago who said: "The Communist road to Paris lies through Peking and Calcutta."

He charted the course and he pointed the way. Europe was to be taken by coming around through Asia, and Peking already is a part of World Communism.

Shrewd, patient, cruel, Russia works steadily at her goal of taking the world. At the moment Russia, with China, is maneuvering especially toward India, for India means Asia. After Asia comes Africa, and then, with these masses of people under her control, all these raw materials and markets under her control, Russia will be in a position to advance along the southern flank of Europe and open the road to Paris. With Europe neutralized and South America exploited, Russia then can move more openly against her final objective, the throttling and the overthrow of the United States.

While Russia now edges on toward her goal, she lulls the United States and deceives all others, who are foolish enough to believe, with her endless talk of peace, disarmament, and coexistence.

10

After finishing my assignment in Calcutta I had a break in my schedule, and for the first time since getting to India I had a few days off. We had been looking forward especially to this time, for we had made our plans to spend it in Nepal.

It is a small kingdom, only a sliver of earth high in south central Asia, the home of Mount Everest and higher than anywhere else, the cap of the world. A good many places are not so interesting as they are reported to be, and travel about the world to see the famous sights can be disappointing. Dr. Johnson once said that there are places worth seeing, but few of them are worth *going* to see. There is one place, though, that we found to be worth going almost any distance to see, and that is this kingdom of Nepal.

It has been shut off, its outside contacts almost completely forbidden for centuries, and only recently has it been opened so that people could go there. These visitors, however, have been few, and they have made little difference in the lives or ways of the people. The small mountain country today is just the same as the Nepalese have enjoyed it for centuries. The laws and restrictions of government are almost negligible, and even these are conveniently ignored by the people. There is little schooling or study of books to bother men and confuse them. And religion in Nepal has no rules and no threats; religion is a festival. The country today is unwashed, illiterate, and magnificent.

A year or so ago I read about Nepal in the *Reader's Digest,* and the story made it seem like a wonderful place; but it was so far away and so off the line of travel that I almost forgot about it. Nepal remained only a name in a magazine and vaguely the place where Mount Everest is, until the last night that my wife and I were in Tokyo on this trip.

We were traveling out of Japan, heading for Manila on the Dutch air line, and the Dutch, being hospitable people, had said that while we waited for the going of their plane they would provide us with a drink, anything we liked. I was thirsty and asked for a bottle of beer; but when they brought it, it was jug size and I couldn't drink it all. There was a man seated across the waiting room whom I had looked at more than once and had wondered where he came from. There was a touch of the Mongol about him and a touch of the Indian, and I couldn't figure him out.

Now that I had the beer, he was looking at me, and I guessed that possibly he might be thirsty, too. I found another glass and went over and asked if he would do me a favor and help me finish the beer. We drank it, drifting into talk until I got around to asking him where he came from. He said that he was from Nepal, from Katmandu—and "Katmandu" was lost on me. He said that he was a doctor and had been in the United States studying malaria control. There were malarial districts in Nepal, and he was a member of a commission that was trying to clean them up. He had traveled over a good part of the United States and he thought it the finest country he had ever been in, and all the people had been so good to him. "Doctors would let me come into their office and talk to them," he said. "And famous men gave me time."

After we had discussed my country, I asked him about his, and he told me of Nepal. I listened, then beckoned for my wife to come and listen, too, for I knew that we were going there. Here was a country covered with Himalayan snows and so lost in the past that time seemed only to have waved at it.

Our trip to Nepal took some arranging after we were in India, for Nepal lies at India's northern border, in an almost inaccessible region between India and Tibet. There are no trains in Nepal, and whenever the Nepalese want to get anywhere, they walk. Ordinary loads they carry on their backs, in huge baskets. When there is more than they can carry, they use mules except when they are going over the high mountain passes, and then they use goats. We could get to Katmandu only on the one small plane that flies in and out of India each day.

On the day that we flew over the mountains and into Nepal there was a dust haze, a bright glint in the air that closed us in. I was disappointed, for I wanted my wife to see the Himalayas. There is nothing like the majesty of these mountains when they are seen far off, and nothing like their jagged fury and terror as one flies among them.

The little airport at Katmandu is only one short landing strip, and we came low into the valley out of the haze and landed not far from the one frame building beside the strip. There were a few Nepalese standing around, the men short but strong, and they have such dignity that they seemed hardly to notice us, looking past us toward the mountains. The women wore loose blouses of bright colors and a kind of billowing sarong for a skirt. Some of them wore ear pendants of silver, and some wore nose rings of gold. Their features were a mixture, but there was more of the Mongol than of the Indian in their faces.

Off at one side of the field stood a large airplane, and we were told that it was the king's airplane; it had been given to him by the Russian Government, but since there was nobody to fly it, it just stood there. We drove a long way from the airfield to our hotel, and it turned out to be a resplendent building of marble and stone that once had been the palace of a maharaja. Here in this palace we were told that Nepal is ruled by a king, but also it is ruled by a Little Goddess. This country, as the man in Tokyo had said, seemed to be something out of Aladdin's lamp, its door only slightly pushed open, having skipped five hundred years to come directly from the Middle Ages into now.

We were here during the Festival of Holi, the Hindu festival of spring, and the people all threw brightly colored powder on each other, streaking and splotching their clothes, and the girls and young women came out in gay attire, with vermilion in their hair. This festival is for the people, but also the gods must not be slighted. So Ganesa, the pot-bellied elephant god, sat cross-legged in his shrine and he was red and blue and yellow all over from the powder, the color smeared thick on his huge ears and his snout. Hanuman, the monkey god, son of the wind and a monkey nymph, was wreathed and adorned with flowers, and his long, curling tail was colored to the tip.

The houses here in Katmandu are so old that their bricks are crumbling and their balconies sag over the miniature streets, but the window frames are wooden and each householder, when each house was built long ago, was able to carve the frames to suit himself, with a story of the gods perhaps, with flowers and birds and arabesques perhaps. It is under these balconies that the people constantly pass, bent under their loaded baskets, or walking upright and herding their sheep, their cattle, and goats.

The little streets, uncertain in their going, weave their way into the center of Katmandu, to the cluster of the tiny shops, each no bigger than a stall, where the shopkeepers sell salt and candles, hides and tallow, brass pots and blankets. The farmers, moving about in their open market in the very center of town, sell rice and chilies, buckwheat and garlic, mustard, and white radishes two feet long. Lordly bankers sit around the edge of this market, each with a board in front of him and his coins in little stacks on the board, his fingers lightly riffling the coins and clinking them as a trader goes by.

We wandered along the wavering streets and on through the market, and we came to a temple. We couldn't tell what kind of temple it was. What was the religion here? We asked a Nepalese, who had come with us from the hotel and who could speak English, what kind of temple this was. He said that he didn't know.

Did it matter? A man might want to worship as a Hindu one day. He might want to be a Buddhist another day. Did it matter?

In one temple, as we crossed the threshold and entered the courtyard, I pointed at a statue of Athena. What was this Greek goddess doing in a temple in Nepal?

It seems that an Englishman who had lived in Katmandu long ago had a flower garden, and he had brought a marble statue of Athena and put it in his garden. Then the Englishman went away and the Nepalese looked at the poor goddess living off by herself, and they thought that she must be lonely. So they had a feast and a procession, and they carried this unknown goddess to the temple and they gave her a place along with all the other gods. And when we saw her, Athena was just as streaked with candle drippings and just as smeared with red and blue and yellow powder as even Ganesa or Hanuman, the monkey god.

There are other temples and shrines scattered about in Katmandu, standing on a street corner, beside a road, in the market place, and carved on them and painted on them are completely informative sex scenes. Open as the morning sun and totally exposed, some of these carvings are monstrous in their size, and some are fragile, but all the sexual equipment of any man or any woman is fully sculptured here and precisely painted. The people go by, passing what is known to them, and accepting it as they accept the sun and the rain, the moon and the stars.

But the traveler, seeing all this for the first time, stops and looks. The art of these shrines is notable for the perfection of its form and color, but even more memorable than these reproductions is the unlimited imagination of the artists. They depict in vivid detail all the ordinary activities of any man and woman; they then loose their imagination and portray, in equally vivid detail, all possible variants and contortions of man, woman, and beast.

There are no veils here, no shadows, no misunderstandings. One might as well be standing on a street corner, reading public notices on a bulletin board.

The Nepalese are such gentlemen that no one seemed surprised, and no one noticed or even glanced at us, when my wife and I, awe-stricken, walked slowly around these shrines, unbelieving. The Nepalese think that what is here, natural or unnatural, is for any visitor to consider, for enlightenment or worship.

We walked the streets of Katmandu with our private minstrel, a lean man with a one-string fiddle, playing a gay tune as he led us about the city. Whenever we stopped at a shop, at a shrine, he stood behind us. But when we were ready to move on, he took his place in front, his fingers dancing lightly over the string, fiddling us on our way.

We came to an open square where there was a crowd. We saw huge umbrellas hanging high at the top of poles, and as we looked, the umbrellas opened slowly and colored powder spilled out and all the air suddenly was a rainbow, red and blue and yellow, and the children were dancing in it, holding up their hands to catch it.

And then, suddenly, our minstrel caught me and shook my arm, almost dragging me along to where the powder was still in the air. He put his fiddle under his arm, so that he could have both hands to pull at me, though now and then he would loose one hand and point, almost distracted that he couldn't make me understand. There was an Englishman there, and I asked what the man was pointing at and the Englishman pointed, too, at one of the buildings, and he said: "The little goddess. She is there."

So long ago that no one knows how long, a little goddess lived in the palace of the king of Nepal and she advised the king; but she told him that no one else must ever see her, and the king warned the queen never to go to that room and never to open that door. But one day the queen opened the door and looked, and the goddess disappeared.

The king was sad and he begged for her to come back. He begged so hard that finally the gods told him that while he could never have the same little goddess again, he, and all the other kings who came after him, could choose a goddess and she would always be found among the little girls of his kingdom. The king then sent for his wise men and his astrologers and they searched the kingdom and found a little girl, seven years old, and she came and lived in the palace and she was the little goddess until she was twelve. But then she was too old and she must leave, and another little goddess was found, and there has always been one, and there is one now.

She lives in a palace of her own, with other little girls to play with her, and she goes out twice each year, riding on her flowered cart, and the king and all the people bow low as she rides by.

There are many windows in front of her palace and all of them are square except one, and that one is oval. This is the window that only the little goddess looks out, and she was there now, seeing the fall of the colored powder. She may have been ten years old, and she had on a golden headdress that was high and golden earrings that were long; her eyes were darkened, and her black brows were painted and tilted sharply up her temples.

I stood there looking at her, and suddenly she looked down at me, and caught me gazing at her. She looked a moment longer, and I don't know why, and maybe it wasn't quite the thing to do, but I winked at her. I could see her catch her breath, astonished, and then, not knowing what else to do, she stuck her tongue out at me and bobbed out of sight.

And now, long after, when things are difficult and other men seem to be going by me, there is comfort in knowing that few of them, possibly no other man in *this* world, has ever had a little goddess stick out her tongue at him.

One night at our hotel at Katmandu, seated by the wood fire, we heard the news. The Chinese were moving into Tibet, just across the border. And that night the oil lamps burned in the monasteries and the hollow sound of the long horns mourned into the night as the Buddhist monks blew their lament.

The next day the news came again, and before many days we had learned that China had taken all of Tibet. It was then that the men of Nepal looked at one another and wondered what this might mean to them. There had been only a border between Nepal and Tibet, and no man really knew where it was, and no man had worried about it.

But there is cause to worry now, for already, after only this short time of coming into Tibet, China is building roads across Tibet that lead toward Nepal. Already there are maps coming out of Peiping that show Nepal as a possession of China. China has begun to claim Mount Everest as a part of her territory, and the maps show that soon she will be claiming all of Nepal. With Tibet in China's power, only Nepal now lies at this border between the Red Chinese and India.

The morning that we left Katmandu, driving along the narrow dirt road to the airport and seeing the people going about their daily chores, there was for us something of the lonely feeling that one has when he is leaving a very old person, that he will not be there next time.

When we flew out of the little country, the air was clear and the jagged mountains thrust their eternal white into the sky. Whatever else there might be for me as I looked back, there was still the hollow sound of the long horns blowing the lament on the night that Tibet was taken.

11

We came back into India and went to the city of Benares. By this time we had traveled over most of India, visited the large cities, seen the countryside, and knew something of the villages. In noting the changes in the country, I had found that there were many of them, some of them deep and significant—the new national pride, the individual self-respect—but there was no change in the one factor that is the most confusing in the thinking of the West about India, and that is the Hindu religion. Of the five most prominent religions, Christian, Buddhist, Jewish, Moslem, and Hindu, the Hindu religion is so completely different from the others, so nebulous and so all-inclusive that it, of all religions, is least known and least comprehended by other men. And the center of the Hindu religion is the city of Benares.

A cathedral, a synagogue, a mosque, all are holy places to some men, and therefore they are places of respect for all men. A city, too, can be a holy place, if some men say so. Other men who come to the city may find it bizarre, extravagant, even fantastic, and there is nothing wrong with this; but when they find it repulsive or ridiculous there should be shame, for one man's worship in whatever form it may be is never fit subject for the scorn or ridicule of another. And men who come to the holy city of Benares and seek to belittle it are unfortunate in their own lacks. To draw back from the lepers and festering sores of

Benares, the monkeys and the bulls, is one thing; but to question the holiness of this Hindu city is to give too great surety to one's own belief.

There are fifteen hundred temples in Benares and hundreds of thousands of pilgrims come every year, sleeping where they can, eating where they can, and bathing in the sacred waters of the Ganges, drinking the water and taking little brass pots of it to throw on Ganesa, and on Siva, and on the golden bull. To die and be dipped in the Ganges and be burned beside the Ganges are a way to salvation, and many an old person comes and lives in Benares, waiting to die and be cremated in the ghats beside the river. To die with one's feet actually in the river as he breathes his last is the open and waiting door to immediate salvation, and why this is true these devout men of India cannot make clear to everyone, and they seldom try. It remains confusion in the minds of most Westerners, but the Hindus believe it, and that is enough. Sometimes they, too, ask questions, wanting to know about other men who also touch themselves with water, or keep their hats on, or take their shoes off, and the answers they get do not seem entirely clear to them or to clarify what they ask.

The Hindu religion became less difficult for me when I was in Katmandu, for there is a temple in Katmandu, a single temple, where live all the Hindu deities—all 90,000,000 of them. Going into this temple and seeing only the bare and empty room, seeing no image and no person and hearing no sound, one pays his respects to the deities and comes away knowing that he has done his best, and knowing that he doesn't understand, and probably never will.

Benares is a turgid city and even one who has respect and wants to ask no questions will find wonder here. A man, naked but for his loincloth, walks round and round a tree. His forehead is marked with painted symbols, and in one hand he holds a staff which will never touch the earth, and in the other hand a brass pot, and he walks round and round the tree, chanting. A young

Indian explained to me: "Lord Siva is in the tree. And this man is worshiping."

I watched a man, tall, his body magnificent in form and strength, a fragment of cloth at his loins, as he walked on the top of a pedestal. The pedestal, built of stone, rose high out of the waters of the Ganges and he walked the circle of the pedestal, his feet tracing the outer edge, until he had finished the circle, and then, facing the early sun, he stood on his head. Still facing the sun, he stared at the sun, unblinking. He remained rigid and staring, as fixed as the stone column itself, until he dropped to his feet once more, walked the circle of the pedestal once more, came back, and stood on his head once more. "That," my Indian friend explained, "is worship-cum-exercise."

These forms of worship, no matter how strange they may seem at first, will lose some of their puzzlement after a while; but there will always remain in Benares many practices that confuse and even upset the Westerner. There is, for instance, the whole matter of the treatment and the disposal of the dead.

A Westerner, accustomed to everything quiet and hushed, closed in with the dead, is somewhat startled as he rides along on a clear and lovely day, chatting with his friends, and looks out of the window of his automobile into the face of a dead man beside him. The body lies on a wooden platform, built like a litter, and tied there with the feet, the head, and the chest exposed, beads and flowers wreathed about his neck and yellow paste smeared on his forehead. The litter is borne on the shoulders of his friends, and the little procession moves along at a jog. Often there is someone to throw rice into the dead face, and often there is singing, and almost always there is chanting. Sometimes there is music, sometimes a band.

The religious law and the custom of the Hindu people are that they burn their dead, and in the cities there are established places for these cremations, a small stretch of bare and open ground with piles of wood beside it. One comes here with a body and says how much wood he will buy, the kind of cremation that he can pay for. In Calcutta, for instance, if he wants the best cremation, he buys five dollars' worth of wood and it is stacked five feet high and then the body is laid on it, and the eldest son lights the fire. But if five dollars is more than can be paid, then the relatives pay two dollars and a lesser amount of wood is placed at the bottom of a hole in the ground, and the body is stuffed in, where the burning will be hotter. There is a society of benevolent men and women in most cities who maintain a fund so that everybody can have a cremation of some kind.

When a man dies during the night, his cremation fire must be lighted before daybreak, and this is why so often on the streets of a Hindu city one sees the little jogging processions going on all through the night. In a city there is no problem about cremation, but out in the country the religious law of lighting the fire before daybreak can be a terrible burden, for while the law in this hot country is a wise one, there is always the question of where the wood is coming from. There are vast areas in India where there are no trees, and some villages sit in open plains that are bare for miles around. If a man dies here, what can be done? The getting of wood is difficult even when a man lies ill for a long time and gives notice of his dying; but when he dies suddenly, when there has been no chance for his family to travel and gather wood, then whatever there is at hand that can be burned must be burned, no matter if it is a part of the household equipment and needed.

The most-wanted place for cremation, of course, is Benares and beside the holy river, but taking a body there from somewhere else is impossible, and only those who die in the city itself can be dipped into the water and burned on the bank of the Ganges. This is why so many who are old and feeble come here, waiting their time, and why every morning there are funeral pyres burning beside the river. Throughout the day other fires are lighted, and the blue smoke almost always can be seen, even from far off, ascending in columns to the sky.

Besides the public cremations and the seemingly almost casual disposal of the dead there is another matter in this Hindu country that compels the interest of the Westerner; this is the attitude of the Hindu, which is so strange to us, toward cows and bulls, their urine and their dung.

Some persons come to India and go away remembering perhaps above all else the sight and the smell of cow dung, which is as much a part of India as the air that one breathes, for it is in every city, in every village, always the acrid smell of the old and burning dung.

To raise questions about this is to forget the Indian's reply: What else can we burn? And to forget that Americans, praised and honored by us as our forefathers, traveled westward over plains where there was no wood, and they cooked their food over fires of buffalo dung and kept themselves warm by these fires.

In India today, where wood is so scarce and so precious, children and women go into the streets and into the fields, wherever animals go, to collect dung as a woman or a child in the United States might walk out into the woods to gather sticks and fuel for the stove or the hearth. One sees these children and women walking the streets, following the paths of the animals, and gathering their droppings, scraping them up with their hands and putting them into baskets, each child and each woman putting her basket on her head and walking on, still watching. Sometimes a woman without a basket will see a pile of fresh dung and she will stop and gather it, molding it into a large ball and carrying it home in her hand, from time to time patting it and reshaping it as she goes.

I sat one day at a watering place in a small Indian town, a stone well where wandering cows and bulls come, and here the workmen bring their draft buffaloes each noon for water. The women were washing here, slamming the garments on the stone platform beside the watering trough. The buffaloes came in thick at noon, the huge animals pushing and grunting, their horns striking and clattering. Some had horns so long and so spiked that they had to be led separately to the trough, the other animals driven back to make room for them. The women washed, and when a buffalo stopped and urinated on their wash stones, a woman would splash a handful of water on the urine, partly clearing it, and wash on.

Three little boys and one little girl, she being probably twelve years old, were there, and each had a basket. When one of the animals, a cow, a bull, a buffalo, relieved itself, the children would gather around. Squatting over the steaming pile, they would divide it into four smaller piles, laughing and reaching for more, redividing when one thought that it was not fair. They showed the little girl a nice courtesy and allowed her always to choose her pile first.

Then she would take it to one side of the watering place where there was a stone shelf, and there she would empty the dung and knead it as if it were dough. She would work it into little balls, rolling it round and round in her hands, then putting it on the shelf and kneading it again, pressing it flat and working out the moisture. When it was dry enough to hold its shape, she would flatten it like pancakes and lay these cakes along the shelf in the sun to finish their drying, so that she could stack them in her basket and take home her findings and her work for the day.

She was a pretty child, slim and fair, her features small but neatly cut, and as she was busy at her work, kneading and pressing, she would pause now and then and push back her hair with the back of her hand, or push up her bracelets that kept slipping down and getting in her way. Once, when one of the boys brought her a joint of sugar cane, she stopped her work long enough to peel it with her teeth and chew it as she went on kneading.

Such cakes as this child made I have seen plastered against the sides of a thousand Indian homes. I have seen them piled in the yard, stacked on the steps, waiting to be burned. I have seen, beside the road or at the edge of a village, mounds of dung as big as a haystack and a column as tall as a man. Some of these mounds and columns have been decorated by some rural sculptor, he having seen a design that he liked at some temple, or at a wayside shrine, or he himself had imagined a pretty pattern, and had fashioned it with his work knife while the dung was still moist.

Some village people sprinkle cow urine on the floor of their houses in the morning, for it is healthy, so they say, the ammonia being good for them. Everything that comes from the cow, the milk, the urine, the dung, is good for them, and the cow for ages has been sacred. Millions of these gaunt beasts, cows and bulls, unowned and unclaimed, roam Indian cities and wander over the countryside. They eat the grass that the land needs, grazing it close and baring the ground for the monsoon rains to swirl and erode and ruin, sinking India deeper into her land difficulties. But the cow is holy and must not be interfered with. To kill a cow would be like killing a saint. The cow must not be touched with any sign of anger, or touched at all except for the milking, wringing a few cups from the stringy black udder, or touched in reverence and worship.

All this of cows and bulls, both living and in golden statue, and all that it signifies, is beyond our understanding; and the center of all this is Benares, the holy city of the Hindus. Here the bulls wander in and out of the temples, the floor awash with water that has been brought from the Ganges in little brass pots and splashed on Ganesa, splashed on Siva, and it is awash, too, with the urine and the diluted dung of the animals, and no man as he wades in the wash would think for an instant of driving the animals out. And the monkeys, too, give their part to the sloshing on the floor, perched on Siva's brow, sitting amid the tuberose garlands that wreath his neck as they scratch and crack their fleas.

It is a strange place, this Benares, with the river and the dead, the reeking temples, and the begging whine of the lepers, the mutilated, and the deformed. It is darkness to Western eyes, but it is the Hindu city of worship, where they come to pray and to die, and as such it is a place for no man to question.

12

Most of these things, the strange practices at Benares and all matters pertaining to the cow, I had seen before; but this time, traveling for the State Department, I came across a good deal that I had not known about. India is an open pageant to anybody, any traveler can come here and see the color of its life and glimpse the curious things that go on, but moving about as I did this time, and despite believing that I had a fairly good idea of India, I was set back and left confused by some of the things that happened to me.

I knew that the strict custom in the Hindu religion is against killing any animal. The Hindu will go to any length to avoid even accidentally killing an animal, and some of the people of India go so far as to wear a mask to avoid breathing in any kind of insect and thereby killing it. Never mind themselves, they aren't protecting themselves against breathing these bugs, they are just taking care of whatever is in the air that they might happen to breathe. Also, some of them will eat only when the sun is up, because at night, or even at twilight, they might fail to see a bug in their food and eat it; for this same reason, for fear that they might not be able to see clearly and might eat a bug, they go without all food on a cloudy day. (I have often wondered just how they reconciled all the care about killing no animal, or even an insect, and their going out and murdering a whole trainload of Moslems.)

The refusal to kill any animal of course leads them never to eat meat of any kind. Every time I went out to a buffet dinner at the home of an American in India, and when there were to be Hindus present, I noticed that the hostess always had two tables, or that a large table was divided in its servings, and she would move around among her guests, notifying the non-meat eaters which table, or which part of the big table, was vegetarian. Some of these people are so strict that even the sight of a boiled egg sliced on top of a salad will turn them from the salad, away from even any part of it hidden down at the bottom, and for them to find out that an egg has been cooked into a dish causes them to refuse to taste the dish. This limitation on their diet has its effect on their health, and a person sees more skinny people in India, not only because of poverty but because of diet restrictions, than anywhere else.

Knowing about this attitude toward the killing of animals, I respected it and did my best not to offend anybody about it. The obvious customs of any religion, such as taking off shoes when entering a mosque, or a woman putting on a headpiece when going into a cathedral, are nothing to puzzle about because they are customs that are generally known and a person just observes them. But it is the little side issues, the taboos, that get him into trouble, and some of these offshoots of the Hindu religion can completely floor an unsuspecting American.

I knew about the Hindu's regard for animals, and that the taking of any life is evil; but one day when I was teaching at a large university I crossed the limitation with no thought whatsoever that I was even near it. The lecture was on American poetry, and things were going along fine. I had selected some poems that I believed would be of particular interest to the Indians, not only because the poems themselves are good but because they tell about the United States. One of the poems that I had chosen was Carl Sandburg's "Chicago."

The students had been interested, and the professors had been paying close attention, and I was pleased that they were enjoying these poems about the United States. Then I read "Chicago," and

I felt the whole room freeze. It was as if they had slammed a door and left me outside. I was aware that something had gone wrong, though I had no idea what I had done; all I knew was that my lecture from that moment was a failure. The students and the professors simply sat there, polite, distant, uninterested.

Afterward I found out what had happened. An Indian, who worked at USIS, had accompanied me to the lecture and as we drove back to the USIS office he casually mentioned that he had enjoyed all the poems except "Chicago." He was looking directly at me when he told me that he just did not like that poem. And as he said it, I understood. The opening line of the poem, "Hog butcher to the world," would finish any poem for a Hindu audience, ruin any lecture, and slam the door on any man who would quote it.

This matter of animals and the sacredness of all life can show up in the strangest places. I was in a small town soon after I had come to India, and I opened the door of my room at the hotel and the floor was covered with ants. I waited outside in the hall and called for the bearer. "Get rid of those things. Have you got any Flit?"

He was an old man, his beard white, and he looked at me, and then he looked at the ants. "They will go," he said.

I asked him where they would go, and he pointed at one hole in the floor, and then another. "Perhaps there," he said. "Perhaps there. They will go."

I was in a hurry and didn't debate it with him, walking on into my room and stepping into the midst of the ants as I did. I went on to the bathroom, and when I came back the old bearer still was standing there, looking down at the footprint of dead ants that I had left on the floor.

"The next time . . ." the old man asked, gently, "will the Sahib step over?"

I knew that he was an old man and a bearer, a servant, probably uneducated and superstitious, and I didn't pay much attention to him, but I did humor his request, although I considered it only the whim of this old man—because I was new in India again and had not reaccustomed myself to its ways.

Thinking of what had happened as only a little thing, but considering it an interesting story, I told it a short time afterward when I was teaching at a university. I had just come from delivering my first lecture and was having tea with the vice-chancellor, the dean, and a number of professors. We were a small group, seated about a table, and in the easy and enjoyable conversation of the room I remembered the happening of the old man and the ants, and I told it as an entertaining story.

Again there was that chill in the room, and again I felt the door slam. In the sudden stillness and quiet the dean went on stirring his tea, but no one looked at me.

After a moment, though, and the tenseness in the room became obvious, the dean tried to ease it; but he was still stirring his tea and looking down at his cup, not at me, when he said, "When the ants come to our house, my wife always puts out a few grains of sugar to make them happy."

That taught me my lesson about insects and animals, and I did not offend in this way again, but there was still a lot more that I had to learn about getting on with these people because now I was associating with them more closely than before, and I wasn't always finding it easy to know just what to do, or how to carry out just what was expected of me. Take the simple matter of making a speech in India—I found out that it can be very unlike what I was accustomed to at home.

One of my first speeches was to a Rotary Club, a large one, and I wasn't particularly worried about making it because I knew something about Rotary Clubs and how they carry on their business, since I had visited a good many of them in the United States. As the speaker of the day, I sat at the head table in ease and confidence while the president made his announcements and the committees made their reports. Then, after these announcement and reports had been completed, the president turned to me and for several minutes he told of my past and he praised me, saying that he and the club were proud to have me for their speaker of the occasion.

After such a gracious introduction I stood, hitched my lapels, cleared my throat, and was taking my time, giving them a good look at me, trying to impress them, before I headed for the speaker's stand to make my speech. But as I moved toward the speaker's stand, an American, who was sitting three chairs away, leaned over and grabbed my coattail, jerking me back. "No!" He jerked again. "Not yet," he whispered. "They introduce you now, and you make your speech later. You just stand up now, take a bow, and sit down again."

I thought that was a crazy way of doing it, but I took my bow and eased back into my chair, red faced, and I sat there twisting my glass and swinging my foot. They went on with further reports and announcements, and they read the birthday list and sang "Happy Birthday" to all members whose birthdays had been that week, and then the president again turned to me, and this time he said, "I now call on the speaker to deliver his address."

I stood, hitched my lapels, cleared my throat, glanced back at my coattail, and again headed for the speaker's stand. I took my position, looked at the clock, and got ready. But at that moment the vice president showed up. He was carrying a garland of flowers, tuberoses and daisies and tinsel, and he looped it around my neck. While I was looking down at the garland, he put a bouquet in my hand, marigolds and lotus leaves.

This was my first experience with these flowers, and I didn't know what to do about them. I thought that if I took off the garland, I might be considered rude and unappreciative, not knowing that a person is supposed to take it off and lay it on the table. So I stood there, and from a mass of tuberoses in that hot room I made my speech.

An Indian audience may listen, or they may get up and walk around, crack peanuts, tell jokes, wave to their friends, saunter out, and they may, or may not, come back in again—all this while the speaker is delivering his address.

After this had happened to me a few times, I was upset about it, thinking that the people weren't interested in listening to me and that I was a failure. And then one evening I attended the graduation exercises at one of the big Indian universities where the commencement address was to be given by a man who holds one of the top positions in the Indian government, an international figure. He was introduced and he started his speech, and I was sitting only about ten feet from him, and even that close I couldn't begin to follow him; there was so much noise, so much going on in the hall, people moving about and talking with each other, that I couldn't hear half of what he was saying. Even the vice-chancellor, who had introduced him, had turned around and was carrying on a lively conversation with somebody else. *Nobody paid any attention to him.*

Of course it isn't always this way, and many a lecture is listened to with almost tense attention; in fact, most of the lectures that I gave after I had been in India for a while, and had found out what I was supposed to do and how to do it, were received in this way. But a man must learn to watch an Indian audience and control it, quickly halting any sign of inattention from anywhere in the lecture hall. This is an added strain on a speaker, but it is necessary.

There are times, however, when there is nothing that a speaker can do about it, and he might just as well relax. There was that evening, for instance, in Hyderabad when I spoke to a club of businessmen. After I had been introduced and had sat down again, the social chairman rose and announced that this meeting was the anniversary of the club, and that they had a birthday cake. Having said this, he pointed toward the center doors, and they swung open. Two cooks bore in a chocolate cake so big that it needed both of them to carry it. The name of the club was mounted in pink icing and fifteen candles blazed.

The cake was placed in the front of the room, standing on the floor and just in front of the speaker's table, and partly hiding that table. It was where everybody could gaze at it and imagine its rich chocolate flavor.

The chairman then called on ten young ladies, beautiful themselves and with flowers coiled in their hair, to come forward and cut the cake. They were beautifully dressed, too, their saris draped with care and intention, precisely molding the silken gleam of their figures as they moved.

They cut the cake and they served it, gliding about among the audience, passing out the cake and exchanging little jokes with the men they served. While these pretty girls continued to go about, laughing gaily with the members whose eyes followed them about the room like radar, and while the forks and plates were clacking and clattering, and everyone had forgotten my introduction or that I so much as existed, the chairman rose and turned to me. "I now call on our speaker to give his address on 'American Business and How It Operates in the American Democracy.'" I could have delivered Spartacus' address to the gladiators and nobody would have known any difference.

Even this speech, though, lost in the clatter of plates, and ignored in the swing of silken hips, was less an occasion for me than an evening I spent in a North Indian city when I was to speak on American poetry to a society of scholars and savants. On this evening I climbed the hill completely at ease, heading toward a large hall at the top. I believed that I knew my subject sufficiently, I had spoken to a number of Indian audiences, and I saw no reason to be bothered.

The floor of the hall was bare and most of the audience were elderly men, many of them white-bearded, and they sat cross-legged on the floor. There were also a few younger men, and then there was a bevy of small boys, ranging in age from eight to twelve years. I wondered why these children were there, but they had been playing at the bottom of the hill, and having seen the lights, they had come up to investigate and had taken their places in the audience, sitting on the floor wherever they could find room among the gray-bearded men.

I was introduced, received my garland, accepted my bouquet, and began my address. The old men and the younger men listened, and the boys sat still for a while. But soon they began to fidget, and then to squirm. Not for them Walt Whitman. Not for them America singing or the lilacs that bloomed.

They twisted, and they shifted, glancing at each other, until finally one of them tiptoed out, and then another, until they all were gone, and I thanked a merciful heaven to be rid of them.

In the new stillness and dignity of the room my speech was picking up, and I was gaining confidence, when the door to the balcony creaked open and the boys filed in. They sat for a moment, and then one of them leaned over and whispered to another, and he whispered to another, and they got up and started a game of hide-and-seek.

One of them counted while the others hid, and they all squealed when they were caught, and shouted as they ran. This kept up in the balcony until one of them had an idea, and he came back downstairs. Easing open the door, he tiptoed in and found a place among the old men, huddling down and hiding under a shawl, while I read on, now the poems of Emily Dickinson.

But the boy had been seen, and soon the door eased open again, and another boy who was "It" tiptoed in, searching among the old men, crawling about, lifting their shawls, and peeping under. When he made his discovery, they both raced for the door.

The new hiding place was popular and other boys came in, and still others came in to find them, creeping about and searching, while I read on: "Inebriate of air am I, and debauchee of dew."

And then, from outside and along the wall of the building, there sounded a bumping and a scraping. A cow was going along the narrow passage. She slowed down at the window, turned her head, and then went on again, bumping and scraping.

The old men seemed to notice nothing as they looked up at me and listened to the sound of our poetry. The Indian people and their Hindu religion have a tolerance, and a patience, and an acceptance of all things.

After one has been in India for a while, he begins to get some of that feeling for himself, a tolerance and an acceptance, and I came to the place, finally, when I believed that the Hindu religion is a gentle and a wise religion. I never understood it, but I came to the greater understanding that this does not matter, and I was interested without trying to explain.

Certainly I could not explain what my wife and I saw one morning on a street in Calcutta. We saw a carefully dressed man, perfectly tailored, hurrying into a large bank, yet even in his hurry he paused long enough to step to the edge of the sidewalk, lift a cow's tail, kiss the tassel, drop the tail, and hurry on into the bank. No one seemed to notice him except my staring wife and me.

I cannot explain the emptying of half the sewage of the city of Benares into the Ganges, the washing of the city's clothes and the dipping of the dead into the river, and the people all bathing in the water, drinking it, and continuing in good health. While my wife and I were in India, a member of the Indian Parliament raised the question of the people of Benares drinking this water with half the sewage of the city in it. Was it not a risk to health? He was answered quickly and angrily. If *all* the sewage of Benares was emptied into the river, the water would still be pure. Did not the Ganges rise in Siva's head and flow from Siva's head? How could the water possibly be impure?

These things that astonish us are a part of a life that is set apart from us, outside the comprehension of an ordinary Westerner, and he is wasting his time in trying to figure them out. He might as well give up trying because that night at the most formal dinner, given for the social and intellectual leaders of the city, he will sit next to the man who kissed the cow's tail, and the man will carry on a conversation, in any of half-a-dozen languages, on any subject from philosophy to mathematics, from world politics to music.

And the lady he saw that morning drinking the water of the Ganges, standing in the river only a few steps below the dripping bodies of the dead, lifting the water with her bunched fingers and pouring it into her mouth—he will see that same lady standing with her husband at some fashionable bar that evening, sipping her Martini with discrimination, and wondering, as she smooths the silken folds of her sari, if a Gibson might not be preferred.

These things, and so much more, we do not understand, and again it does not matter; for the surprising and the bizarre in India are less than the learning, the sense of beauty, the tolerance, and the patience of these people. These are the qualities to be remembered about India and her people.

I learned something of the enduring quality of India from an unexpected teacher. He was the old man who had asked me to step over the ants, but the more enduring lesson that I learned from him had nothing to do with these ants.

On the day I arrived at the small hotel where he was a bearer, I unpacked my belongings and started to go out, then I noticed that there was no lock, and I called for him.

He came in, this old man with the white beard, and he listened as I told him that there was no lock, no way to protect my belongings and myself, as I slept that night.

He looked at me for a long time, he looked at my body and at my possessions, my clothes and all that I had brought with me, and then he turned back to me again, puzzled. "Lock, Sahib?" He lifted his hand. "What is there to lock?"

I glanced at the old man standing there. A lock could safeguard only a man's body, only his possessions, only these physical things.

What is there to lock?

13

New Delhi was my last assignment in India. I had started here and now I had come back to this capital of the country, and I was thinking about some of the things that I had learned as I had traveled in India.

One of my most important lessons had been in Bangalore where the lawyers had been so courteous to me personally but had shouted and banged their fists about the United States. After that had happened, I decided on different tactics. Having found out that I was likely always to be asked about our sending arms to Pakistan, about segregation, probably about our stand on Kashmir, and possibly something about our foreign aid, I made up my mind to head off their shouting and their finger shaking. I didn't like it for myself and I wasn't going to put up with it for the United States, so I managed somewhere in my speech, or certainly somewhere before the questioning could get started, to let them know where I *personally* stood on Pakistan, Kashmir, or anything else that concerned their country and mine. There was nothing new or unusual about what I said, but I told them honestly what I thought, establishing a clear relationship between us, and between our nations, and it worked.

I had found out as far back as the Philippines that in dealing with these people of other countries straight man-to-man talk is the best. I didn't start out on the trip with any idea of ducking or dodging anything, but at times I had caught myself being a little careful and weighing my words, thinking that I should be circumspect in talking with foreign audiences. Before long, however, and especially after the Philippines, I forgot about playing it safe and when I was sure that I had an opinion, and was sure that I believed in it, then I said it. This is the best way to get along with them. These people of other countries, the Indians in particular, often are forthright to the point of bluntness, and they recognize and appreciate complete frankness, no matter how wide the disagreement or how sharp the argument that may follow.

After Bangalore I made certain in every speech to settle another thing, too. I let them know that with me the United States came first. Where the United States was concerned, even indirectly, I had one interest—the good of my own country. After that was settled, I could become interested in their country, but India and India's problems were completely second with me to the needs and problems of my own country.

This put things on a different basis. Actually, I don't think that many of them had ever stopped and given the United States a thought. The United States was a mass, a force of billions and billions of dollars, and it didn't consist of people, of just ordinary men and women, and all that ordinary men and women have to contend with. (I believe that this is true in many countries, and that we, who individually are the most friendly and kindly of men, have not managed to establish in the minds of other men that our nation is made up of this kind of people.)

Nor had it occurred to them that India could be second to anybody. Young as a nation, vain and selfish as the young often are, they wanted what *they* wanted, and they didn't like being crossed. That the United States would dare to bolster Pakistan, their old religious enemy, infuriated them. It didn't matter to them that the United States was trying to protect herself; this didn't interest them in the slightest, and they brushed it aside.

But I found if I let them know what we are doing, just stood there and made plain to them how things are, reminding them that the United States is a nation, too, and that we Americans are men and women, too, and that we will listen but that we aren't going to be told, that we can be reasonable but that we can be tough—I found out that when I told them this, then the whole feeling of a room could change. I could see the men in the room sort of settle back and glance at each other, and occasionally there would be a glance almost of surprise that they had overlooked that fact that the United States is just people. After this shift, and it was invariable, we discussed the issues of Pakistan, segregation, Kashmir, or anything else with some show of reason, giving and taking in the argument; and while the argument sometimes could get strong, nobody shouted, and they weren't red faced, and they didn't beat on the table.

I doubt if anybody was completely convinced and satisfied about the issues themselves, but I am certain that a lot of them caught on that here is a nation, the United States, that has its national lacks and its national problems, as well as all its money and its strength. They began to realize, too, that the men and women of this nation have some of the same personal worries as Indian men and women, and that Americans deserve to be recognized and considered, and that India and Indians were not always to come first.

The question about aid and money was always a touchy one, but there wasn't any use in dodging that either. I mentioned that the only aid that we Americans had, when we were starting out as a nation, was when we ourselves reached for a bigger ax.

I let them know, too, that hard work wasn't just at the beginning for the United States. We in the United States still have to work hard; either we work for what we get, or we don't get it. The wife of the United States senator from my state operates a business of curing hams and bacon. I didn't want to offend anybody by mentioning the curing of meat, but that was the way we lived, and a United States senator's wife has a ham-curing business, and she runs it herself. The state senator from my district has a broom factory, and he makes mops, too. And my banker has a farm. There is nobody in the United States who is too good to work, and work with his hands.

As for the actual money that we individual Americans have, despite our riches as a nation, I told them that my wife was wandering around in the shops of their city that morning, seeing things that she and I wanted to buy but that we couldn't afford because so much of our income had gone away from us in the form of taxes. Some of this money that had come out of our pockets had been sent on to India, and was helping in India now; helping, incidentally, to keep *their* taxes down. Some of the money that had come out of *my* pocket was, at this very minute, in *their* pockets.

I wasn't objecting to this because I knew that this was the way that it had to be, and I believed in it; but there wasn't any sense or reason in talking about more American aid to India, or more American aid to anywhere else in the world, until we sat down and had some hardheaded bargaining, made some contracts, and *knew* what we in the United States were going to get back. The time had come for us to be certain of what kind of partnership, financial and moral, we were getting into.

We didn't mind working, reaching for a bigger ax, curing hams, making mops, and we didn't mind sharing with the nations of the free world, and we would go on sharing whenever we believed it was sensible and to our common advantage; but we wanted some understandings, and some clearer agreements, and to be downright honest about it, we wouldn't mind just a little appreciation.

When I had first known that I was coming to India there were three places I was sure that I wanted us to visit. One, the caves of Ellora and Ajanta, we had seen while I was in the Bombay area, for they are not far from Bombay and are near the city of Aurangabad.

Caves and rock carving are almost as common as ruins over

the earth, and the experienced traveler learns to shy away from them, since so many aren't worth looking at. Many of them, too, are in the same pattern and are monotonous, but nowhere else in the world is there anything like these caves of Ellora and Ajanta, and they are worth *going* to see. Their interest is not only because they are huge and somewhat fantastic, but they are beautiful in their design and godly in their purpose, and one feels this, and he may have seen many things over the world, but he will remember these caves.

They are man-made, cut back into the rock, and some of them are two thousand years old. At Ajanta there are thirty caves. They once formed a Buddhist monastery where the monks ran a college, and the scholars lived, and studied, and worshiped in the caves with the monks. Each cave is cut back into a rock cliff that stands above a ravine and over a river, and some of the caves were dormitories, with stone beds and stone pillows, and some were classrooms with stone benches and stone bulletin boards. Often in front of these dormitories are broad verandas, the roofs supported by stone pillars, and here the scholars studied and the monks could sit and look out over the ravine and meditate.

Besides the dormitories and classrooms at Ajanta there are caves that were meeting halls, chapels, and chapterhouses for the monks, some of them cut back seventy feet deep and twenty feet wide, and here are carved images of Buddha that are so restful, so serene, so sure of eternity, that one can understand how these men worshiped here. Also there are frescoes, scenes of this earth and of heaven, that are beautiful in their conception, their drawing, and their coloring. They are flaked and chipped, but they endure.

The other caves in this area are at Ellora, only a short distance from Ajanta, but they have nothing to do with the monastery and the college. They are rock temples extending a mile and a quarter along the face of a hill, and some of the temples are Buddhist, some Hindu, some Jain, and the most remarkable of them all is a temple of Siva, the most remarkable structure that I have ever seen, more than anything in Angkor, more than anything in Greece or Rome.

For this temple, the builders adopted a plan different from any of the others; they did not cut back into the face of the hill and make a cave, instead, they started at the top and cut straight down into the rock on four sides, leaving a huge mass of stone standing alone and completely detached. They then started cutting into the stone, working in from four sides, to make their temple.

As they moved in, carving as they advanced, they created this miracle of architecture. Some of the galleries and corridors were started from opposite sides, and they met in the mass of stone at the fraction of the inch that had been planned for their meeting. In front of these galleries and corridors that run throughout the temple, often crossing each other, is an open courtyard, and here are elephants carved life-size, and yet the massiveness of the whole is so great that the elephants are not unduly noticed and they simply blend into the vast temple. There are towering obelisks, and vestibules and passages adorned with images of Siva and Parvati, with statues of Siva slaying his enemies, Siva meditating, Siva as the gigantic masculine symbol of creation.

The banistered stairway leads from vestibule to vestibule, from balcony to balcony, until it arrives at last, in the center of the temple, ninety feet high, at the holy of holies, the image of the sacred bull.

The other two places that I wanted us to see were Jaipur, the Pink City, and the Taj Mahal. Both of them are near New Delhi, and after we were back in New Delhi, our time in India getting short, we planned our trips to go to see them.

Some two and a half centuries ago there was a ruler named Jai Singh II, and he was a warrior, an astronomer, a mathematician—and he loved the color pink. No one knows why this man was so fond of this color, but he decided to build a whole city of pink. He laid it out himself, and every house, every shop, every palace was pink.

It is still pink, and a person might believe that a whole street of pink buildings would be too much, like a sudden flight of flamingoes, but these pink streets of Jaipur are really very attractive as well as being very unusual. One walks along here, past the houses, past the palaces, and he sees this strange continuous sight in pink; but whatever he may see, or however it may interest him, there is always in his mind, more than any wonder about the color itself, his questions about this curious man who fought his battles, studied the stars, and then decided—for what *possible* reason?—that he wanted a city all in pink.

There are a few modern side streets in Jaipur now, and a few new areas, that have deviated from the will of the builder. They have used ordinary colors, the houses and the buildings like anywhere else, but one hurries past them without even a glance, wanting to get back to where all is pink.

Not far from Jaipur is the ancient city of Amber, and we went there one morning and hired an elephant to take us up a hill too steep for us to climb, so that we could visit the old palace at the top. We were riding along past a gorge when we looked up and saw a line of camels near the palace wall, and we thought it strange that a caravan should have come here.

When finally we came to the top, our elephant moved out into a mob of men, women, and children. Jaipur and Amber are in the state of Rajasthan, and the Rajasthanis are among the most picturesque of all the Indian people in their attire. This day they were arrayed in especially colorful dress with gaudy skirts and blouses, bright headpieces, bracelets stacked up their arms, loops of silver in their ears, and their anklets jangling as they walked. We had heard that J. Arthur Rank was in the area, filming a picture called *Northwest Frontier,* but we had not known that he was to be at this ancient palace with these hundreds of Indian people and all these animals hired for the big scene.

Unable to ride through the mass of people and the pack of animals, we climbed down off our elephant and left him beside the wall and walked up to the top where we could watch the filming of the scene. It was a flight scene, the people running in panic before their enemies, crushing their way through a narrow pass. The director told the interpreters, and the interpreters explained to the people that they were terrified and were fleeing for their lives. They were in complete panic, cringing from the death behind them, and racing to escape.

When finally all was ready, the director checked once more, the cameraman checked, and the interpreter checked, making completely sure that these people understood their terror.

There was a moment's pause, for one last look at everything, and then the signal was given!

The people, looking back over their shoulders, surged up the hill to escape the death behind them. A herd of goats raced through the passage, the goatherd running with them. A bullock cart strained through, the white-bearded driver leaning forward and lashing his animals. An elephant lumbered past. And then a camel came on.

It just so happened that this camel was carrying, as a part of his load, a large tin trunk, which, since it was only a bit of the show, was empty. It also happened that just as this camel came opposite the cameras, the trunk slipped out from under its ropes, slid down the camel's side, and nicked him as it went by.

That camel then stopped and backed up. He looked around slowly, judging his distance and taking good aim, then he lifted his hind foot and kicked that trunk clear out into space, sailing it and spinning it toward the bottom of the gorge.

The other camel drivers, still fleeing for their lives, still running from the death behind them, came through the pass doubled up with laughter, a mahout almost fell off his elephant, and the other refugees couldn't hide their laughing.

The movie director called it off. They would do it all over

again when these Indians, running in terror for their lives, weren't having such a damn good time.

Three centuries ago lived a woman named Mumtaz Mahal and one day she was seen by the Emperor Shah Jahan, the Mogul emperor of Delhi, and he loved her and took her for his wife. He called her Taj Mahal, "Crown of the Palace," and she bore him thirteen children, then, in 1631, she died.

Soon the emperor, who had loved this woman more than he knew, called for the artists of his own country and sent messengers abroad, requesting that designers and builders come to his court. They came, bringing with them their dreams in stone and marble, and among them came Ustad Isa, and whether he was a Byzantine Turk or a Persian no one knows for sure, nor does it matter. He brought a model, made of wood, and he showed it to Shah Jahan. The emperor liked it and told him to begin his work.

He built in pure-white marble, building the broad sweep of the terrace in marble, and the great center dome in marble, and the smaller domes and slender minarets. He inlaid with agates, with bloodstones and jasper, placing them in wreaths, scrolls, and frets. He pierced and carved until the tracery was like marble lace. He worked for seventeen years, and with him worked a French goldsmith, Austin of Bordeaux. Then the tomb was ready, and Mumtaz Mahal was laid to her permanent rest.

Shah Jahan went about the business of state, building the Mogul power to its greatest strength, destroying his enemies, caring for his people, and building, always building—the Pearl Mosque at Agra, the palace and the great mosque at Delhi, the Peacock Throne.

And then he fell ill and his son, Aurangzeb, imprisoned him. But even this son was merciful and he put the old shah where there would be memories. Outside the room was a balcony and there, on moonlight nights, the shah could sit and look across the land, and across the river, and see the white tomb of his wife. He remembered wars and victories, but he dreamed of a woman and of a voice at night. Then one day he ceased to dream, and they came and carried him across the river, and across the marble terrace, and down the marble stairs, and they put him beside this woman that he had loved, and they are there now.

The building that he built for her is more beautiful than has been written or told. It has been pictured so many times that one can at least imagine the beauty of its design, but not even imagination can conceive of the interior with small flowers inlaid in their natural colors with precious stones, and the larger flowers, life-size, carved in the marble so perfectly that even the stamens stand clear.

One must come in the daytime to see the details of the interior, but the beauty of the building as a whole is lost by day, for the blaze of the marble is too white and one cannot look. Even by the full moon it is too white. I have seen it by the full moon, and it is there for one to see, but it is too plainly seen and too clear.

But when the moon is a bit old and the night begins dark, and one sits at the far end of the garden and waits, he will see it before it is there, because he knows it is there. And then, slowly, it comes to the call of the moon, drifting up out of the darkness, but never coming quite clear, and he never sees it plainly but he will see it forever.

It was getting on close to the time when we would be leaving India, and we went back to New Delhi again. It is a pretty city with wide and slow-curving streets, parks and generous playing fields, and almost everywhere that one looks there are flowers along the way, abundant and rich in their colors. Dominating the city are the government buildings, huge and of red sandstone. They have a sweep and a strength and a simple beauty that make them impressive and memorable.

They have been put up by the Indians themselves since the Republic, and I asked a man about the size of these buildings and how much they must have cost. He admitted their cost, but he said that India is a young nation and that many of the people are illiterate, and that they had lived for so long under the English that now they must have something that they can see, something to prove to them that their government is big and strong. Each year the government debates the money for putting up the lights on Republic Night, knowing that they need every rupee they can save, but always they put up the lights. The people, so many of them simple in their ways and almost childlike in their thinking about their nation, have to be shown again that they really are independent, that now they have taken their place among the nations and rule themselves in a democracy, and here are the buildings, and here the lights to prove it.

I have walked through these government buildings and talked with government men, and we in the United States probably cannot comprehend, no matter how clearly we are told, what these people are up against. India's population already is dense, and yet it is increasing. Illiteracy of the nation is 80 per cent. (United States: 3 per cent.) *The life expectancy of an Indian is twenty-seven years. His average annual income is $60.00.*

Confronted with these barriers, and always with the Communists adding to India's burdens, the Indian leaders are doing just about all that men can do to develop and stabilize their nation. They are making birth control a prime teaching, they are extending general education, increasing hospital and nursing service, enlarging farm demonstrations, and encouraging cottage handicrafts. They are doing their utmost, and no man can hold back his esteem from these Indian leaders for what they are doing *inside* their country for the betterment of their nation.

It is one of the most puzzling contrasts of our time that these same men, so wise and so courageous in their internal program for India, should sustain the shortsighted and dangerous plan of "nonalignment" in India's foreign policy.

With things as they are with India, and with all the world today, the international stand of her government is impossible to agree with or to honor. India's government is a Socialist one, and her political leaders have chosen for her this policy of non-alignment, giving as their reason that India is a peaceful nation, wanting to stay outside the power struggle of the world, and that she must expend all her energy in building up her economy at home.

This is all that any nation would like to do, but somebody has got to face up to the fact of Russia, Red China, and World Communism, and it is no credit to India that she prefers to let somebody else do it, while she herself enjoys all the benefits of continuing as a free and non-Communistic country.

The expediency of her political philosophy, and her selfishness in treating both sides equally, both World Communism and the world democracies, and her accepting aid and benefits from both, endanger India herself and make just that much harder the tasks of the democratic nations that are keeping her free. Everybody recognizes the need for India to build up her economy at home, and nobody asks her to supply one man, one gun, or one rupee; but her Western friends, on whom her independence depends, and to whom she entrusts her national freedom, could use her openly declared and unrestrained moral support, and she should have the national courage and political integrity to give it.

We stood at the window of our hotel that last afternoon and saw the dust storm like a red wall, heaven high, coming toward us across the plain. It tore down the trellises, slammed benches against the building, skidded bicycles along the street, and then closed in, and we could not see the street. Within minutes there was a red film on everything in our room, although we had shut the windows tight. It had been dry and burning hot all the morning, and now this dust storm in the afternoon—yet we still did not want to leave India.

There was a curious lonely feeling about our going; just why,

I cannot explain. There had been days when I had wanted to get out of India, out of the heat, away from the dirt, and free of these contradictory and, at times, exasperating people.

I had been surfeited with their talk about Pakistan. I did not believe for one minute that Pakistan was ever going to use the arms that we are sending to them for anything so foolish as to attack India, and I didn't believe for one minute that the Indians thought so either. It just gave their demagogues a bloody shirt to wave, and their rednecks, whether they wore morning coats or loincloths, an excuse to shout.

I had had more than enough from them, too, of their pious hypocrisy in criticizing the people of the United States about our shortcomings in segregation while they continued their caste system.

But in spite of their national smugness and, at times, their personal flight from reason, friendships with men and women in India can become a close and treasured thing, and an interest in India and a concern for the nation can become true and lasting.

What India and her people can do to a man is difficult to discuss and impossible to make plain. Some say that it is the ageless beauty of India, some say that it is her tolerance and enduring wisdom, some say it is her mysticism. Whatever it may be that holds a man to India, whether the beauty of the land or the lure of the religion, the gods or the people, one cannot be sure; but as I made ready to leave, I was more certain than ever that India is the most colorful, the most provocative, the most fascinating country on earth.

14

The almond trees were a lavender haze over the hills of Kashmir as we flew in for a landing. It was early April, and we had left New Delhi that morning, and already, this early in the year, the heat was closing in at Delhi and the dust storms were blowing and summer was pressing. It had been shirt-sleeve weather in New Delhi and we had said good-by to our friends in the shade, waiting as long as we could and slow in saying good-by to these people who had been so kind to us, and then crossing the open strip of the airfield fast to get to the plane itself and out of the heat.

On the way up from New Delhi to Srinagar, the capital of Kashmir, there had been two landings, and at both of these cities, still on the plains of India, the heat had been close and soggy and again we had stayed inside the terminal buildings in the shade. But flying on north over the mountains, the Himalayas again and their snow, we were cold inside the plane, and when we landed and were on the ground at Srinagar it was sharp cold, the wind with a real sting in it, and we put on our overcoats, hurrying into the little wooden shack that was the air terminal to wait for the automobile that was coming for us. We shook a little from the cold, even inside the shack as we waited, but we grinned at each other, and it was good to find that there could be cold again after the months of steady heat in India.

The way from the airport at Srinagar was long and twisting down from the hills and on across the open countryside, the land rolling and broken by rocks and gullies, and it was early spring here in Kashmir, and so much that we saw reminded us of home, for so much here was like spring in Georgia.

It had seemed to us, all the time that we were in India, that the calendar and the countryside were in curious disagreement, because even though the months had been January and February and March, the flowers that we had been seeing in India were the summer flowers at home; but now here in Kashmir we had gone back to true spring again, and it seemed as fresh and clean and pretty as a young girl. There were jonquils as yellow as churned butter, some of them scattered almost wild along the road, and some growing in rows in the gardens of the Kashmiri people, and here, too, in these gardens, were beds of pansies and banks of forsythia. The pear trees were in full white and the apple blossoms were fringed with pink. There were orchards of almond trees, and their blossoms were too pale for lavender, now that we were on the ground and could see them better; but whatever their delicate color, they were pretty in their faint pastel as they lifted on over the hills. And I kept looking at the small streams, breaking so fast over the rocks, because the water was clear and cold. It was green as pure jade, and clear as the snow it came from, and for so long we had been seeing only the slow, broad rivers of India, warm and muddy.

Our hotel again was a maharaja's palace and this was the third of these palaces that we had stayed in: in Katmandu, in Jaipur, and now here in Srinagar. Life for the maharajas of India has changed considerably in recent years. First, the national government abolished the princely states, thereby dethroning the maharajas and ending their rule. Then the government took their land and apportioned it among farmers and men who would work it, paying the princes a token fee but giving them no choice but to sell.

Next, the government put a real squeeze on the maharajas, for it told each of them that he could keep one of his palaces, a place for him to live in, but he could have no more than one. The others, the summer palace, the winter palace, the hunting palace, would have to be put to some use; they could not be left empty and idle throughout most of the year, unoccupied except for the short seasons that the princes had been living in them.

The government went even further, and it told each maharaja, most of whom up to now had done little but play with their pearls, their polo ponies, and the ladies of their courts, that he could do one of two things: he himself could go to work and open these extra palaces as hotels, in which case they would be his business to run as he saw fit, for his own profit or loss, or he could give them up and the government would take them and run them as government hotels. There was a pressing need for hotels in India, and the Indian Government was not standing back on any niceties about who owned what, they were just seeing to it that the palaces were taken out of their dustcloths and put to work, along with everything else in India that could be used for the benefit of the nation.

Some of the maharajas walked out, indignant at this treatment and insulted at the suggestion that they should run a hotel, but a few of them took a long-range and more practical view of the national situation and their own position, and they formed companies and went into the hotel business. In Jaipur, for instance, the Rambagh Palace, a gorgeous place with an unbelievably beautiful garden, is now a fine hotel, run by a company headed by the maharaja and with his family as stockholders. All the comforts of any hotel are here, and they are emphasized because the maharaja used to entertain in style and suites are more common than rooms. My wife and I asked for just an ordinary room and that is all we expected, but it turned out to be a large and airy sitting room looking out on the garden, a huge bedroom, a bath that an old Roman could have gotten lost in, and a carved ceiling twenty feet high. Of course the gardeners did arrive before daybreak and they sat under our window and talked and woke us, but we forgave them for that because the smell of the flowers is sweetest at daybreak, and then, too, we could watch the sun as it first touched them.

Besides these comforts in our suite there were even more resplendent touches of the old days—the marble roof garden, the chandeliers with their myriad crystals, and the dining room that used to be the maharaja's banqueting hall; on the floor of this room is a Persian rug that was specially woven for it, a single design in a rug from wall to wall, fifty by thirty feet.

Now that we had come to Srinagar, we were to stay at the palace of another prince, the former maharaja of Kashmir. It is a stately building with a lawn spreading wide down to a lake, and beyond the lake are the high, white mountains. It is a place of rarest beauty, but we wondered how anyone could have endured it in the freezing winters of Kashmir, for there was no trace of heat in our part of the palace and our room was as cold as the wind down from the mountain snow. We asked what could be done, and before long the bearer, a fat and genial man, came in with the best that he could do, an electric heater no bigger than a man's hat, and even the bearer was shaking his head when he turned it on. It had no effect in the huge room, and we called for brandy and reached for our coats and blankets.

This princely state of Kashmir that we had come into has long been one of the major monkey wrenches in the machinery of the United Nations, and it has been, and is now, a constant irritant to the United States, one of the continuing reasons why we are disliked and distrusted in this part of the world.

The story of Kashmir has a close sequel, fantastic and somewhat amusing, if you like, in the bizarre story of Hyderabad, also a former princely state. Together, the two states form another of the innumerable paradoxes that is India.

When Russia makes a land grab, or snatches a state and a community of people somewhere, and then justifies it with some sanctimonious and high-flown tale, even Russia, along with everybody else, knows that Russia is lying. But the Indians are not like this, and herein is a part of the difficulty of getting along with them.

They think it perfectly sensible and entirely proper to take one stand when it suits them, then turn right around and take exactly the opposite stand when it suits them; and to them, both stands are entirely right and are not to be questioned because each concerns *them* and *India*. Try to sit down with them and show them that they are changing face simply because they want things this way, and at first they are indignant, and then furious, and then, once they are crowded with unanswerable facts, they just withdraw into nirvana, that wonderful world of the spirit where each man can create whatever it is that he wants for himself, or his nation, and his wanting makes it true. Our difficulty in dealing with them is that we continually suspect that this is a dodge, a device, a trick; but to the mystical Indian it is *true*, and once they have gone into their strange retreat, we of the West cannot follow. We can only stand outside, frustrated and annoyed, unable to go in ourselves, unable to send in any facts, or to get at them with either reason or logic.

When India, back in 1947, was unscrambling her old provinces and princely states, getting ready to make a nation, she came across the large state of Hyderabad in south-central India. The ruler was Mohammedan, but the people were chiefly Hindu. India simply took over the state, disregarding the protesting Moslem ruler, sending in troops and brushing him aside, saying that of course the people must rule. Since the majority of the people of Hyderabad were Hindu, then Hyderabad of course must be a Hindu state and become a part of India.

Now for Kashmir...

Seventy-seven per cent of the people of Kashmir are Moslems, but the ruler was a Hindu, and India said that of course a ruler must decide where his state should go. Since the ruler was a Hindu, Kashmir of course must be a Hindu state and become a part of India.

However, they hit a snag in Kashmir because it lies between

India and Pakistan, and the people of Pakistan said that it was a Moslem state because most of the people were Moslems, and therefore it should join Pakistan. Each side sent in its troops, a sheer power play by both India and Pakistan, a grab for the land, and they fought a small war to see which of them would get it.

The United Nations stepped in and ended the war, drawing an armistice line, but this did not end the quarrel and Kashmir today is split between India and Pakistan, each side accusing the other of having stolen the land it now occupies and each side demanding that the other side get out.

Both India and Pakistan, under encouragement from the United Nations, have agreed to a plebiscite; but India has never been willing to agree to terms, for India knows how the people, overwhelmingly Moslem, would vote. India keeps her troops in strong garrisons in that part of the country she holds, and Indian troops are frequently seen in Srinagar, the capital and central city of the country.

The biggest park in Srinagar has a huge sign over it, "NEHRU PARK," and one Kashmiri, a dignified and ordinarily a very reserved gentleman, told me that every time he saw that name and that sign he wanted to vomit.

Kashmir is a place to go and look, and see how beautiful a country with lakes and mountains and gardens can be. It is no place for hurry, for engagements or appointments, or what do we do tomorrow? One gets up, and here is the day again, and he drifts through it.

There are lovely gardens in Srinagar, the Mogul gardens, and one of them is Shalimar, which means "Abode of Love." And one is the "Garden of Pleasure." And one is "Royal Spring." These are poetic names, but they are not too much, for the gardens are as pretty as the names.

We went to the new city of Srinagar and to the old city, and it is very old, with houses that teeter on the brink of time and other houses that are roofed with a sod of grass, each housetop covered over thick with green, and now and then one sees a wild iris or a buttercup blooming on a roof. We went to the Floating Gardens, which of course aren't floating at all, and it is only a name; the vegetables grow on the small land plots that have been built up until they are just out of the shallow water, and the gardeners go out in boats to tend to their plantings.

We went to the country club and had tea, and the Moslem men sat around with their hats on. They complained that Kashmir, a Mohammedan country, is ruled in large part by the soldiers of India, by the Hindu guns. Why didn't the United States come in and settle the Kashmir question? They accused the United States and blamed us.

There is no reason whatsoever for the United States to take any action regarding Kashmir. Kashmir is an international issue that has long confronted the United Nations, and still confronts that organization, and the American responsibility is no more than that of England, France, or Ethiopia. Yet throughout India, and now here in Kashmir itself, I was hearing the United States blamed for not settling the Kashmir question. I had argued this issue so many times before, and I saw no reason for arguing again, for spoiling a pleasant afternoon in this country with the lake outside the window and the white mountains in the sky.

I asked these men at the country club what would happen if there were a plebiscite in Kashmir, how would the vote go. They reminded me that the country is three to one Moslem. How would I expect it to go? That was why India was blocking the plebiscite. She had stolen the land, and she meant to keep it.

"The people, of course, would vote to go to Pakistan," one man said. "But that is not what we really want. We don't want a plebiscite. We want independence—an independent Kashmir."

They all want independence these days, any group that can possibly arrange itself into any kind of national form is wanting independence, without regard whatsoever for the realities of independence. Since World War II new nations have been blown like bubbles in the Orient, and their strain and danger of breaking are adding to the economic imbalance and the political tensions in the East.

I asked the man if he believed that Kashmir had a sound and independent economy. Political independence is good only for a flag and some shouting. How were they going to pay their bills? Could they maintain themselves?

"We would have to build up our national economy," he said. "It would be difficult at first but we would expect the United States, of course, to help us get started."

They look to us for everything. They blame us for everything.

This is one of the puzzles that we people back home can't figure out. Just how did we get ourselves into this international mess, forever playing the role of both Santa Claus and whipping boy, fronting over the world for everybody's debts and everybody's failures?

In the struggle between the United States and Russia for the dominant place in the world, in the efforts of each of these two leaders to guide its side to the defeat of the other, and then move on in world influence, both the United States and Russia are making constant use of foreign aid, and we in the United States, in our senate, in our banking circles, in our labor and farm councils, in our women's clubs, are harping on how much we spend. But how much we spend is not the paramount factor. It is where we spend it, what for, and how.

No sensible businessman would start spending his money until he had looked over the ground mighty carefully, knew a lot about the people he was going to deal with, was thoroughly and specifically acquainted with the project he was undertaking, and had figured as close as he could what profit he would make. Russia follows this plan.

In the first place, she knows the countries and the people, making it her business to learn everything about them, the strength of the people, their weakness, their needs, their wants.

Her aid is patiently planned, well ordered, and usually it is something tremendously big and impressive, something that the people can see and be proud of, and that they will brag about, always mentioning the name of Russia. She goes in and she builds a steel mill, a dam, doing one specific thing exactly as she has contracted for it, making sure beforehand that she can keep her word to the fraction, and positive that she can make the mill work just as she has promised, allowing no chance for a breakdown so that people could criticize or ridicule Russia. Invariably she does this on her own terms, always knowing what she is going to get back, always making sure that there will be something in it for Russia, and benefit and encouragement for World Communism.

The United States, generous and bighearted, comes in openhanded, and starts a *program,* a health program, agriculture, teacher training, animal husbandry, beetle control. It is well meaning and in the long run would be helpful, but an illiterate people just sampling independence have nothing to compare it with, it is too complex and too long range, and they misunderstand and mistrust. Let half your land lie idle! A fat chicken for a scrawny one! What are these Americans up to? These things that we undertake cannot be quickly seen or completely realized. We have not yet caught on to the need for immediacy and the justifiable benefits of the obvious—these are the reasons that the government of India built the huge buildings, even while they were needing every rupee for something else, but knowing that they had to *convince* the people.

The United States has gone over the world, and in so many places, and in so many ways, we have undertaken so many things. We have set out to teach men how to breed cattle and how to plant wheat. We have told one nation where it needs a road and another that it needs fertilizer. We have been doing everything for everybody, and now everybody looks to us for everything. When the tractor that we gave them needs a nut or a bolt, and we aren't standing right there to hand it to them, they blame us for the whole thing, even the tractor in the first place.

It is curious that our lending has so often brought us blame for failures, and our giving has returned us international disloyalty and distrust.

On the lakes of Kashmir are taxiboats, ordinary small, flat-bottomed boats, called *shikaras,* and one gets into them for a ride or a journey as he uses a gondola in Venice. The boatmen will take a person anywhere he wants to go; but since so often in Kashmir one doesn't want to go anywhere, and wants only to drift, the boatman always is more than willing to join in the ease, and he lies back, too, and lets the boat and the wind have their way.

Then there are the famous houseboats of Kashmir that are rented for a vacation, or for the whole summer. They look like large automobile trailers and they are parked along the riverbank, side by side and close together, and all around the edges of the lake. The larger ones have two living rooms, three bedrooms, and a bath with hot and cold running water. They have their own terraces and gardens, and at the back is a smaller boat for the four servants that are standard for such an establishment. Now and then a person who lives in one of them goes by small boat across to the land, and on into Srinagar to buy, or his servants go in for supplies, or the farmers from the Floating Gardens come along in their *shikaras* to bring the fresh vegetables and the really excellent fruits of Kashmir. It is an easy and a lazy and an enjoyable life.

There are few places so pretty to look at as Kashmir, and so perfect to deny the sovereignty of time, but there had to be an end to it, for even before we had left India I had heard from Washington again, and now they were asking if I would go on to Pakistan, to Afghanistan, and to still other countries for USIS. I had agreed to go, and the time had come for us to take up that work again.

We were slow in our packing that last afternoon, for our room had been changed to where there was heat and we could sit in the alcove, warm and drinking our tea, and look out at the lake with its houseboats and the *shikaras* slowly moving, and we could see the mountains and their snow. It was not easy to go away from this, to leave a place that was so quiet and so restful, and go back south again, to take up a scheduled life in the heat and the clutter and the push of the cities again.

15

The way out of Kashmir is south and back over the mountains once more and on to the city of Amritsar. We landed there and right away stepped back into the rivalry and contention between India and Pakistan. When seen from the United States or from any other country far off, or known only from newspaper accounts and books, the quarrel between these two countries seems to be one of the most foolish and most futile of all the cantankerous squabbles now going on between nations, and it is. But to one who comes here, who hears the Hindus scream their hate and the Moslems mutter their curses, who knows of the trainloads of dead and the murdered people, this is nonsense and futility all right, but it is deadly.

It can seem silly, and it is; petty, and it is, but live with these people for a while and one begins to feel the force and the constancy of this issue. Religious hate is the most persistent and venomous of all, and it has been so since man first began to subdivide his god and assume interpretation of the parts, but nowhere else in the world of religious contention has there been such intense and lasting hate as between Hindus and Moslems. There probably never will be a declared war between India and Pakistan, for their leaders are not that suicidal, but there will continue to be a token killing here, a murder there, and now and then a crumpled man with a gaping throat will be found. One who knows this will understand that even incidental happenings between Hindus and Moslems always have this background of religious violence. It is the pall that hangs over this part of the world, evil and destructive, and it can never be disregarded.

Amritsar is in India, and from there we were to cross over into Pakistan, going on to Lahore, a distance of twenty-eight miles.

We hired an automobile to take us to the border, and there it would stop, for no automobile is allowed to cross over, and there is no dealing or transportation here of any kind between the two countries, no taxi, bus, or bullock cart. Yet here is a wide and once important highway over which goods and trade went back and forth, and people traveled, and its benefits were shared by everyone. It is still here, but now it lies empty and stretches on through vacant land, and we saw no one, either coming or going, as we approached the border.

As we sighted the border and its barrier across the road, our driver slowed down, saying that he didn't want to get too near and he stopped. He himself was an Indian, and we, of course, were on the Indian side, but he just didn't want to get too close to this border.

Our car had hardly stopped rolling when fifteen or twenty men came up from beside the road, from out of the grass itself so it seemed, and they were instantly swarming about us, snatching at our clothes and catching hold of us, each banging his skinny chest and bragging about how strong he was and what a load he could carry. The shouting and the grabbing continued, until from out of the general scramble one man emerged, tall, soft-spoken, and the others fell back. This man was the head porter and he stated his terms: we would pay him and he would appoint the men to carry our bags.

Seldom has there been a more forlorn procession than marched that macadam road that day. It was oven hot, the sun baking down, and there was no sign of shade, not a patch, for every tree and every bit of undergrowth had been cut back from the road to prevent an ambush. I was leading, going on toward the barricade, my wife trailing me by some half-dozen paces, a folded newspaper held over her head, and behind us were strung out six barefooted, gaunt, and ragged porters, moving in a silent line, each with a suitcase on his head. I called back to my wife a comment about a safari, but she didn't answer.

We came to the first barricade, and the Indian guards admitted us past their post, on to the customs officer, the passport officer, the currency-control officer where our money was counted and if we had had more than fifty rupees, it would have been taken away from us. No one goes out of India with more than fifty rupees; the government takes the rest.

We filled out forms and answered questions, until finally the Indian authorities signed our papers and waved us on toward Pakistan. Outside the building we found the porters squatted like six frogs beside our suitcases, and at sight of us they put the suitcases on their heads again, fell in line, and we marched on, crossing the no-man's land that separates India and Pakistan, a quarter of a mile wide and empty of everything.

Here are two countries that are irrevocably bound to each other in their geography, their economy, and their culture, yet they have turned their backs on each other. India produces coal, but Pakistan won't buy coal from India; she must send to China or to Poland to get her coal, and pay the extra cost. Pakistan produces jute, and jute is essential to India's mills, but India won't buy from Pakistan, scouring the world to find her jute, no matter what the extra cost.

These people have lived together for centuries, and together they make one nation, yet now, at a time when unions of nations are essential and no nation on earth can retain its freedom alone, these people, who together might have made an almost impregnable stand, have split in arrogance and old hates. The loss is not theirs alone, for the division of these two countries increases the risks to all the democracies.

On across no-man's land we trudged, the porters marching in file, their impassive faces carved in brown marble, their eyes cast down, seeing only the heels of the man in front, our suitcases steady as stone above the pliant swing of their necks. After a quarter of a mile of this dead land we came to a second barrier, and it was exactly like the first, the same poles, same wire, same sentry boxes, only the guards here were different, for here they were Pakistanis.

The Indian porters could not cross this line and they took the suitcases from their heads, set them down in the road, and again instantly flushed around us, this time holding out their hands for baksheesh. Once they had it, they turned back toward India, strung out in single file again, stalking back to their country. Pakistani porters then stepped into no-man's land, picked up our suitcases, put them on their heads, and filed into Pakistan. If we had not known, we could not have told that there had been a transfer.

Once more we saw the customs officer, passport officer, currency-control officer, filling out the same kind of forms, answering the identical questions, and once more our papers were signed and once more the authorities waved us on, this time admitting us into Pakistan. It had taken us better than two hours to get through the two blockades.

An officer from USIS was waiting here on the Pakistan side to drive us into Lahore, and he drove fast to get us there in time for my first meeting, a talk with the newspapermen of the city.

Lahore is a crowded city of a million people, and I saw no major difference in this Pakistani city from the cities of India, from Bombay or Madras or Calcutta, except for the dress of the people. Here in Pakistan most of the women are veiled and most of the men wear the distinctive turban of the Moslems, white and full in its wrapping. Their robes, too, are white, and the old men are white-bearded. One sees them hurrying along to the mosque, their slippered feet urgent upon the stones, while high from the minaret the unsatisfied muezzin calls them again to prayer, summoning them again to the washing and to their praying.

Five times each day they pray, facing Mecca. Wherever they may be, in whatever part of the Moslem world, they face toward Mecca when they pray, and it is strange to go from east to west of Mecca, from north to south of Mecca, and see them shift in their facing as they pray. Mecca is fixed, whatever the stars or the seasons may be.

It is strange, too, to walk into the washroom at some airport or railway station or hotel and see some man, his foot lifted and in the washbasin, washing his feet and making ready for prayer, for always they must wash before they pray. It is risky, too, to drive too fast on a mountain road in a Mohammedan country because at sunset one may swing around a cliff and there will lie a Moslem, prostrate in the dust, making his prayers toward Mecca. It can be a pretty sight, though, to see some shepherd boy, with the sun low behind him, lay aside his staff and unwrap his shawl, spreading it and smoothing it, and kneeling there to pray.

Five times each day the muezzin climbs into the minaret and sounds the call to prayer. *La Illaha illa Allah* is his call, and throughout the world of Islam, from Indonesia across Asia, on across Africa to Morocco, 350,000,000 Moslems prostrate themselves toward Mecca. It can be disconcerting when this call sounds in the midst of a lecture and a good part of the audience gets up and walks out, coming back later.

Lahore is a city of universities and colleges, and in this city Rudyard Kipling's father once was curator of the museum. Today in a grass plot not far from the museum there stands the most famous cannon in the world, Kim's cannon, *Zam Zama*. In Lahore is the newspaper, the *Civil and Military Gazette,* with a plaque on the wall saying that Rudyard Kipling once worked here as a reporter. This was before the turn of the century, and the editor told me that not even the old men now remember Kipling.

I went to Rawalpindi, in the north of Pakistan, and stayed at the headquarters of the General Staff of the Pakistani army. The officers were young, intelligent, and vigorous, and I felt a strict training and discipline, as if the Pakistani army were dependable soldiers and desirable allies.

My talks at this headquarters were about current life in the United States, letting the Pakistanis know more about us, and I was surprised one evening after a reception when I was asked to talk to the officers and their wives about American literature. I was astonished later, during the questioning, when I found out how much they know about our literature. It is somewhat worrisome to discover how much more the peoples of the world know about us than we have bothered to learn about them.

I was here among these Moslem soldiers during the month of Ramadan, the ninth month, which is the most holy of all because it was in this month that the Koran was revealed to the Prophet Mohammed. Every day throughout this month of Ramadan there must be a total fasting from all food, from water and women, and this fasting is from the first moment each morning that a white thread can be distinguished from a black thread, until again at night the threads cannot be distinguished one from the other. This is a time of trial and strain for the Moslems, and it is a delicate time, too, for any unbeliever who is among them, for he must guard against any display or ostentation in his eating or drinking.

The end of Ramadan is on the night when the new moon of the incoming month is seen, and this moon they call the Id moon; but merely because the astronomers say that the moon will be in the sky, that their calculations have told them that it will be there, means nothing, for it must be seen by men. He who sees it first cries out, and when it has been seen by two others, then Ramadan and the month of fasting are over.

On the night that the Id moon was expected in Rawalpindi we were outside, a hundred of us, men and women, all searching in the evening sky for the sign that would release them, and they could go back inside the building and drink the tea and eat the cakes that had been prepared but that they could not touch unless the moon was seen.

And then suddenly a young officer cried, "There! There is the Id moon." But I could not see it, and I asked where it was and he came behind me and fixed my head, holding it, and he said: "There! Look! The Id moon is just beyond the garden and above the lemon bush." And there it was, a hair of gold on the floor of the sky, and we all went inside and had tea and cakes, even though it was not yet dark and we could still tell the difference between a white thread and a black one.

One of the officers was a young captain, and we came to know each other. He visited my room one evening, and as we talked I happened, for some reason that I don't remember, to mention Lucknow, which is in India. He touched his sleeve, as if to brush something off. "You have been to Lucknow?"

I had been there only a short time before.

"I was born in Lucknow," he said. "Tell me about it."

So often these people who have hurried from one country to another, hastening to some strange city across the line, listen as if their whole childhood were here again, their home and their family, as they hear someone tell of the place that they know best. This is perhaps the most saddening part of all this brutality and nonsense, when some man or woman sits still and listens and remembers, and anyone can see their loneliness and feel their longing.

While most people fled to the country of their religion at the time India was partitioned, some Hindus and some Moslems stayed on in their homes and risked the fighting. Today, in some of the larger cities of India, one occasionally sees the white turban of the Moslem man and now and then a veiled woman. In Pakistan, too, one sees a Hindu now and then. They go their way untroubled in business and in worship; but when they worship in the opposite religion, they are in second place in the country, and need not aspire to too high a place or expect power in the national government.

At the time of partition, the land as well as the people had to be divided, and the result is a nation, Pakistan, with almost a baffling geography. The division of the land was made according to religion, and there was a concentration of Moslems at the northeast corner of India and another concentration at the northwest corner, so they just cut these two corners off and called them Pakistan, a nation with its two parts a thousand miles away from each other, and with the enemy nation, India, lying in between. There is no way for a Pakistani to get from one half of his country to the other except by land across India, by air over India, or by sea around India. It is as if 1,000 miles of Russia lay between New England and Texas, and the total unreality of the arrangement indicates the impetuousness and stubbornness of the men who planned it and signed it.

In Pakistan, whether one is in the eastern part or the western part, whether in the city of Dacca or Karachi, he hears the same talk that he heard in India, only now it is reversed. In Pakistan I was asked again and again and again: Why does the United States send economic aid to India? Why do we strengthen India, when she is only waiting to attack Pakistan?

Sometimes I could close my eyes and say it with them, just reversing the names. I had heard it so many times before.

We send arms to Pakistan, and India is furious.

We send economic aid to India, and Pakistan is suspicious.

One reason they are angry and suspicious is that nobody from the American government, nobody who has the full authority of the American government, has gone into these two countries, put aside the hampering formality of diplomatic talk, and looked them straight in the eye and told each country exactly what we are doing, why we are doing it, and that we are going to keep on doing it until we ourselves decide that there is something else that is more suited to our interest. We will listen to them, we will work with them, but until they convince us that some other way is better for us and for all the democracies, we shall continue what in our judgment is the best plan.

A person who travels between India and Pakistan and listens to the talk in the two countries, hearing it exactly reversed, the aggressor now the innocent, the warlike now the mild, is getting a pretty good example of man's ability to dupe himself into believing that all righteousness resides with him, and that all evil is with somebody else.

There is, for instance, this matter of certain rivers that are supposed to form the boundaries between the two countries. The hurried and flustered men who drew the lines at the time of partition forgot about the habits of these rivers, for they are in a low, flat country and sometimes they wander. According to rainfall, they may change their beds from one season to the next, and the people who live in this variable area sometimes find that their farms that they have worked for so long, are now over on the other side of the river and in the other country. This shifting of farms from one country to another makes for confusion and irritation, and occasionally some man whose farm has left him may fire a few protesting shots across the river at the man over there working the land and getting its benefits.

This is a fairly common occurrence, and I have read numerous accounts of these flurries. I have read them in Indian papers and in Pakistani papers, and I have yet to read that the shots ever came from anywhere except from the other side.

This endless accusing and bickering are a part of the contention between the two countries at a time when their joined strength is so much needed by each other, and by all the nations of the free world, in the massed struggle for Asia.

But the contentions at the border between Pakistan and India, the endless quarrels about water supply, and who shall control Kashmir—all these are causes of friction, but they are the lesser reasons that divide the two nations.

The actual reason, the consuming reason, is that each morning at sunrise half of all these people face toward Mecca and the other half come up out of the Ganges carrying little brass pots; half of them pray to Allah and the other half splash water on Ganesa the elephant god, and toss flowers on the dancing figure of Lord Siva.

16

New countries, those that a man has not seen before, are of particular interest to him, and I had not been to Afghanistan, and I was glad that I was going there. Usually there is pleasure in going back to some country where one has been before, but on such a trip there is a lack of anticipation, an absence of that gentle excitement that goes along with him as he travels toward a new country. Going back to London or Paris, for instance, is sort of like going home again, and it is astonishing how quickly, even before the day is out, that one *is* home again. No matter how long since he has been there, years perhaps, the changes are not so many and he walks the Strand and wanders about the Place de l'Opéra, and it seems that he has never been away. Cupid still draws his bow in Piccadilly Circus and down the way Lord Nelson looks out to the sea. The musty old opera house still stands as the center of Paris, and the waiters stack the cognac dishes, as always, at the Café de la Paix. Nothing, it seems, has really changed. But a new place and a new country can only be imagined, for they can be anything.

Before I had left the United States there had been correspondence with the State Department about my going to Afghanistan. The president of the University of Kabul had been to Washington and had visited the International Educational Exchange Service, and he had said that he would like an American to come to his university and lecture on American literature and talk to his students about the United States. The students in Afghanistan, he said, were interested in the United States and he would like them to know more about it. He himself was a graduate of the University of Illinois, and he thought that it would be worth while if the IES would send an American to Kabul. This had been mentioned to me, but nothing had been settled before I left home.

I wanted to go to Afghanistan, this obscure kingdom in southwestern Asia, for I had read about it often and had been near its borders several times but had never been inside. Then, too, Afghanistan seemed just so far away.

How far away it seems is a part of an American newspaper tradition. Most newspapers in the United States want to keep their editorial pages close to home. They want to discuss the problems of *their* town and *their* state, and what directly and immediately concerns them. An evaluation of national affairs now and then is all right; but if an editor goes too far afield, discussing events in some foreign country, then his editorial may be branded by the office wits with the slurring name of "Afghanistanism." The editorial has wandered off and lost itself in some hazy, unlocated country called Afghanistan. They don't know, and even now they probably won't listen, but Afghanistan today borders their American state and is a part of their American city, whatever their city or state may be.

Instructions had come to me while I was in the south of India that I was to go to Afghanistan. I was to complete my work in India and Pakistan, then fly from Karachi to Kabul. I was warned about a visa. Afghanistan was not fully open yet, and one could not get into the country so easily as he might travel elsewhere.

I managed a visa and finished my work in Pakistan, and then one night I went to bed in Karachi knowing that early the next morning I would fly to Kabul. But at four o'clock that next morning Pakistan Airways telephoned to inform me that the flight to Afghanistan had been called off. It was raining in Kabul and the field there is only a small dirt field, and no plane can land on it when it is wet. All air connections with Kabul had been canceled. I asked when they might be opened again. Pakistan Airways didn't know when it would stop raining in Kabul, and air connection with Afghanistan had been canceled indefinitely.

At such moments in a man's life coffee can be a help, and the bearer who had been sleeping on the veranda outside my room came in, and he and I had a conference. Before long coffee was on my table and beside the pot was a map of Asia. There was no way to get through directly from Karachi to Kabul. The straight distance is about eight hundred miles and there are mountain passes and glaciers that even goats can't get over. And there are no trains in Afghanistan.

But I was supposed to be in Kabul the next day and was scheduled to speak the next night at the Institute of Education. Pakistan Airways said that their planes were flying to Lahore and on to Peshawar, which is a city near the mouth of the Khyber Pass. The plane would leave that afternoon. My wife and I decided that she would not go. Instead, she would go on to Persia and wait for me there.

But my Afghanistan visa read that I was to enter the country by air, and I had no idea what they would say about my wanting to change and go in by land. Leaving my hotel early, I was sitting at the Afghan embassy waiting when it opened. My visit started a series of interviews, from the ambassador on down, and called for a flurry of conferences, discussions, and debates; but in the end they revised my visa, stamped my passport, and we all shook hands and were happy. Even those Afghans at the embassy who could speak no English stood and smiled and waved as I hurried out.

This, however, did not satisfy all official requirements. Pakistan, too, was concerned and I would need permission from the Pakistani police to leave their country. But there was no time to see the police in Karachi and I left there in the early afternoon for Lahore, and flew on to Peshawar, arriving after dark. And it was in Peshawar, this town at the northern border of Pakistan, that a hotel bearer and I searched for two hours in the back streets and alleys, being sent from one place to another, until a little after midnight we found the home of the chief of police and persuaded him, a sleepy and grumpy official, to sign my papers and grant me permission to leave Pakistan.

The next morning I hired an automobile to take me to the mouth of the Khyber Pass, and there I sat and waited. It was sometime around ten o'clock that I saw a cloud of dust approaching, and then a station wagon came around the curve. I stood as straight as I could, gave the driver my best smile, and thumbed.

The automobile slowed down. "Where are you going?"

"Afghanistan," I said.

He opened the door. "Get in."

He was a Frenchman, a geologist, and he was leading a caravan of ten trucks driven by other geologists and engineers. They were a work party, sent out by France, to search for uranium in Afghanistan. He told me that the trucks behind us carried their equipment and supplies, and then he pointed to a suitcase that was packed and puffed. *That,* he said, carried the papers of the months of negotiations that had been necessary before he and his associates and their trucks had been granted permission to cross one country and go on into the other. I thought of my one visa and could only imagine his trouble in getting clearance for his trucks.

We drove on through the Khyber Pass. At times the cliffs at each side were so steep and high, and the way so sharply winding, boxing us in between turns, that I had to lean out of the window to see the sky. Along the way, sunk in the rocks, were plaques with the names and records of British regiments that had fought in this Pass—the old Khyber Pass of India, so famous in Indian history and fiction, but now a part of that northwest corner that had been cut off and was Pakistan. It is a valiant record, written there in the rocks, and one can look around and see why the fighting was so fierce and why not even England could conquer the wild tribesmen of this mountain area. Soldiers going through the Pass, and it was the only way through, were marching to their certain death. The tribesmen among the rocks on the mountainside could take their time and prove their marksmanship each time they fired.

Even now these tribesmen live outside the law, and I saw them at road stations where we stopped for endorsement of our passports and papers. They are tall and upright men, each sufficient to himself, looking past a stranger and ignoring him. Each of them carries his rifle, long rifles with heavy barrels and out of date but shining clean, and each man wears a bandoleer looped over his shoulder and filled with cartridges.

At one station, as I was on my way to a wall at the back that was the urinal, I passed a group of these men and no one turned his head, no one glanced or seemed to know that I had passed. When I came back, I asked a question, and one man pointed but no one spoke. I watched these men as they came and went at this station, and often they passed each other without speaking or any sign of recognition.

Along the road one sees these men from time to time on points of lookout as sentries, a thin scattering of outposts for the Pakistani army, and now and then one sees a changing of the guard at one of the tiny forts that are built high among the rocks, sometimes only a single room plastered against the mountainside. It is an area of its own, lawless and haughty, barriered off from the rest of the world, where even the soldiers are tribesmen first and the rifle still rules the Pass.

Beyond the Khyber Pass the country eases back somewhat and there are stretches of almost level ground, the mountains always keeping close but still with places here and there wide enough for a man to graze his sheep and even farm a little. We traveled on through this country almost due north through Pakistan, the road rocky and dusty but wide enough for automobiles or trucks to pass each other, and we continued on until we came to a sagging chain across the road that marked the border between

Pakistan and Afghanistan, with sentries and a military post on each side.

Hitchhikers can't be choosers, and I sat back and waited while the Pakistani border authorities examined every paper in the stuffed suitcase that the Frenchman opened. They had never seen such a collection of papers and they had a wonderful time, turning through them and searching for still other places to stamp and other places to sign their names.

But I was not the only one who waited. A half-dozen Pakistanis wanted to get back into their country, and some Afghans wanted to go on across the border and into their country, but none could be admitted or cross until he had had his papers stamped. And the clerks were having far too good a time burrowing in this mound of hitherto-unseen documents to be bothered with just ordinary passes.

Now and then, though, some one of the officials would notice the waiting men and demand their papers. He would examine them, and if they were in order, he would make ready for them to be signed. Since none of these men could write, the official would lift the ink pad, hold it out in front of him, and blast some spit on it. Then he would place it on his desk again, press the man's thumb on the wet pad, and press the thumb on the paper, making everything official and proper, and giving the man permission to cross the line.

Some of these men and I, as we waited, and others who were just sitting around loafing and doing nothing, struck up a friendship, for these were men of the valleys and not the mountain tribesmen, and they were a smiling and a congenial lot. We did some good communicating with gestures, frowns, grunts, and a few drawings in the dust, using a stick or a finger. We got along so well that when an old man, about noontime, appeared at the door of a small building that I had hardly noticed and yelled the call to prayer, they motioned for me to come along with them, and, loosening my shoes and stepping out of them, I entered the shabby little room and we all faced the west.

I had brought my lunch, which the hotel at Peshawar had prepared for me, and the Frenchmen had brought theirs, and we ate boiled eggs, and opened small jars of preserves, and we had bread. Each of us had a bottle of soda, and the men standing around stared when we pulled off the tops and the water boiled out. What kind of water was that?

After lunch, and after having finished their requirements with the officials, it was the Frenchmen's time to sit back and smoke and joke me as I had to go through the formalities, signing all the books and having my passport and papers stamped. At many of these frontier posts, where only a few travelers cross, the requirements can be intricate and prolonged. At last, though, all was finished and the Pakistani authorities, and the Pakistani soldiers, and my friends among the loafers, all came down front and center and saluted and waved as the chain was lowered and we drove out of Pakistan and crossed over into Afghanistan.

The control on the Afghan side was less demanding, and besides the Frenchmen had an Afghan traveling with them who was married to a Frenchwoman, and they gave all their papers to him and he talked his way through in a hurry. The Afghan officials couldn't quite figure out what this American was doing along and they kept pointing at me, but the Afghan told them something and they all grinned and shrugged and signed my papers. I never knew what he told them.

We left this border station and started north again, but we had gone only a mile, or a bit more, when we swung around a sharp corner and there was another control, the soldiers across the road, set up as a double safety about who was coming into their country. Again the Afghan talked, showing our papers, and again they passed us on.

Here in Afghanistan the mountains had moved back completely and great valleys spread green as far as we could see, except directly to the north, where the snow mountains now were beginning to appear. On each side of the road, as we traveled, there was full and fertile land with well-kept farms, and terraced farms moving up the slopes of the hills. Now and then on the upper land, and particularly when we passed steep areas, the broadtail sheep were grazing and often we saw the black tents of the nomads, their cook fires burning in front.

The valley farms and those on the hillsides were laid out as perfectly as land could be used, and the water from the swift rivers was eased into it through canals, the water blocked here and turned there by dykes of stone, feeding it to wherever it was needed. Wheat and barley and lentils were growing, and they make two crops a year on this land. Next autumn they will gather their rice and cut millet and sorghum; they will get maize and tobacco and turnips.

Each farm spreads out in all directions from a center cluster of dwellings, usually the home of one man and his family, but his family will consist of all his sons and all their wives, all his relatives, and all the relatives of their relatives. The family in Afghanistan extends on until the man at the head of it is really the head of a clan, with all others owing him respect and obedience.

The dwellings are large and comfortable, and the thick walls, made to block out the winter cold and to hold in the night coolness of summer, are built of stones that are piled and shaped and then held together by mud, and the sides of these walls and their tops are covered and smoothed over with mud as if they were plastered. In addition to the houses there are shelters for the animals, for all the sheep and the cattle, and often there is a silo rising high for the storing of the grain. Usually, too, there is a thick wall built around the whole settlement and one thinks, as he looks at it, of some medieval town, fortified and walled in.

Always in the dwelling of the head of the family, and usually in the home of each son and relative, there is a large samovar where the green tea is prepared for the household and also quickly made whenever a guest appears. These hospitable men and their families are independent, self-respecting, and healthy, their lands yielding good crops and their homes clean. Their children are shy at first, but after they have peeped around the corner for a while, they come out to be seen.

In total contrast to this farmer, with his tilled fields and community life, is the nomad of Afghanistan. He goes where he wills and he carries his world with him. The weather tells him when to move and a pleasant sun lets him know when to stop. These nomads live in the open, under tents made of hides, and they have milk and butter and solid balls of dried buttermilk, their plates freshened with whatever green things their women can find in the far spread of the land that belongs to nobody. I have watched a whole line of these women, eight of them abreast, as they moved over the land, each woman with her basket and all of them gathering as they went. In this way there would be no waste of some woman coming along later where other women had been, for they all gathered the green things together and they curried the land. Now and then the nomads, for a feast, slaughter a lamb and enjoy in particular the rich fat in his broad tail. But usually they eat only milk from their sheep or what their women find.

When it is time to go again, and the old man of the camp has decided, they strike their tents and load their belongings—mercifully free of the hamperings of comforts—onto their animals, and they move out into the road once more, continuing the journey that began the day they were born and that will end when, beside some road, they are buried. Most of their things, their tents, bedding, and pots, go onto the camels, but the newborn lambs and chickens are tied to the backs of the donkeys, while the old people, the very old, are helped onto the horses, and then the caravan, with the sheep in the midst of it, goes on toward where the sun is warmer, or, if it is summer, to where the winds are cool. This nomad, with his wide black turban and long black shirt and baggy trousers of varied colors scorns a house and literally has no word in his language for "hearth" or "fireplace." He admits no control and he acknowledges only one obligation, that the sun never rises or sets but that he is prostrate toward Mecca.

The spread of the land grew less as we traveled on north, the hills closing in, and then the hills themselves were turning into the high rocks of the mountains, and the fields were gone. Once more the cliffs rose beside us, and we were traveling in a gorge until we began to climb, slowly at first, hardly noticing the rise, knowing only that when there was a break in the rocks ahead of us we could see more of the snow mountains, white against the blue. But this climb became steeper until it was sharp up the mountain, the road cutting its way through passes that walled us in until suddenly, around some curve, one side would not be there and the drop would be sheer into the gorge.

And then we came to the river. It was no such river as I had ever seen before. There was no flow to this river, it surged and it crashed, breaking against the huge rocks in its bed, and the spray shot up, the whole gorge a swirl of diamonds, the gleam holding fixed for an instant before it fell back and then shot up again.

This river at times was a tumult beside us and then we would turn a bend in the road and there would be a waterfall, so sudden and so close that one would draw back from it, thinking that the water would fall on him before the road could turn away, bending from the roar and the spray and the surge among the rocks.

We followed this road and traveled beside the river, constantly climbing, and then, all of a sudden, it was the strangest feeling, after having seen the force of the river for so long, to come out on higher ground to a place where the river spread out through a valley, as peaceful, as quiet as the green fields beside it, hardly a sign of its moving, the water as clear and almost as still as a lake, and without our knowing it both of us lowered our voices as we spoke.

It was getting on toward night when we came up over a steep brow and leveled off and there, stretching on before us, was a wide plateau. Far ahead on this level land we could see the lights of Kabul, not many of them and none of them strong, nothing like the night glare of an American city; but there were lights at the street corners and in some of the houses, and we could see, in the last of day, the silhouette of the tower of Radio Kabul.

We drove on until we came to pavement, and the Frenchman said that he had been to Kabul before and that he knew the way. He would take me to the American embassy and leave me there.

The city of Kabul is a *complete* surprise. Before arriving there, a person probably will be influenced by the same kind of thinking that prompts the tag of "Afghanistanism" in some American newspaper offices. Kabul is just *so* far away, so out of anybody's ordinary path, that most of us probably tend to put it in a world somewhere off by itself. What's more, a person who recently has been to Katmandu in Nepal, and Srinagar in Kashmir, is likely to have further misconceptions about Kabul. Katmandu is as medieval as chain armor and crossbows, and Srinagar has not entirely left this era. But Kabul in its streets and many of its buildings is as modern as any town, and there is a lively, up-to-date air about Kabul in the way that the people walk, in the brisk trading at the market, and in the swing of the automobiles that keep a man watching out at street crossings. Kabul is a frisky place.

The main streets are as wide as the boulevards of Paris, and as clean, bending with an easy curve one into the other. And through the city flows the Kabul River, the same river that one sees as he travels up through the mountains; but here in Kabul the river is small and flows at a steady pace, the fury coming sometime later after it has been joined by other streams and all their water is packed together into the gorges. One can walk the central street beside the river in Kabul, or follow the streets bending off, and so far as the streets themselves and the buildings are concerned he can almost feel that he is in some middle-sized city back home, except that here in Kabul almost anywhere he looks he will see the domes of mosques and their high minarets. The large banks of Kabul, the Parliament building, the Ministry of Mines and Industry, the Ministry of Education, the headquarters of the Afghan Red Crescent Society, all these buildings, along with the numerous factories in the city, compare in modernity and usefulness with similar buildings anywhere. Actually, I have seldom seen an American Red Cross building more suited to its purpose than the building of the Red Crescent Society here in Kabul.

This does not mean that all of Kabul is modern. There are streets and lanes where one sees the slow caravans of camels coming in, and they are loaded with silks and carpets, cotton goods, dyestuffs, and hardware; and when they go out again, they carry dried fruit, asafoetida, spices, hides, and wool. One watches these caravans as they move, the camels in line, and he sees the slow meandering of their necks, hears the squush of their cushioned feet, and these back lanes are more suited to the camels than to any automobile. No car here dares go faster than a creep, a driver easing in and out of the holes, wondering even then when he will break a spring.

This is a part of the town that has come down from the past and has been untouched by the progress of the city. Here is the ancient Kabul to which the conquerors came, Alexander the Great, Genghis Khan, the fierce Moslem and Mogul invaders, and all coming with sword and fire—but still Kabul has survived. It was a rich prize for the conquerors, for Kabul back then was a center of trade and travel, an assembly place for goods and caravans coming up out of India and for traders coming across from China; all the people of the far Orient brought their goods here, sending them on to Persia, to Baghdad, and to Constantinople.

But suddenly a new way was found, and the trading ships sailed for this southern cape, and the caravans no longer came to Kabul. The busy and wealthy center of trade was ignored and left to dry up in its own dust. Yet while all this of conquerors and mighty kings is gone, and gone so long ago, one even now in the small shops of Kabul can feel a touch from the past. In these shops he can go in and bargain, taking care and making sure of what he gets, but if he knows what he is after he may come across a Greek coin or a Thracian coin, found in the dust of Kabul, and now and then he may see a coin from Bactria or even from the land of Kush.

Long ago and today are so near each other in Kabul that contrasts are common, and one of the most memorable is at the university. I was invited to the office of the president of the university, and I called on him. As we talked, we were interrupted again and again by the telephone, for the president of the university and all officials of Afghanistan, even cabinet officers, must answer their own telephones. For someone else to answer would be an intrusion and impolite, even though the person calling is speaking only over the telephone, and not actually entering the room himself.

After this visit was ended and the teacups had been carried away, the president took me to his outer office and there he showed me the model, in its wide glass case, of the university that is to be built. Here was the great library building. Here the recitation halls. There the science buildings. Here the gymnasium. There the dormitories. He had been to the University of Illinois, all right! And he dreamed of an American university with all its buildings and all its equipment—he wanted one just like it here in Kabul. He dreamed, too, of more than buildings, and he told me of the faculty that he planned. There was hope, and almost belief, in the room as he talked.

Then he took me to my first lecture, leaving his model and his dream and going with me to the university that is now. We walked into the old and scarred building and on into one of the large rooms, unheated and cold. I stood on a dirt floor as I lectured, and the students' chairs were on the ground. When I tried to write a name on the blackboard, the chalk was of such a quality that it crumbled in my hand. And yet, before long, the floor might have been made of oak and the room was warm as I told them about my country, and the literature of my country, and the way we live, and they leaned forward as they listened.

Afterward they blocked my way from the room, none of them realizing how they stood between me and the door. Then we went outside and they came along and stood beside my automobile in the dust of the lane, and we kept on talking. These students at the University of Kabul, stirred by some American teachers who are there now, were more persistent in their reaching for knowledge than any students I met anywhere else. Their English was not always sure, but their desire was endless. When time came for me to leave Kabul, I found that leaving them was with a feeling of something unfulfilled and with a kind of sadness that surprised me.

I met other students in Kabul. There is a college there, Habibia College, which we in the United States would call a high school, since the students are of that age and that academic progress. USIS asked me to talk to these boys about American sports, and I have never spoken to a more eager audience.

There were some two hundred of them and they didn't wait for me to finish my talk before they began their questioning; they couldn't wait. I saw them squirming until finally one boy bounced up and asked me to tell them more about basketball. Were all the basketball players in the United States seven feet tall? "What about me? Could I play in the United States?" He didn't look much over five feet and my spirits sagged as I thought of what I must tell him, then they rose again as I remembered Davey Banks of the old Celtics, one of the greatest of them all and a man of short stature. I told them about Banks and they, most of them short even for their young ages, poked out their chests and swaggered.

They wanted to know especially about wrestling and boxing, tennis and handball, the individual sports where one man is on his own. They haven't yet developed the full feel of team play, even though they do play soccer, volleyball, basketball, and hockey. But these sports do not have such standing with them as they have in the United States, for the Afghan is still primarily an individualist, still a man of intense personal pride, and he prefers a sport where he himself, and he alone, can prove his prowess. Many of them are descended from the mountain people, and their ancestors were better in the fighting when each man with his own rifle found his own target. Drill and mass formations have never been popular with the Afghans.

My next job in Kabul was at the Press Department of the School of Journalism. I went there expecting to find undergraduates, young men preparing for newspaper careers, such as one finds at most schools of journalism at American universities. Instead, these were the actual newspapermen of Kabul, the reporters and editors, and they were considerably older than undergraduates. I had to speak through an interpreter because these men did not have the knowledge of English that I had found at the university or even at Habibia College. Despite this bother of language, the newspapermen of Kabul turned out to be an interesting lot.

I started out by diagramming the newsroom of an ordinary American newspaper, telling them about the managing editor, the city editor, the copy desk, and I was tracing the flow of news through the newsroom when a man held up his hand and spoke in Afghan. The interpreter said that the man wanted to know who controlled the newsroom.

"The managing editor," I said, and went on with my story.

Another man held up his hand. "Who controls the managing editor?"

I explained that on some papers the newsroom is independent, at others it is controlled by the editor.

"Who controls the editor?"

"The owner of the paper makes the final decision. It is his property and he has a right to control it."

Another hand went up. "Who controls the owner?"

"Nobody," I said.

They looked at me. They looked at each other. From then on they looked at the table. They just sat there, staring down, and said nothing.

I figured that something had gone wrong, but I didn't know what. Maybe something I had said. Something I had done. As one travels from one country to another, and from one religion to another, he can never be sure when he has violated some religious law, some custom, some taboo—"Hog butcher to the world"—and that evening I talked to friends, both Americans and English-speaking Afghans.

I found out that the newspapermen believed that I had lied to them. So far as they knew there is *nothing* associated with a newspaper that isn't controlled. On their newspapers anything from a one-inch story of two bicycles running into each other to the lead editorial of the biggest newspaper in Afghanistan is censored, controlled, and ordered. The censor of the national press and radio, an officer of the national government, can say what news is to be printed and what is to be left out. He can tell what editorial stand will be taken on any issue and what stand will not be taken.

When we came back together the next day, I was ready for them. I took off. I soared. I let them know about the freedom of the American press. I let them know that there can never be a free country without a free press. The American press is a basic part of the American democracy, and no American government, of whatever party in Washington, would dare touch or tarnish this press freedom. I let them have it, and when I had finished, a little carried away myself by my own oration, I rubbed my hands and caught my breath, getting set for the discussion that I knew would follow. "Are there any questions?" I asked.

A man held up his hand and the interpreter listened to him, then turned to me. "He would like to know who controls the owner of the newspaper."

I tried, but there just isn't a lot that a person can do. Before we parted I think they had decided that I wasn't lying to them about an American newspaper being able to say what it believes, and say it without any government control; but they had lived for so long the other way, and so completely the other way, that they didn't understand and they couldn't understand. After a while we decided that we would get along with each other without arguing this point any more, and we left it and went on to other things.

It was interesting a few days later to be talking to the censor of the national press and radio, the man who controls the newspapers, and have him, who had been at none of these meetings, quote me repeatedly and speak of various things that had happened. He made no show of knowing about it and called no particular attention to his knowing. He seemed to take for granted that I would understand what he would do—that he would have someone at each meeting to take it all down, and then come and report it to him.

The students I had taught at the university had been men, there had been only boys at Habibia College, and now here again at the Department of Journalism there were only men. I had met no women in Afghanistan and twice I had been to dinner in the homes of Americans, when Afghanistan men were among the guests, and the American wife had not appeared.

In this Mohammedan country such complete separation of men and women was to be expected, and the total covering of an Afghan woman whenever she appeared on the street, or anywhere in public, was not only a custom but a part of religion. Afghanistan is one of the strictest of all Moslem countries, and its national laws are founded on the religious laws of Islam. The king must be a Moslem and before his coronation he must pledge to the people, in the presence of Parliament, that he "will protect the true religion of Islam." In a country so dedicated to Islamic law one might look for women to be veiled, and on the streets of Kabul I saw no Afghan woman throughout the time I was there who was not totally covered with the *chadri*, the long, loose garment, like a flowing sack, that comes down over the top of her head, covering her head completely, with only two small holes for her eyes, and usually even these holes are latticed. The garment hangs over her entire body to below her ankles, and sometimes it drags the ground to hide even her feet.

Women are not discussed in the ordinary conversation of men in Islamic countries, and there was a momentary strain in the office of a government official one afternoon when we were talking about various features of life in Afghanistan, and I asked about the *chadri* and if it might someday be abolished. He glanced at me quickly, then looked away and said something in a vague way about doubting that it would be done away with. Somehow we continued to talk about these veils and I said, with no purpose and only as a comment, that it seemed strange to me to come to a country and meet so many interesting men and to talk to no woman. Soon after I said this the conversation shifted and we talked of other things.

The next day a government official, an associate of the man with whom I had spoken the previous afternoon, called on me, and I supposed that he had come on only another of the courtesy calls that one receives now and then from officials in these countries. We began our talk by exchanging the usual formalities that are expected, and then we discussed the countryside of Afghanistan, and the people of the countryside, seemingly without point, until he asked me, with an offhand carelessness, if I would come to his home for tea. I was surprised, because I had been told that it was unlikely that I would be invited into the home of an Afghan. I accepted, of course, and later, as he was leaving, he mentioned that his wife would be there, and there would be other lady guests.

When I reported this to friends, American and British, they said that it was impossible. No American, and a stranger at that, would be invited into an Afghan home for tea where there would be women. They would have to be unveiled. It could not be.

But it was, and the next afternoon I had tea in an attractive home with a delightful garden, the home perfectly furnished, both with comforts and luxuries, and among the guests were four beautiful women. Their dresses must have been from Paris, and there was a suggestion of shadow about their eyes, and it was a downright sin to cover such figures in a loose sack. They all spoke good English and one was a teacher of French at the college for women. We talked about Afghanistan, and about travel in Asia and in Europe. They hoped someday to visit the United States. Later I asked one of them, as we stood by the window, if she thought that there was a chance of the veils being abolished. She waited for an instant, shrugged, half-smiled, and didn't answer.

This was in the spring, and I had thought that the tea was only a courtesy, arranged for me by the government official who had decided, perhaps, that he didn't want a visitor to come to his country and go away without seeing how beautiful the women could be.

The tea, however, was only a preliminary to far more important events, for already the Afghan government was planning to abolish the *chadri*. Later in the summer various ladies of the leading families, always with their husbands, began to appear in public without the veil. Teachers and students also began to come out without it, at first wearing a scarf over the head, dark glasses, and a dark coat, but soon the glasses were discarded and all pretense done away with, the women then walking in public with their faces fully uncovered.

The change was instigated by the government partly to liberate women, but even more because the government needed men, and wanted women to release men from office work and other jobs. This need of the government played its immediate part in abolishing the *chadri,* but there are reasons even more important. For some time now, the progressive women of Afghanistan have been working to do away with this sign of imprisonment and symbol of inferiority, and these courageous women deserve full credit for their part in breaking the unvarying rule of the veil.

The *chadri* probably never will completely disappear from Kabul and other Afghan cities, just as it is still frequently seen on the streets of Pakistan and in the Moslem area of Indian cities, but its use will become less in Afghanistan until only the more timid Moslem women will wear it, or the more sternly orthodox men will demand that their wives continue its use.

The change, however, this partial abolition of the *chadri*, has not come about lightly, and since it affected religious custom and Moslem law, there have been riots and fighting. Two weeks after President Eisenhower had made his tour of the Orient, to bring American good will, visiting Afghanistan among the other nations, a mob in the Afghan city of Kandahar, stirred by the mullahs, the Moslem priests who were bitter against the abolition of the *chadri*, began their rioting by beating an American. They then moved on to the home of another American, destroyed his automobile, tore his dog to pieces, and threw rocks through the window of the house.

Before the rioting was ended, men had been killed, power lines cut, buildings burned and others demolished, and unveiled girls had been caught and mutilated.

Why the rioting began with an attack on Americans, why the mob went first to the homes of Americans, one cannot say for sure, but that it should happen so short a time after Mr. Eisenhower had been in the country to establish a closer relationship between them and us goes to show that all the cheering and the throwing of flowers do not prove anything. We would be wise not to be lulled into any belief that our stock has gone up in the East merely because our President was accorded a tumultuous welcome. More than a brisk visit of state, no matter who the person, or how vast the publicity of the moment, is needed to bring about any useful relationship between us and the peoples of these countries.

My time of leaving Afghanistan was in April, and on a Friday, when all offices and shops were closed as usual in this Moslem country, some American friends invited me for a picnic. We drove out forty miles to a village, and near there we had our lunch. We spread a blanket and ate beside a small stream that came down fast from the mountains, the water as clear as air and cold as snow, glinting when the sun touched it through the leaves.

After lunch we went for a walk to the edge of the hill and there, far across from us, were the snow mountains of the Hindu Kush, and below them, but rising high under the crest of white, were other mountains without snow, black and broken and jagged. Down in the valley was the far spread of the fields, and they were green except for one lake, and except for the red of the poppies and the tulips that swayed with the wind, and there was lilac in the wind. Coming up the hill toward us, up from the valley, were the apple trees, and the wild peach, and the redbuds in bloom. I have never seen the earth and its growing things so beautiful.

On the last day I was to be in Afghanistan I called on an official of the government and we talked about his country. There was so much for us to talk about, and chief among all this was Russia. Russia forms the northern border of Afghanistan, only a river away.

I asked about the Russian roadbuilding machinery that I had seen at work on the road as I came up to Kabul. I asked, too, about the Russian engineers and supervisors that I had seen at various points along the way.

What of the Russian helicopters that I had seen at different fields?

I asked about the pilots of the Afghanistan Air Force who are now being trained in Russia, and trained on Russian planes.

There is an airfield that the Russians have built immediately outside Kabul. Jets can land there. No one else from any other country is allowed near this field, only Russians. What of it?

And what of the only paved, straight highway in Afghanistan? It is directly down from the Russian border and it is wide enough, and kept in good enough condition, for endless mobile units to be moved over it.

He listened attentively to me and to my questions.

But these things, he told me, are evidence of Russian friendship. The two countries are neighbors.

I asked about the economy of Afghanistan. I had heard that the Afghan trade is turning more, all the time, to the north. I had been told that Russia, in luring this trade, is paying *above* the world market in her buying from Afghanistan. In her selling to Afghanistan, Russia is selling *below* the world market.

I had seen the shops of Kabul, and shops in other towns of the country, filled with Russian goods, packed to the door with them and stacked on the walkways outside. Was Afghanistan becoming dependent on Russia for its trade—as Afghanistan already is dependent for its air force? Was Afghanistan placing itself in such a position that Russia could have her way in the country, whenever and whatever that way might be? Already Russia could throttle the Afghan trade, disrupt the economy of the country, and force Afghanistan to do Russia's will.

As I continued to ask my questions, particularly about the trade and the economy, he shifted some papers on his desk and he looked at me, and he spoke quietly. "Patriotism," he said, "is an elusive force except in times of war. And now that we are at peace, and are concerned chiefly with prosperity, I have heard that even in your country the national interest is quickly forgotten whenever your businessmen can make a profit." He paused and again he looked at me. "We can make a profit with Russia."

The next morning I was to leave Kabul, and our plane circled above the valley where I had seen the poppies and the tulips.

This morning, too, the wild peach and the redbud were in bloom, and the sun on the Hindu Kush was bright.

There, across the river to the north, is Russia. There, to the south, is Pakistan, and on beyond to the south is India.

The way to India lies through Afghanistan. And Afghan airmen are in Russia. And Afghan traders are crossing the river, back and forth. And the road is straight and clear down from the border.

I saw the flash of the sun on the snow, and then the pilot banked his plane and all was shut out behind me.

17

The land west of Kabul is mostly desert and we were traveling west, flying toward Iran. The desert here is a pale tan color, streaked and splotched white by the drift of the sand, and it blazes under the sun. There were hills and mountains, all of them rock, bare and lifeless. Now and then we flew over a village, a cluster of brown, mud-covered houses, but these villages were far apart.

There is a landing field in the desert near the city of Herat in western Afghanistan, four hundred miles from Kabul, and we came down here to change from the small plane to a bigger one of four engines. It would take us on to Teheran. These large planes cannot get in over the mountains and down into the boxed-in field at Kabul.

Here in Herat we were in the heat again, even the soft wind of the desert was a burning wind, and we felt it particularly after the coolness that we had left in Kabul. Nothing was green at the airport at Herat and there was only the pale and empty land, far and flat except where it was ripped and broken by the rocks.

The desert was still beneath us as we flew out of Afghanistan and on into Iran, and we flew for four hours before we saw the city of Teheran sprawled out on the desert, tall buildings in its center and sand at its edges. Close by the city is the startling sight of black mountains rising from the desert and covered with snow. And at the airport was the happy sight of my wife again.

Driving into Teheran, I knew that I had come into a different world from the Far East. Kabul was more than a morning's flight away, and I was on another planet from Benares. The shrines of Nepal and the shrines of Nikko, the Shinto priests and the Hindu holy men were infinitely far behind me, for this was a Western city, and I had seen nothing like Teheran since I had left Honolulu. In some of the cities of the Orient one can see the pavement and the buildings of the West, but always the people wear the garments of the East and the bullock is passing with painted horns, his flower wreath about his neck, and one can hear the faint tinkle of the camel bell. But there is none of that here, and these men of Teheran wear American suits and American shoes. The women, too, wear Western dress, though they do make a gesture to Moslem law by draping their heads with a black cloth. All the bewildering beauty of the East, its mysticism and its fantasy, is gone and this is bare, cold, and commonplace.

This feeling of coming into the West again was partly influenced, of course, because my wife was waiting for me here in Teheran; but she was not the main factor in my feeling that I was getting nearer home, coming back to my own land again, approaching Europe and America once more. Teheran is intentionally like a Western city, for the Shah of Iran, some fifty years ago, tore down the old Persian palaces, throwing away the brilliantly colored tiles, and pulling down the mud huts of the people. He set out to build a modern city of buildings and businesses and factories, sensible and praiseworthy, and he did it; but a traveler is just not too interested in finding a city, even in Iran, with all the physical attributes of Cincinnati or St. Louis, no matter how ancient that city's past or poetic its tradition. One takes a walk in Teheran, goes for a ride in Teheran, and goes back to his hotel and reads.

What the city lacks in interest for the tourist I found for myself in my work in Teheran, especially at the university. In other countries, I had been coasting along and enjoying myself in the classroom, dealing with enthusiastic students who were easy to get along with. But the first day I lectured at the university in Teheran I found that I was dealing with a different crowd. I began my lecture on time, although the interpreter said no. I should wait for the students to get there. One didn't begin a lecture on time!

But we did, and I had only a sprinkling of students. After a while a few of the others began to drift in. They looked at me in some surprise, not knowing that a stranger would be lecturing in their class, and even more surprised that the class should have been started before *they* got there. They kept straggling in until a batch of them came in about fifteen minutes before the hour was to end, and I asked if they went to school here or had just dropped in for tea. The interpreter turned crimson and stood there. I asked him to translate it and he shook his head. "They might be offended," he said. "They might leave."

That wasn't my idea of a classroom, or a university, and of students working, so I told him to translate it. If this bunch of stragglers wanted to leave, it would suit me. It was their university, but this was my classroom, and as long as they were attending my classes they were going to do it, within reason, in my way. He did translate it, and they sat there, looking around, astonished and indignant, but they sat there, and they didn't leave, and before our time with each other was ended we were friends. They turned out to be a group of pleasant and intelligent men, although they never did catch on to what I meant by *study*.

I went to Isfahan, a city to the south and once the capital of old Persia, and I traveled to other cities over the country, particularly to Meshed, far to the northwest, up near the Russian border. It is a nineteen-hour train journey from Teheran, for there are no planes that go there. Most of the way is through desert country, though now and then the train stops at some small town or village, and I would see the men of the village waiting at the station and occasionally a man would have a rose tucked behind his ear.

In the compartment with me was another American, and he was in Iran on the agricultural program fostered by the United States. As we rode over the flat country, so much of it bare and desert, we saw the shepherds now and then with their great flocks of sheep, and he told me of his dealings with them. One of the troubles, he said, was in getting them to cull the black sheep. "We have told them over and over again that the black wool does not bring so good a price as the white wool, and we keep telling them to cull the black sheep. But they say that a flock of all-white sheep is not pretty."

Meshed is a holy place, a shrine for thousands of Moslem pilgrims to come every year, and until the railroad line was built many of them died in the long crossing of the desert. Even now some who set out with camel or donkey do not reach the place of worship, but this, too, is salvation, for to die on the pilgrimage is blessed. Here in Meshed is buried the Imam Riza, the eighth in the line of succession after Mohammed's cousin and son-in-law, Ali. Here the people come to worship at his tomb and in the huge mosque that has been built over it, the center dome of gold.

The USIS representative in Meshed had approached the authorities of the mosque before I arrived, asking that I be allowed to visit some part of it. The shrine itself is, of course, forbidden to any except Moslems, but occasionally an unbeliever is admitted to some parts of the mosque, and it was agreed that I might come.

On the morning appointed, and at a time exactly halfway between the times for prayer, I presented myself at a side entrance. A guard was waiting, and he escorted me, through back ways, to the office of the secretary of the mosque. There tea was served and also the sweet cakes that are usual. The various compliments and thanks that must be exchanged were spoken, and then, again through back ways, I was escorted to a passage that led up to the roof of the mosque, and from there on up into the high minaret where the muezzin stands when he calls to prayer. The golden dome was bright, and the colored tiles gleamed on the sloping roofs and walls of the mosque, and down below us lay the city of Meshed, stretching on to the desert, and most of its streets were narrow and sharply twisting. Next to Mecca itself here is one of the most holy places of the Moslems.

I was allowed to look down into the courtyard outside the actual shrine itself, but care was taken that I did not approach where I might glance in. Not even the glimpse of an unbeliever is permitted. I saw the worshipers enter the courtyard and prostrate themselves as they approached the entrance of the shrine, kissing the doorposts and kissing the stones that led inside.

As we were leaving, through the same back passage again, someone opened a door and I was exposed for a moment. An old man, bent, and walking with a high stick, caught sight of me, an infidel within the mosque, and he raised his stick and threw back his head and bellowed. One of the guards slammed the door and hurried me on, the old man still crying out behind us.

In the office of the secretary once more, tea was brought again and again the sweet cakes. Again we exchanged compliments and I spoke my thanks, taking especial care to say what it had meant to me to have stepped on this ground, so near the shrine of the Imam Riza. I was grateful.

The secretary of the mosque nodded. "We do not doubt your feelings," he said. "We know them. And the Imam knows them."

The turquoise mines of Iran are near to Meshed, and there was a dealer who had a stone that I wanted, but his price was too much for me, and for days we bargained. With this stone on the table between us, placed there on white satin by the dealer so that the color might be even bluer, we talked of everything except the stone, while he brewed his tea, and how many times we emptied the pot and he filled it again I do not know. I know only that on the day before I was to leave Meshed, and after I had strained as high as I could, he took my hand and turned my palm up, and he laid the stone in my palm and, still holding my hand, his lips moved, selling me the stone but giving me his blessing.

The long journey back from Meshed brought me into Teheran in the late afternoon, and I was to meet with the newspapermen of the city that evening. I had found, as I traveled, that talking with newspapermen usually was an enjoyable experience in whatever country I might be. We always started off talking about newspapers and invariably they wanted to learn about papers in the United States. Sometimes the questions were technical questions about newsrooms, composing rooms, pressrooms, but more often they just wanted to know about the kind of newspapermen we are.

The more I traveled the more I became convinced that the best way for us in the United States to make friends in other countries is just to sit down and tell them about ourselves. That is what they always ask about. What kind of people are you Americans? How do you live? That is what students, newspapermen, businessmen, and women ask about and want to know. They want to know about *us*. The best product that we can export around the world is ourselves.

Our skyscrapers, our luxury trains, our wheat fields, all play their part, and they make good movies. Our educational system, our law courts, the plan and the structure of our government, make good subjects for speeches. But when the movies have been shown and the speeches made, I found that they came around my desk, and walked along the street with me, and came to the hotel later to ask about *us*. If we would just tell them the kind of people we are, instead of letting them think in terms of stock markets, billionaires, and missile bases. We send out so much that only misleads and confuses them, and all the time they want to know who we are. How did we make this country? How do we keep it running? Who lives next door to you? What did you have for breakfast? How did you cook it?

They all want to know about us, and then after they have asked and talked about the United States for a while I found that they always wanted to tell me about themselves and especially about their country, and what their country is up against. When they talk to an American, they seem to feel that they are talking to an international partner, perhaps the senior partner, and they tell their fears and unload their worries.

There is a good deal of fear and worry in Iran. Russia forms the northern land border of Iran and Russia has been trying for so long, and is trying now, to take the country. Russia is always probing, seeking a way, and Russian agents are living among the people now and the Russian radio keeps up its constant attack. The Shah must go! The government must be overthrown! A good government, a Communist government, must be put in.

One of the shrewdest moves that Russia has made in Iran has been the "repatriation" of the Kurds, the fighting men, the war-like tribesmen of northern Iran. These men are wanderers, and Russia has been searching for them in Turkey, in Iraq, in Russia itself, and once they have been found, wherever they are, Russia has set about converting them to Communism, then sending them back into Iran. Russia says that she is doing the kindly thing and helping these men find their way back to their homes, but the people of Iran know that the Kurds are being sent in to stir up discord and to lead the fighting when it starts.

I heard in Iran the usual, and so it seems almost routine, criticism of our aid program. So much of the money that we send in, earmarked and directed for aid, is syphoned off by the politicians and finds its way into the pockets of the men with influence. One Iranian told me that we Americans are a generous people, but that we are so foolish in trying to buy our way, and so loose with our money, throwing it broadcast without knowing where it is going, that he, and other of his countrymen, look on us with "good-natured contempt."

I had come to expect this talk, and I often heard it; but here in Iran I heard something else, something entirely different, a cause of pride and an answer to bureaucrats—and it concerned an American girl.

My wife and I had known this girl at the University of North Carolina in Chapel Hill, and when we arrived in Teheran we went to the information desk at the embassy and asked the lady there to look up the address of this girl. But she didn't have to look it up. "Everybody knows her." And she told us where to find her.

We went there and an Iranian nurse said, "Of course we know her. Everybody does." And she told us that our friend was out in a village that morning, but she would be back later, and then the Iranian nurse began telling us about this American girl.

She was in the American Health Service in Iran and one day she heard about an orphanage in Teheran and she went there, and when she came out she walked as far as the gate and then she leaned up against the wall and sobbed. The next day she was back again, this time taking pictures, and I have seen those pictures of children with stomachs as big as pumpkins and legs like broomsticks, these starving babies.

She took her pictures, and she took her story, and she started out. She went to Americans in Iran. She went to Europeans. She went to Iranians. She went to the Queen.

Public responsibility was slack and private participation was negligible, but this one girl knew only one answer.

She got the Americans just to come and see. She got the Europeans to come and see. She got the Queen to come and see.

Working after hours, entirely on her own time, she got the money and fixed a house into a nursery, and they took fifty of these potbellied, dying children into this house and began to feed them. The American women began to come to help. The Europeans came. Then the Iranians, finding out about this new thing that was going on in their country, began to come.

Something had to be done about these babies, and talk of adoption was started. This was something that was new. Adopt a baby!

But they did adopt them, and a hundred babies have gone out from this nursery. Today, their adoptive parents send back pictures of healthy, happy children. Are they any more? Could they have another?

We saw our friend, after she came back from her nursing duties that morning in the village, and she took us to the nursery, and when the door opened and they heard her voice, the children came running and they swarmed over her like ants.

She is only a young woman, but I would put her up against any of the multimillion-dollar programs that we have poured into Iran. And so would the people of Iran.

18

We left Iran and came into the Middle East, landing first at Damascus, and immediately we ran into the conflict that now dominates the Middle East, shaping its thinking, its economy, and its politics. It was here that we first glimpsed the Moslem's determination to end the state of Israel and the Jew's determination never to yield one inch of the land that is Israel, or to budge from this country that now is his.

Before we landed at Damascus we were told that all passengers would be required to surrender their passports, even though they were transients who were flying on with this same plane after its half-hour stop. Usually the passports of transients are not examined, but when our plane landed at Damascus and we came to the bottom of the steps, there was a Syrian officer and he took all passports.

As we walked away from the plane, I asked an employee of the air line why this was done with people who were going on through, and I was told that officials of this Arab country would examine all passports for any Israeli visa or any sign of a person's having been to Israel, or planning to go there. Such a person would be returned to the plane immediately and not allowed in the waiting room. Also, notice would be sent ahead to Lebanon, the plane's next stop, and to other Arab countries. *Any* relationship with Israel bars a person from entering an Arab country and ends his contact with the Arab world in the Middle East.

The plan of the Arabs is to shut Israel off, to box Israel in, and to deny that Israel exists. The purpose of the surrounding Arab countries—and they do surround Israel on all sides except for the sea—is to hamper Israel's economy, restrict her development, and if possible strangle the country. I heard only one answer when talking with Arabs about Israel: Israel must be driven into the sea. Even the most enlightened Arabs, scholars and travelers, men who know the course of history and the forces shaping the world today, will say, and say again, that Israel must be driven into the sea.

This is not the wild and inflaming talk of fanatics and would-be dictators in the Arab world. The Arab world is split on some issues, but not on Israel, and throughout the Middle East one hears from the Arabs the most binding and compelling oaths that there shall be no recognition or acceptance of the Jewish state. One hears from them only one wish and one promise: Israel will be driven into the sea.

As a person begins his travels in the Middle East this is the prime fact that confronts him: The Arabs will not yield to Israel. Israel will not yield to the Arabs.

This is the basic fact of the Middle East, and we in the United States have not been sufficiently informed of the feelings and the fervor of the Arabs to use every influence, every force that they can command or rally to break the Jewish state, drive out the Jews, and take back the land that they believe was stolen from them. To this end the Arab world is dedicated in its economy, its military development, and in the oath of its people to their Prophet and their God, swearing that they will drive out the Jews and exterminate Israel.

The plane from Damascus is hardly in the air before it has crossed over the mountains of Syria and is flying above the valley of Lebanon, but this valley is so small that the plane cannot dip down from the mountains and land at once, and it must go on and swing out over the sea. However, one scarcely notices the valley at first, for he is looking at the Mediterranean. Having flown for so long over the desert, over the tan-colored rocks and the blazing heat, he stares at the far stretches of this water and at the deep blue beneath him.

The swing out over the water not only gives a sight of the sea, but as one comes back toward the land he has a full view of Beirut, Lebanon's capital, and now he *knows* that he is out of the Orient, for this surely is the south of France, somewhere on the road from Cannes to Nice to Monte Carlo. Here is the same storybook look, the same setting for a light opera, the houses pastel in their colors and their roofs bright red and blue, the tiles gleaming in the Mediterranean sun. Many of the houses are built on the side of the mountain, their colors scattered bright in the slope of the green.

There were friends to take us for a drive, and to their beach cottage, and we went swimming in the sea. All this was so easy and so ordinary that it was like being home again. It is pleasant for a man to come home, but always he asks what of those lands that he has left. What of their people? Does one ever really leave where he was? What of the Parsee women? What of the vultures that wait? What of Krishna's flute at the temple under the water? Is there still lilac in the wind down from the Hindu Kush? Coming back home, one puts on the old suit, I suppose, and wears it; but it never fits quite the same.

After our swim and our lunch we went for a drive and we saw the place where the marines had landed. This is a tricky story about the American marines in Lebanon, and it can be told in a number of ways. We can take credit for what we did, heading off confusion and stabilizing a government, and especial credit for how we did it; but in fairness and in quiet honesty we might consider its implications and how it looked to some other people.

It had been a local war here in Lebanon, almost a city war in Beirut, a civil war for control of a very tiny country; but it was the match near the powder keg, and the big nations were watching. Egypt to the south was flicking her dragon tail, and Russia in the north was waiting for carrion. The streets were barricaded and the fighting was going on until it became clear that the side favorable to the West was losing, and that side got word to the United States that it needed help, strong and quick, and the United States sent in the marines. They came in so fast that some elements of the Lebanese army were unwarned and almost fired on the marines, and if this had happened, only God knows the extent of the calamity.

The marines came on, and it was a sheer power play, the might of the United States moving into a small country and taking sides with its force of arms, settling an internal issue by American tanks. Had Russia done this, we would have protested. If Russia today were to move into Cuba, for instance, to settle an internal issue, even though the Russian marines were invited to come in by the Cuban government, we would protest. Just as we would protest if Russia began building missile bases and air bases in Cuba and Guatemala and other countries near the United States; although we have built and now maintain a number of such bases as close to Russia as we can get, useful for our military forces, of course, but evidence in the eyes of millions of men over the world that we are a warlike and an aggressor nation. In the leveling off of the power nations, in the balancing of international strength and influence, the peoples of the world now are judging the United States and Russia exactly the same, and they see no reason why we should have missile bases at Russia's border, and then talk about the Monroe Doctrine for ourselves.

The entry of the United States marines into Lebanon was welcomed by the Lebanese that it benefited; but the other side in Lebanon, and men elsewhere throughout the Middle East, and on into the Far East, looked on this move by the American marines in the same way that they regard the attack by England and France against Egypt. The French and the English went in shooting; we didn't, but we were ready to shoot, and the spirit, so these peoples of the Eastern countries believe, was the same—a stronger country exercising its will and having its way by the strength of its arms. This is the spirit of colonialism, which is so hated in the East, and this is the estimate, by most people of the East, of the entry of the United States marines into Lebanon.

It is to the eternal credit of these marines and their officers that nothing went wrong, for it is God's mercy, along with the strict training of the United States marines, that nobody pulled a trigger. One frightened boy, one blustering fool, and the United States would have been in war, the mighty United States invading and attacking a country the size of a postage stamp.

The center of our life in Lebanon was at the American University in Beirut. I taught here for long enough to come to know the officials of the university, a number of the faculty, and a good many students. I saw the university at work, in the classroom and on the campus, and its students are from the far countries of the earth, women from Pakistan and men from Ghana, from Ohio and France.

Here is a really wonderful example, both in method and result, of American money used for the good of peoples of other countries, and also with some sense about our own advantage. This is a model of what can be done by the considered advance of American money spent under intelligent and demanding supervision. Here is where Washington, and all agencies concerned with our foreign aid, could learn so much.

This university, the largest American educational institution outside the United States, has the standards of instruction of any other American university, and except that it is in another country, it *is* an American university. The language of instruction is English, the basis of instruction is American, and students from over the world get a chance to see how hard some American men and women, their teachers, can work. They also find out what is expected and required in the highest standards for American undergraduates. They go home with revised ideas about the United States, taking a respect for the classroom demands and an appreciation of the campus friendships, of these American teachers and administrators who direct the university. This university at Beirut is known and talked about throughout the Middle East, and it has done much to help the American position in that part of the world.

There are places to see in Lebanon, and their number is surprising because the country is so small. Lebanon is only one hundred and twenty miles long and thirty-five miles at its widest. But in the north are the cedars of Lebanon, a memorable sight, and whether any of these trees now standing were among the original cedars, as some men claim, does not matter. One can believe it so, and it is a pleasant belief that here are the trees such as Solomon used, and that were used by builders before Solomon, trees to build their temples, to roof their palaces, and to send as far away as timberless Egypt to be traded for grain and olive oil.

To the north also are the ruins of Baalbeck, with a temple that one will remember, and twenty miles from Beirut, at the village of Jebeil, are other ruins that are memorable. At this village, some thirty years ago, there was a landslide, and no one knew that there were any ruins here, but the slide bared a sarcophagus and then exposed a whole royal burial ground, and the archaeologists came quickly and went to work.

It proved to be the site of Byblos, a city that was here fourteen hundred years before Christ, before even Tyre and Sidon, and as the workmen dug, they uncovered one civilization beneath another, always going deeper and always moving back in time, until they came to the homes and the markets of the Phoenicians, and on below them to still other civilizations. As one stands here now, time loses its pretense, for Rome was yesterday and the Crusaders today. It is a disturbing place and it plucks at a man's sleeve as he looks.

Coming back from the trip to Byblos, we drove past a shambles: boxes roofed with tar paper, crates covered with rusty tin, and in them live the Arab refugees from Palestine. There are thousands of these refugees here, living where a man would not put his dog. Filth and vermin are in these places, and a stench to gag a person at the thought of food.

In the fighting in Palestine, before the armistices of 1949 ended it, the Arabs were driven out of the region that now is Israel, or they fled of their own accord, running before the advancing Jews. For all the years since then the refugees have lived off the care of the United Nations. It is impossible not to pity them; it is difficult not to criticize them. Why don't they go to work? Will they sit here forever?

These are obvious questions and are quickly asked by an American. But the answers don't come quickly, and they are not easy to understand. These families had homes and these men had land over there across the line where now is Israel, and where other families live today and other men work the land and gather the crops. This was the land and these the crops that the Arabs once owned, and this the land that their fathers owned before them, and they swear by the beard of the Prophet, a frightful oath, that they will return. They will go back into their land, they swear, and they will drive the Jews into the sea.

They will not consider going to any other land, no matter how easy the going might be made for them or how fertile the land might be. They will go back to *their* land. It is more than earth to them; it is their honor, their pledge. If they were to go to any other land, they would not only surrender every chance of ever returning to their homes, but they would sacrifice their honor in the violation of their pledge. They will wait, for a man can be patient as he broods, but they have sworn to wait no longer than they must, and then they will wade to their thighs in the reddened sea as they drive the Jews before them. They will wait, but not too long.

And while they wait, they grow thin and their women look to the south with blank eyes and their children wear rags. These men are among those who have been washed up on the skeleton shores from the seas of hate. Their brothers are in the back alleys of Seoul. And others climb the waterless, stinking cliffs of Hong

Kong. And still others infest the hovels across northern India; and in Pakistan they curse even as they tell their beads. These men, these millions of men, may not be on the conscience of civilization, but they are on the record.

I met with a group of Arabs, men of learning, at ease in many languages and at home in the capitals of the world, and I asked them about these refugees. Could nothing be done to persuade them to go somewhere else, anywhere, and begin work? "We would not persuade them," one man answered. "We would not ask them to lose their souls. They have made a vow."

"But the Jews believe it is their land," I said. "Promised to them two thousand years ago...."

"Do not say this." He spoke quickly. "You are an intelligent man. What of this old tale of the Hebrews? If Iroquois chieftains were to come back today to Broadway and Forty-second Street and say, 'This is our land. It was promised to us two thousand years ago by the Great Spirit....' If they did this, and started setting up their wigwams, you would lead them away to the insane asylum. And if they started brandishing their tomahawks, some Irish cop would knock them in the head.

"This talk of the Lord and of his promise is sheer propaganda and nonsense. The land now is simply real estate. And it is ours. Ours it will always be. And not all the money of the rich Jews in America—who financed the land in the first place, and brought their political pressure in the United States, and who still maintain Israel today—not all their money, or all the money from anywhere else, will keep our land from us. We will take it back, and we will drive the Jews into the sea."

This is the talk that I heard from the Arabs, and this is the only talk that I heard from them. They say it almost as a ritual, as a chant, about the state of Israel and its people—"We will drive the Jews into the sea."

The Arabs say, no matter what the British may have promised, however many White Papers were prepared, that Britain was promising land that did not belong to her; and when the Jews came in, they were nothing more nor less than invaders, driving the Arab people from their homes and taking their land by force. The Arabs also contend that the recognition of Israel by the prominent nations, the United States among them, has no significance or justification, and these nations are merely playing to the politically powerful Jews in their own countries.

Whatever may be right in the Middle East, whatever may be just, whatever may have been the eternal promise of Jehovah concerning the return of the Jew, none of this affects the record in the slightest so far as the Arab sees it. So far as he is concerned, the Jew is living where he has no right to be, and the land does not belong to him.

The taking of this land by the Jews is more than the loss of the land itself, for the Arab is a man proud in his person and unyielding in his religion, and his religion is of the sword. His hatred is deepened, and continues as a part of his faith, because the Jews not only took the land but they broke the sword of Islam. The land might, in time, be forgotten; but never this defeat by the Jews, for this is more than a military loss, it is a disgrace in the eyes of the Prophet and it must be wiped out. Whatever the cost, whatever the delay—the Jew must be driven into the sea.

There are many Christians in Lebanon, almost equaling the Moslems in number, and they live in fear that the fighting will break out again, and that the Moslems and the Jews will tear the Middle East apart. This fear is justified because no matter how quiet all may appear to be, one senses that the fighting is imminent and poised, and that the Jews and the Arabs would like to get at each other again. The Christians of Lebanon believe that time may adjust the boundaries and force the acceptance of the state of Israel, but not even time can lessen the hate between these people, or do away with the enmity of their religions, or wipe out the threat of the fighting.

I talked with a good many of these Christians and learned

some things that we might well consider in our dealings with other people, for often it is these little things that can help or hurt us most. They told me of some high-school boys and girls in Beirut who had formed a study club and were going to discuss "International Relations," and they were very serious about it. A committee of these boys and girls called at the American embassy, planning to invite an American to come and speak to them. They waited so long that they were restless, and when finally they were seen they were told that there were no American speakers for this purpose.

So the committee decided that they would go to the Russian embassy. They were met and escorted to a room where they were served fruit juice and cakes. A few minutes later the Russian ambassador himself came in and sat down and talked with them. He thought it a fine idea, and one of his best men had just come back from Russia and this man would come and speak to them, telling them about students and student life in Russia. The man did come and he made the speech, and these students in Beirut now are wondering if they might not like Russia. They might like to enroll in one of the Russian universities, and what about all this criticism of Russia and Communism anyhow?

I also heard about the people of a village not far from Beirut, and the difficulty they were having in raising money to buy a church bell. Then one morning a delegation of Russians came and presented them the money for their bell. Now every morning they hear the tolling, and they are reminded of how kind the Russians are. Each Sunday as they go to worship, listening to the sound of the bell, they wonder who could have said that the Russians are a godless people.

I heard about another gift, this one from the American government. Sometime after the fighting in Lebanon, and after the marines were gone, an American official came to a banquet. He reminded the Lebanese of all that the United States had done for Lebanon, all the help, all the aid, and he quoted the figures. Then he announced still another contribution, and he produced a check. And my Lebanese friend told me: "Every Lebanese in the room felt the humiliation of accepting these alms from your government. Couldn't this American official have figured out some other way to present his check, some way to save our pride? We have things to sell—why couldn't he have bought our Lebanese apples, no matter what he might have done with them afterward. Did he have to parade again just how much money the United States is *giving* to the world? It is embarrassing to be given anything, and you hate a man who calls attention to it."

Beirut is more of a European city than any other city of the Middle East. The French stayed here so long that they made Beirut into a little Paris, and it is that now. The streets and the shops, the cafés and the night clubs, are European in appearance, and many of the people are European in their ways. It is a cosmopolitan place, gay and bright, even though in Lebanon itself there is always the friction between the Christians and the Moslems, and at the border of Lebanon there is always the hate between the Moslems and the Jews.

19

When time came for us to leave Lebanon, we were faced with a problem. My next work for the State Department was in Israel —but how was I to get there? There are no trains and no bus services between Lebanon or between any of the Arab countries and Israel. There is no airplane service, no plane of any kind takes off from an Arab country and flies to Israel, and no boat goes from an Arab country to Israel. This closing of the borders in every possible way is part of the Arab plan to seal off Israel and to try to blot out the Jewish state. I found out that there is not even telephone or telegraph communication, and no mail service, between any of the Arab countries and Israel. The Arabs just pretend that Israel isn't there, except as a dishonor which they intend to wipe out.

This impasse is hampering, of course, to everything in the Middle East, and it looked as if it might block my getting to Israel; but I had a schedule of work waiting for me there, and I had to go. But how? This was no casual question, for I was told by men in Lebanon that I could not get to Israel, that I was foolish to try, and that I had better disregard it and go on somewhere else.

I took my predicament to the air line, and the man at the counter flinched. He wanted no part of it. Our round-the-world tickets called for us to select our route of travel, but these airline officials, who represent one of the biggest world-circling air-line companies, wanted nothing to do with the tickets of people who were trying to get out of an Arab country and into Israel. But whether they wanted it or not, I showed them our tickets and I asked them to figure out a way. I didn't want to embarrass anybody, but I had to get to Israel.

They figured, and they finally came up with a solution. To get from Beirut to Tel Aviv in Israel, a distance directly south of about one hundred miles, we would have to fly west out over the Mediterranean for a distance of two hundred miles to the island of Cyprus. There we would change planes, and change air lines, and then fly back some four hundred miles southeast to Tel Aviv.

What's more, none of this could show on our regular tickets, for we would not be able to get out of Lebanon if it were known that we intended to go on to Israel later. If this were known, no air line that flies out of Lebanon would carry us anywhere. They would have nothing to do with us, and we could just sit.

So it was arranged that each of us was to be issued two tickets, one of them a fake so that we could get out of Lebanon. This ticket would schedule us from Lebanon to Cyprus and from Cyprus to Egypt, showing our destination as another Arab state, and therefore the Arabs of Lebanon would deal with us.

But at the same time a second ticket would be issued to each of us, and this one would be under the counter and secret. It would show our destination as Tel Aviv. Once we were out of Lebanon and had landed in Cyprus, we were to tear up the tickets to Egypt, produce the tickets to Tel Aviv, and fly on to Israel.

While all this make-believe was going on, all this subterfuge and trickery, I talked with an American and told him the troubles that we were having, and he said that there might be another way to get into Israel. If we would go to Jerusalem, now a divided city, he had heard that there is a gate that we might get through, crossing there from the Arab side of the city over into that part of Jerusalem that is in Israel.

I wanted my wife to see Jerusalem and since I had been there only during the war, and with no time for sight-seeing, I wanted to go there, too. So we decided to take a chance on getting through the gate, and we washed out our tickets to Cyprus and Egypt. Instead, we bought tickets for the Arab state of Jordan, and we flew to Jerusalem direct, our tickets taking us to the Arab side of the city and our plane landing on the Arab side.

For both my wife and myself our earliest teachings from our parents had been about the Holy Land. We had heard about it in Sunday school and in church, and we had read and studied about it as we grew up. And now, at last, we were entering the Holy Land and there was a humble feeling as our plane taxied toward the building and we saw the sign—*JERUSALEM*.

We had flown down with a group of elderly men and women who were on a tour, and their tour leader stood in the aisle of the plane as we were crossing the field and she told them their schedule. They would be met by the Jerusalem representative of the travel agency, and they would go to the bus, and the bus would go to the hotel, and then they would go to the Garden of Gethsemane.

My wife and I waited and let the older people get out first, and this was not entirely a courtesy, for we wanted to be only with ourselves when we came into the Holy Land. We waited until they all were out and their tour leader was standing at one side of the field shouting for them to come this way. Not that way. This way. And the Jerusalem representative of the travel agency was pointing on toward the bus, shaking his head and waving them on. He would answer all questions later. He would explain everything, where Christ was crucified and everything. Just go on and get in the bus.

We went into customs. A baby was sitting on the floor in its own foulings and an American lady was saying that she just didn't see *why* they couldn't find her bag. It was labeled, and it was on the plane when the plane left Cairo, and just how in the hell did they drop it overboard? And where was the manager?

A large Jordanian policeman, wearing a khaki uniform and a sun helmet with a shade down the back of his neck, spotted us and came through a group of Lebanese pilgrims, led by their priest, and pushing the pilgrims aside to get to us. He spoke excellent English and he arranged for our Jordanian visas, and I paid the fee. He arranged for our baggage to be passed by the customs without even one bag being opened. He arranged for porters to carry our baggage outside, and after I had paid them, and they still demanded more, he murmured a few words and they vanished.

He had influence, this policeman, and I asked him nothing and told him nothing; but I had been somewhat aware of his having had the porters take our baggage to a certain large automobile, where two very dignified gentlemen waited. I had supposed that these two gentlemen were representatives of USIS, or that they were friends of friends of ours in Lebanon, and had been notified of our coming. I had supposed, too, that the policeman's interest in us had been somewhat diplomatic, or at least official. At that time I had no idea that the deal between him and these two gents was strictly commercial.

We drove away from the airport silently, and we were well down the road when one of our companions turned around and with a smile and a bow that would have made Uriah Heep seem like a rowdy, said: "Welcome to the Holy Land."

I returned the bow. "Thank you."

"We are from Murray's Travel Agency." And he presented his card and his documents.

I had noticed that there were other gentlemen, equally dignified, equally suave, with equally big automobiles, waiting at the airport; but apparently they had not made the right arrangements with the big Jordanian policeman, for they didn't get a chance to approach us and we were Murray's, all Murray's.

"You will see—" he said, pointing to the folder.

And we saw: "THE HOLY LAND. Come and Enjoy the Wonderful Views of the Bible History. Your visit to THE HOLY

LAND will Keep in Your Memory Forever. MURRAY'S! offers Qualified Guides. Best Hotel Accommodations. Excellent Transport. Courteous Service. Personal Attention. Moderate Prices."

"These," he said, handing me a card, "are the prices. This is the rate sheet. Now for Tour One..."

I looked at Tour One: Enter St. Stephen's Gate, visit the Pool of Bethesda, Pilate's Palace, Judgment Hall, the Flagellation, Ecce Homo...

"The price for Tour One is $20.00. Now this is Tour Two. We go to the Little Town of Bethlehem. We visit the Church of the Nativity. See the Manger. This is $30.00."

There was also Tour Three. We could go to Jericho, passing the Apostles' Fountain, the Good Samaritan's Inn, and on to the river Jordan. This would be even more, this would be $40.00. Just how much of the Holy Land did we want?

That afternoon we took Tour One, and we saw the curious truth about Jerusalem today, for this ancient city now is cut in half. At the end of the war between the Arabs and the Jews, the United Nations mediator drew a line dividing Jordan and Israel, and this line also divides Jerusalem, running directly through the city—half to Jordan, half to Israel.

Just as there are no dealings between the countries of Jordan and Israel, or between Israel and any other Arab state, so there are no dealings between the two parts of Jerusalem, no trading, no association of the people, no crossing from one side of the city to the other, except through the one gate that we had heard about, the Mandelbaum Gate, which is open at certain times of the day for the passing of certain officials and for the occasional passing of an individual. This gate is always under dual guard, the troops of Jordan on one side, and exactly opposite the troops of Israel on the other. Jerusalem today is two cities, shut off from each other by barricades and sentries, as divided as if there were a wall of fire between.

We took Tour One, which is entirely on the Jordan side of the city, and we drove through St. Stephen's Gate, visited Pilate's

Palace, the Judgment Hall, and kept on going. Our guide was telling it all, talking fast, for he had recited it so many times before, and we were walking along the Via Dolorosa, the Way of the Cross, when he said that right here, Jesus did this. Right here Jesus did that. I asked him how did he know about this. How could he be so certain?

He seemed not to hear my question, and he kept right on talking. Here was where Pontius Pilate stood. Here was where Jesus stood. Here was where the Flagellation took place, this was the rock where He was fastened. Here is where the Cross stood. These other two spots were where the other crosses stood.

"Wait a minute. How do you know all this? That Jesus *was* and *is* is a part of my belief. But belief is separate from geography, and you are making this geography. This happened *here!* On *this* spot. You're showing me a diagram, a blue print. How do you know?"

He spread his hands and tilted his shoulders. "Look, friend, if we didn't say it was here, we'd have to say it was somewhere else. They ask you where it happened. You got to show 'em." He dropped his hands and walked on. "Now we come to the Church of the Holy Sepulchre. Here Jesus' body was brought after the Crucifixion. It was brought in that way, through that entrance, and it was laid here on this slab...."

A priest was standing by the slab and he was burning candles. He looked at me and nodded toward the collection plate.

This Church of the Holy Sepulchre, the most venerated shrine in Christendom, is divided among the Greek Orthodox, the Armenians, the Assyrians, the Roman Catholics, and the Coptics. To make certain that none of these Christian faiths has an advantage, or that none of them takes an advantage, an impartial Moslem has been appointed to keep the keys of this Christian church, and a Moslem always opens the church and always closes it, and always he sits at the door on guard.

Our guide showed us the part of the church where the Armenians worship. He showed the corner that is set apart for the Assyrians. He showed the line that has been drawn for the Coptics, marking off their area of worship.

I looked at all this division, and I thought of Jesus, and the simple completeness of Jesus, and His oneness of all men, and I asked: "Where do Christians worship?"

The guide glanced at me. "I don't know," he said. "I'm a Moslem. Now here is the tomb where Christ rose. Here was the rock, and it was rolled from over there, to right over here...."

The next day we drove to Jericho, passing the remnants of an old building that we were told was the Good Samaritan Inn, and then we went on to the river Jordan. I remember when I was a boy that my aunt had a bottle of the water from the river Jordan. I remember how I had looked at it when she had showed it to me, telling me that this was the water from the river and from the place in the river where Jesus had been baptized. Even now I can remember my feeling, almost a frightened feeling, as I looked at the water. In the way of a boy, and as best I knew how, I worshiped. This has been a precious memory to me always.

So we went to the river Jordan, and when we got there the people who had been on the plane the day before, the group of elderly men and women, were there and their guide was telling them. He was talking fast, getting it over with, but he was telling them. They were hot and they were sweating, and one lady was sitting down and rubbing her ankles; but some of them were making notes, some were taking pictures, and one lady was drawing a sketch of the river. The river is about ten feet wide, and the guide showed them just the place where Jesus had walked down into the water.

A man off to one side had seen us coming, and he knocked on a table gently, not wanting to interrupt the guide who was talking to his tour, but still wanting to attract our attention. We went over to where he was and he had bottles of water from the river Jordan on the table. Each bottle was sealed and the price was marked on it. It looked like a roadside lemonade stand.

After the tour left, our guide began telling us exactly what we had already heard from listening to the other guide, and he told it in the same way, and then we drove on to the Dead Sea. There is a big hotel there and I ordered a Tom Collins before lunch, and we sat in the lounge and watched a fat man with a hairy chest floating on an inflated mattress. Now and then he would reach around behind and scratch.

After lunch we drove to the Little Town of Bethlehem and to the Church of the Nativity. Our guide showed us the Manger. He showed us where the birth took place. It was very graphic.

Back at the hotel late that afternoon, the guide spread his folder again. "Now we come to Tour Five," he said. "Tomorrow we will visit the Tomb of Joseph, the Birthplace of Saul, stand on the spot where Mary and Joseph missed the Child on their way to Nazareth—"

"Wait a minute. You've done just fine," I said. "You're a good guide and I want to thank you. But if you don't mind, let's call it off. Maybe my wife and I would like just to wander around tomorrow by ourselves a bit."

That night, in the lobby of the hotel, we talked to some Arabs, and I asked them how it felt to live in a divided city, when before Jerusalem had been for everybody. They said that it was the Jews. The Jews had come and stolen the land. They had overrun the land, killing people and murdering as they went.

The Arabs would take their land back now if it were not for the United States. "You are backing Israel and protecting the Jews. But not even the United States can stop us. We will drive the Jews into the sea."

The next morning my wife and I went for a walk, and most of the businesses that we saw were travel agencies. There were some stores and a few shops, but most of the signs along the street were travel agencies offering guides, top service, moderate prices.

I felt an embarrassment that I was here, a great humiliation, and I wished to God that I had never come to the Holy Land.

That afternoon we went to the American consulate and each of us paid $2.50. For this money we were given a "certificate" by the American government which, like the tickets to Egypt that had been issued to us by the air line in Lebanon, is a part of the make-believe and subterfuge of the area.

Once we had made this visit to the consulate and had carried out the requirements there, my wife and I were ready, and were armed with the proper papers, to make the crossing from Jordan into Israel. Each of us had a passport, each of us had a certificate, and we set out for the line that divides the city of Jerusalem, and that also divides the countries of Jordan and Israel. We rode in a taxicab through Jerusalem and on toward the line.

At the time of the armistice, in 1949, the Arabs wanted to close the frontier completely and have no passing whatsoever between Jordan and Israel, but the United Nations required that there should be a gateway of some kind, so that officials of the United Nations and foreign diplomats could get back and forth from one country to the other. Jordan acceded to this and a passageway was opened.

This narrow passage that lies across the line in Jerusalem is called the "Mandelbaum Gate," but it is no gate at all and never was. Here was a center of some of the hardest fighting in the Arab-Israeli war, and here a man named Mandelbaum once had a store. But nobody has anything there now, for there is only wreckage left from the fighting, and also some twisted spikes and great blocks of concrete, broken and jagged, that have been added to make it impossible for any armored car to pass or a tank to crash through.

An ordinary person, once he has the proper papers, can cross the line here; but he can go in only one direction—from Jordan into Israel. Jordan allows any traveler to leave her country and cross over into Israel, and the Jews welcome him. But no one, except the diplomats and officials and the massed religious pilgrims at Easter and Christmas, can come back the other way, coming out of Israel into Jordan. Here again is the law of the Arabs: once the touch of Israel is on a person he is barred from any Arab country.

My wife and I approached the Mandelbaum Gate and presented ourselves to the Jordan patrol, showing our *passports* to the Arabs. They contained our Jordanian visas, but no mark of any kind concerning Israel. The Arabs searched them for any word, any sign, any trace whatsoever of Israel, examining each page, but finding nothing, they stamped them and gave us permission to leave their country. They themselves then practiced subterfuge, for they turned their backs and walked away, knowing full well where we were going, but they refused to acknowledge it by watching us go.

It all seemed so pointless, and I wanted to ask them if they didn't think that they, and their nation, were being shortsighted and foolish; but asking them would have been a bit shortsighted on my part, and so I picked up a suitcase, and, my wife beside me, we entered no-man's land between the two countries, a bleak and barren stretch littered with signs of the fighting. It was there, in the heart of Jerusalem, the Holy City, that we crossed over from Jordan to the Israeli side.

As we approached the Israeli outpost, we pocketed our passports and produced our *certificates*. They showed that we were American citizens, and they bore our photographs and the seal of the United States.

The Israeli guards examined them and stamped them, then opened the door and admitted us into Israel.

By using the certificates, we kept our passports free from any mark of Israel, so that the passports would be accepted later, if it became necessary for us to travel again in any Arab country.

20

No matter where else a man may have been or what he may have seen, he will be stirred when he comes to Israel and travels over this country and sees what these people have done. He may have read books about Israel, and seen pictures of Israel, but when he comes here he will stand in amazement before this country.

I saw Palestine years ago for just a short time, but even in that time I saw that it was a bleak and barren country, as rocky and sandy as all the countries in this area, the water scarce and the ground grudging in its yield. The people who lived here dragged along in a shambling way, the houses shabby and the men just scratching at the earth to produce their scrubby crops.

Now go there!

Where the hillsides were rocks, now orchards grow, cherry, peach, plums, and apples. The desert that was sand now yields its crops. You see the people, the men and the women, climbing over the hills, digging out the rocks and putting in the dirt, then planting the trees. You see whole families moving on deeper into the desert, crossing the sand, building houses, stretching the water, turning the dead land green.

They have planted a thousand trees, and ten thousand trees, and made forests where before there was only waste. Their farms stretch to the horizon, the rich black dirt turned and furrowed, and the grain growing and the vegetables growing, where five years ago was a malarial swamp. There is a tradition that the Jew is a professional man or a man of commerce, and not a farmer or a man of the soil. Come and see!

The children are healthy, and the parks in the afternoon are crowded with them at play. The schools are clean and busy, filled with books and machines. I have watched the girls weaving and the boys at their printing presses and metal lathes. *These* children of Israel are no part of an old story handed down from the past; they are writing the record of today.

From a hill high above Haifa I saw mills and factories where a few years ago there was nothing. I saw towering smokestacks crowding the city and moving on out into the Valley of Zebulon, and these are more than mills and factories—here is an old faith and a new vision, and here is determination.

Those who try to belittle Israel do so by saying that any country could do well if it were given millions of dollars by people from outside. Why shouldn't Israel make a good showing? Look at all the money that the Jews of the United States, from South Africa, from Canada, from all over the world, have poured into Israel. Any country could do well with all that money.

But what has been accomplished in Israel took a great deal more than money. In Tel Aviv, in Jerusalem, in Haifa, one sees magnificent buildings, auditoriums, hospitals, community houses, and one knows that money from outside put up the buildings. The names over the doors tell where some of the money came from, and some of these names are well known in the United States. But these buildings aren't Israel. Israel is the people who came here, and live here, and what these people themselves have done with their hard work, their courage, and their determination. Israel is the dedication of all its people to the job of building a nation, their nation more important to them than any personal interest or desire.

In Israel are names that ring down through the centuries—the Sea of Galilee, Capernaum, Tiberias, Cana of Galilee, Mount

Tabor, the Plains of Sharon. In Israel, too, are King Solomon's mines, and they are being reworked today to get what was left and what had been considered too little to bother with. There is also Beersheba, the desert city of Abraham, of Isaac, and of Jacob, and where today Israeli scientists are working on new ways of irrigation, new methods of planting, new crops, all aimed at the desert and all of it pushing the desert back. One goes past Beersheba now and sees where the old line of the desert used to be. One travels on past this line through miles of growing fields, and the scientists point ahead, saying that we will be there next month. And on to there, the month after.

It is a paradox to go to Beersheba, this modern city of science and research, on a Thursday, and watch the Bedouins come up out of the desert on their camels, their long white headdresses flowing, and they themselves as black as the sun can burn them, erect, men of dignity and quality, calm and fearless, their curved dirks at their belts. They have come for the weekly camel market and some of them have brought extra beasts to sell or trade, and throughout the morning they move through the pens, showing little interest as they go, showing no interest at all when they intend to buy. At the end of the morning, and after the camels have been re-sorted and herded again, the Bedouins stalk through the city, their long robes white and clean, and they stop at some shops to buy and at others to gaze, wondering what these new things can be.

Besides Beersheba there are other cities here in Israel from biblical times, and one of them up toward the north is Nazareth. Here is where the carpenter Joseph lived and had his workshop, and here is where a boy grew up. One afternoon in this city of Nazareth I was out for a walk and turned a corner, and there, coming toward me, was a boy riding a donkey. He was sitting back on the hindquarters of the little animal, and he had one leg folded under him, his hand on his knee, just a boy, unconcerned, riding along and looking about him. One couldn't help thinking of another boy who once rode along in Nazareth.

It was on a second visit to Beersheba that my wife and I visited the guesthouse, a stone building with lovely gardens and a good dining room. We were at lunch when three buses unloaded out in front and the tourists came cramming in. Where before there had been only quiet, only the occasional clink of silver or china, only the murmur of conversation, now there was bedlam and the brassy bleat of Brooklyn, tuned to the survival of the loudest.

Two Israelis, with whom we had been chatting at an adjoining table, pushed their cups aside and stood. They smiled as they passed us, and one of them leaned down. "You will excuse us for hurrying," he said, "but sometimes your countrymen can be rather noticeable."

One of these men had been born and had always lived in Palestine, the other was a Jew from the Argentine. There are Jews in Israel today from everywhere. The Israeli Declaration of Independence grants to any Jew the "Right of Return." Any Jew can present himself at the border and as he steps on Israeli soil, and by the one fact that he is a Jew, he is a citizen of the country. Here is the homeland, and any Jew from anywhere is a part of it the moment he returns.

This flow of Jews into Israel is being adroitly used by the Russians in their dealings with the Arabs. One of the fears of the Arabs is that the Israelis will continue to grow in population, both from within and from the influx from without, until they no longer can live and support themselves within their narrow boundaries, and they then will break out and overflow into Arab countries. Having once experienced the loss of land, which they still consider to be theirs, the Arabs believe that the Jew will not hesitate to try for land again whenever he thinks that he can get it. They also point out that every Israeli border, except the sea, touches Arab land and that only the Arabs can lose if the Israelis try to expand.

The Russians, knowing these suspicions of the Arabs, wait until there is some moment of particular unrest in the Arab world, some time of especial hate, and Russia then releases thousands of Jews, freeing them from the satellite countries and allowing them to flood into Israel. Russia then tells the world how compassionate she is, granting the wish of the Jews and allowing them to go to their homeland. At the same time, Russian agents move among the Arabs reminding them that more Jews are coming into Israel. They will have to break out soon, these Jews! The Arabs, if they are wise, will attack first.

Among the Jews from over the world who have come to Israel, some 35,000 were American Jews. But of these only 7,000 remained. The other 28,000 returned to the United States.

One can understand this, for while the basic standard of living —food, housing, clothing—in the two countries, Israel and the United States, is comparable, there is a notable difference in the comforts, and almost a total gap in luxuries. A Jew from Ethiopia or Yemen would find Israel a kind of earthly heaven, with electric lights and plumbing, compared to the living that he has known; but unless a man from the United States has a spiritual dedication to the state of Israel, its meaning and its purpose, he probably will go back to the United States.

Besides losing some of those who come to stay, Israel makes no great appeal to the ordinary traveler, for it is a country with comparatively few tourist attractions and is too busy to exploit even these. Few travelers are interested in coming to see a country's economic and social development, and these at present are Israel's chief attractions. Nor do many tourists want to visit a country and be shown primarily medical centers and housing projects, important as they are—and even though the Israelis who show them are overflowing with pride at what their country is doing.

In Israel one does not see the general run of tourists that crowd the streets of Rome and Paris, and that wander about in the Orient. I asked government men, hotel men, and air-line representatives about this question of tourists in Israel, and they told me that the great majority—some said as high as 90 per cent—of all tourists in Israel today are Jews who have come to see the fulfillment of the promise, and to learn the truth firsthand about their homeland. They come more in devotion as pilgrims than as tourists, and I have seen the old men tremble as they stood before some creation of this modern state of Israel, a school, a factory, a forest.

I saw many of these pilgrim-tourists in all parts of Israel, and perhaps it is a telling fact that most of them are older men and women, many of them in their late fifties and sixties. One sees few tourists in Israel today among the younger people. The dream of the homeland apparently is vivid and compelling to the older men and women, but the younger people may be less concerned.

A person can't help asking what will happen when the older generation is gone. Will the miracle of Israel, and all the present wonder at the creation of the state, dwindle in time until there is only the routine acceptance of its existence? The men who by then will be older—will they, too, return to this land? Will they return in their thinking, their prayers? Will they send money? Perhaps these questions are in the minds of the men who are guiding Israel now and are pressing so hard, trying to get all they can, trying to make the state able to support itself, no matter what may happen in the years ahead.

When one thinks of Israel, he thinks of *Israel,* and of no particular part. Just as when a person looks at a beehive he sees the hive as a whole. A countryside, wherever it may be, can blend into a kind of uniform background, but usually a city has a character and an identity of its own. This is less true in Israel than anywhere else, for here even the cities lose their distinction in the surge of these people, in their hurry and determination to work together in the building of their nation.

Tel Aviv is Israel's most spectacular city, and Tel Aviv is a whirlwind, rising up out of the sheer dust some fifty years ago and still spinning. The shops are busy, the people are working, and the cars line up fast behind each other, waiting for the traffic lights to change. Tel Aviv is like a little New York, intent, ambitious, fast moving. And yet this daily pace, this pressure of getting things done, changes completely at night, and Tel Aviv slips into the casual life of some European city, the people sitting at sidewalk cafés and drinking coffee, sipping a glass of wine, watching the other people go by. The people during the day have earned a pleasant evening, and Tel Aviv is restful and delightful at night.

Jerusalem—at least that part of the city that is in Israel—is quieter than Tel Aviv and moves at a slower pace, but in its streets, its stores, in the ways of its people, Jerusalem, too, is a busy city. One sees the people planning, building, endlessly working together for the making of their country.

Here in Jerusalem one of the great hospitals of the East, and a medical center for training, has just been completed. The new university in Jerusalem has buildings, classrooms, laboratories, and a library that any American university would like to have. Its faculty is made up of scholars drawn from all over the world, men of learning from everywhere who have come here in their dedication to teach for a lower salary and a greater pay. In Jerusalem, too, is probably the best hotel of the Middle East, one of the really notable hotels of the world, the King David.

This hotel, so comfortable, even luxurious without displaying it or insisting on it, is practically on the line between Israel and Jordan. The first time I saw the hotel I was over on the Jordan side, standing on a hill, and my Mohammedan guide pointed across to Israel and said: "There is the YMCA. And there, across the street from the YMCA, is the King David Hotel." The Israeli flag, the Star of David in its center, was bright in the afternoon sun.

Sitting in this hotel, so quiet, so pleasant, one looks out and there, close at hand, is the submerged war—pressure instead of actual fighting. My wife and I often had tea on our balcony in the afternoons, and just under our balcony was a tangle of wire and rubble, and near to us was the Israeli guard walking his post. Slightly across the way, only just over there, the Arab guard walked his post. The mounted guns, in position along the line, were aimed and ready.

It seemed just so damned silly! Of course all war is silly and stupid, but this one seems so completely foolish to drag on.

At present there is only an armistice between Israel and her Arab neighbors. The Jews are ready to settle it, to arrange for a completed peace, and one can understand this because the Jews have won most of what they want, and the victor usually is ready to quit. The Arabs, however, will not agree to the loss of their land or forget that their honor has been sullied and their pride trampled on. And yet the Arabs, no matter what their rights or what the justice of their cause may be, look odd sitting still with their hands folded, brooding and hating, while these people they dislike just go on ignoring them, and building good homes, eating good food, and sending their children to school. After all these years of just sitting, it does look as if the Arab refugees would catch on to the futility of idleness and hate, vow or no vow. And the Arab nations might reread the deal of the cards, and pick up a different hand.

What the end is to be, of course, no man can see, but a person who comes into the Middle East, traveling in both the Arab countries and in Israel, looking about him and talking to men of both sides, is likely to arrive at a very clear belief.

The Arab boycott unquestionably hems Israel in and unquestionably hampers her. The Arabs will continue their boycott, their harassment, their hate, and there will be sniping from both sides, and border clashes, and perhaps all-out war; but no unbiased man can believe that the Arabs of the present, or their sons, or their sons' sons, will drive the Jews into the sea.

The future of Israel, if any man can judge by evidence that he sees, and the more powerful evidence that he feels, is secure. These Israelis are intelligent, and they are determined; they are united, and they are tireless. With them, their nation comes first, and one can believe that they will make it endure.

There are thousands of Arabs today who live in Israel, men and their families who stayed on during the fighting, or who came back after the fighting, and apparently they are comfortable in their homes, satisfied with their work, and secure in their mosques. They are scattered over the whole of Israel and some villages are made up entirely of Arabs. While the men of the Arab countries slam their doors against the Jews, and wipe their lips to cleanse them when they speak the word, the Jews in Israel live with the Arabs inside their country like sensible men, working together for whatever benefits they can get and share.

Arab children go to school the same as Israeli children. Arab families get the same medical attention, the same social benefits. They are free to worship as they please. I saw a good many of these Arabs in Israel, and so far as one can see they seem to be healthy and contented. Certainly, so far as the physical needs of men, they are better off than those who sit and brood, waiting for some miracle to come all the way to them.

I saw one of these Arabs in Israel one afternoon when I was particularly interested in seeing him. We were at Armageddon and the radiator of our automobile, which had been troubling us all the way back from the Sea of Galilee, finally sputtered its last, and I told my wife that that radiator had a nice sense of the fitness of things and had picked the right spot for its final battle. She was a good deal less interested in the setting of our collapse, even in its biblical connotation, than in our getting back to Jerusalem.

Our driver was still tinkering with the radiator when from over the hill came an Arab farmer astraddle his donkey, his donkey so short and his own legs so long that his slippered feet touched the ridges and stirred the dust as he rode in the dirt beside the macadam. He came bobbing on, and he halted opposite. By sight and signs I could tell that he and our driver were in a mild debate about modes of travel, and by the way the Arab was grinning and patting his donkey, I could tell that he preferred his own. Finally, with a parting comment and another grin, he ambled on, his donkey padding along and now and then the Arab's feet stirring the dust. But it wasn't long before he was back, this time trailing a police car that he had hailed at the crossroads and told of our predicament.

The police were sorry that this should have happened to us in Israel, and they halted an express bus and put us on it. The last I saw of the Arab he was sitting sideways on his donkey and he and the Israeli driver still were discussing something, and from the pleased way the Arab was looking, I could imagine what it was. As a matter of fact, even the Israeli was grinning as the Arab kept picking at him.

Back in Jerusalem and at the King David again, we dressed quickly for our dinner engagement. It turned out to be an enjoyable evening at the home of our friends, and we stayed late. Even after we were back in our hotel room, sometime past midnight, we sat talking. It is easy to find things to talk about in Israel, and we were in no hurry to go to sleep.

But finally, though, after I was in bed and had drifted off into good sleep, I was awakened suddenly, and it seemed to me that I had hardly had a moment's rest. The King David Hotel, as I have said, is almost on the line between Jordan and Israel, and every morning before daybreak, just over there on the Jordan side, a muezzin climbs into the minaret and calls the faithful to prayer.

They must have searched all Islam to find this particular muezzin. I have heard them call from Meshed almost to Mecca, and I have never heard another with such powerful lungs. There before daybreak each morning he not only calls the Moslems of Jordan to pray, but he adds an extra flourish to make certain that he is waking every Jew in the King David Hotel, telling him to get up and worship Allah.

Here in this city of Jerusalem, down to the city of Tel Aviv and on to Haifa, over the land with its rocks and deserts, the bending of its grain and the white showering of its apple blossoms, over all this country that is Israel, one feels above all else the faith of a people. The promise for them has been so long, and they believe it, and they will do their part to make it true.

As I looked at Israel, and watched these men and women busy about the day-by-day task of making their country, I wondered if it is only a young nation that can be dedicated to its growth and betterment. And I wondered about us.

Sometimes even the most devoted and the bravest among us doubts that our system of government, loose, changing, democratic, can compete with the exact, fixed, dictatorial government of Russia. Can any government of the people, by the people, the shouted voice of the voters, compete with the massed force of a populace marching in exact step before the pointed finger of one man? Can a crowd stand up against an army?

The answer is here in Israel. The system of government does not decide the strength of a nation, only the people decide.

These people of Israel have one concern, one loyalty—their country. They have one purpose, their nation. They are doctors for Israel. They are ditch diggers for Israel. Personal pay and profits for themselves are needed, but their country is essential. No man works for himself alone, and no unit of society in Israel is so important as Israel.

Their system of government is the same as ours, of the people, by the people, and the strength of their country is in the people.

And what about us? What about us in the United States?

I have heard an old man in Korea, and men in Vietnam, in India, in Afghanistan, and on around the earth, talk about us. They have said that Russia is winning the minds and the loyalties of men away from us.

I have heard them say that Russia can defeat the United States, and *is* defeating the United States.

Do we, now an older nation, have the same devotion to our country and dedication to it as the men who made it for us and handed it on to our care?

Is our nation more to us than each of us to himself, and more than those things that he owns and that pertain to him, and more than the interests and wants of his particular unit of society?

Can there be an enduring nation without a massed purpose of its people and a joined moral force?

Are we so burly, so strong, so sure—"under the terrible burden of destiny laughing as an ignorant fighter laughs who has never lost a battle"—that we can disregard what other men say about us, and live outside the truth that the strength of a nation is in the character of its people?

21

My last assignment for the State Department was in Israel, and we set out for Europe, to travel there just to see. We went first to Turkey, stopping in Istanbul.

One of the first names of a foreign city that I knew, and took for my own, was Constantinople. I read about it and dreamed someday of going there. I knew its place exactly on the map and I built it in my mind, and *this* was the city that it had to be. But I never saw it as Constantinople, and when I went there it was Istanbul, and it was not the city that I had made for myself.

None of the fantasy of the East was there and only a trace of history, only a suggestion of the old Ottoman Empire, and the legends of these men and their wars were gone. They had been wiped out, the past done away with, by a man named Kemal Atatürk, one of the most remarkable of all men, who some thirty years ago simply picked up Turkey by his own strength and carried it ahead, lifting it across a century and bringing it up to now. He swept aside the veil of the women and he threw away the fez, and these were but symbols of what he did, as by his vision and amazing will he brought his country overnight, so it seemed, out of its sloth and decay. He ended corruption in government and restored courage to the Turks, and he brought back their national pride. He made Constantinople into Istanbul and he made Turkey into a nation that is respected and honored and strong. In Turkey today one sees a barefaced bravery that confronts the world and no nation, not even Russia, tampers with it.

There is no particular luxury here, and there seems to be no shameful poverty. The people go their way, nothing flashy about their clothes—many of them, both men and women, wearing black —and nothing flashy about their talk and their manner, only a simple courtesy in their direct dealings, and one quickly learns to respect them.

They are valuable military allies of the United States, and they ask for nothing. They never wheedle. They give and they take. They are partners, an equal in a contract. The United States has guns. So do they. They take off their hat before no man and no nation.

They have no fear of Russia. There is a thin lane of water down from the north past Istanbul. This is the Bosphorus coming down from the Black Sea, down from Russia. And Russia, from the beginning of history, has maneuvered, threatened, fought, and bribed to get control of this way out of the Black Sea, down through the Bosphorus and on into the Mediterranean.

The Turks have always stopped Russia. They stop Russia now. At the mouth of the Bosphorus the Turks keep submarine nets. Also, any Russian ship that wants to pass through the Bosphorus must suffer the indignity of a search. They must stand idle while Turkish officers and guards mount the Russian ships and ride through, watching and inspecting.

One Turk explained to me how Turkey gets along with Russia, after having lived so close and learned so much about Russia. "It is simple," he said. "We believe *nothing* that Russia says. We trust *nothing* that Russia does. And we don't let Russia get by with *anything*."

The two most bustling cities that we saw as we came around the world were Tokyo in Japan and Athens in Greece. In Athens there is more building going on than in any other city that we visited, more sidewalks torn up, more ditches open for water mains, sewer pipes, and power lines. There is hurry everywhere, and people are on the go, stepping off the sidewalks to get along quicker in the streets, risking the whirl of the automobiles and the motorcycles.

The stores in Athens are like the stores in New York, and we were surprised by the number of shoppers, a few of them tourists, but most of them Greeks. They were crowding the stores and buying clothes for themselves, buying for their children, getting household appliances.

The hotels in Athens are full and there are no vacancies at the motels along by the sea. The restaurants are filled and it is difficult to find a table at one of the sidewalk cafés in the afternoon. Athens is a clean and a lively city, the merchants doing well, the students hard at work at their books, and the people themselves keeping busy, in good health and good spirits.

But for all the bustle in Athens and in other Greek cities, for all the improvement in agriculture and economy, the country today still is recognized chiefly for its past, for it was in the past that Greece knew her glory.

In the center of Athens rises a hill, the Acropolis, the supreme testament of the past. Most of the Acropolis is in ruins now, but the Parthenon, the crown of the hill, is probably the single most compelling building on earth, even in its present shattered form.

One walks about this place slowly, for even when the buildings are dust they will speak, and one looks down from the hill and there, spread out before him, is the harbor. There is the grove where Socrates taught, and there the hill where Pericles stood, and from there Demosthenes spoke. Here is more than the glory that was Greece, for glory can be for a day; here the ages gathered, coming out of their past and centering here, remaining for a time, and going on to shape the world. Here was the pinnacle of civilization, never imagined before or achieved since.

On the Acropolis one thinks about ancient Greece, and he wonders about the men who walked here when the city-state of Athens was so powerful. Athens had a big army, a strong navy, and all the latest weapons. Its business was good and Athens was rich. There was a league then, the Delian League, and it had been founded to maintain world security and world peace. Athens was the leader of the democracies.

But as Athens' power and her riches grew, she became involved in her own affairs, concerned with satisfying the wants and demands of her citizens, and her people broke into little minorities that pulled and tugged at her for what they wanted, and Athens lost her meaning as a nation. Weakened by her own citizens, governed by politicians whose purpose was to keep themselves in office, and who had the courage of a weathercock, Athens began her decay.

As one stands on the Acropolis now and looks out, he wonders what some Athenian, at the time of Athens' power and all her surety, might have said if any man had mentioned that Athens someday could lose its place of prominence, and its leadership, and become only a minor state. One can only imagine the astonishment of the Athenian, his indignation and anger that anyone would dare suggest that Athens could ever be overcome, and turned into a second-rate power.

There are two kinds of tourists that go to Rome today, and they are as far apart as the poles. Rome is threatening Paris as the center of fashion, and Rome is now the gathering place for the international set on the Continent. Rome, as any of this crowd will tell you, is now very smart. There was a time, some years ago, when Rome was considered a frowzy place and Paris was chic, but all that has changed now and Rome is *the* place to go.

A cluster of the better hotels of Rome are along the Via Veneto, close to the American embassy, and there the devotees of fashion and the followers of each other assemble each day. Along the sidewalks for blocks are small tables, shaded by brightly colored umbrellas, like beach umbrellas—and there they come in the late morning, and there they sit throughout the afternoon, through dinner, and on into the night. They sip the *espresso* coffee, show their furs, twist their diamonds, and judge the dresses of others as they go by.

It is an interesting place, this Via Veneto, and one sees interesting people, some of them laughing and really gay, and usually these are the young. Then, too, there are the others, the tired and the jaded with hardened faces, painted and plastered against time, sitting in the dull hang-over from the years when they, too, could laugh. They came because the others are here and also, one can believe, to keep a place, no matter how dwindling, in this fashionable display. All are dressed and coiffed in the latest style, and in fact here *are* the latest styles, for here they are made.

Ordinary Americans who come to Rome are interested in this display of fashion, but only as a frilly sideshow to what they really came to see. They came to see the past and its ruins.

Here is the Forum. Here Caesar walked. And Brutus. There, by the tower, the murder was committed. Over there Mark Antony spoke. Cicero came this way, and here he addressed the senate. Here Nero lived, and this is the part of the city that burned.

It is still vivid from Shakespeare's play and through the haze of schoolboy Latin. It comes back, all right, and it lives, and a man wonders what became of all this. Rome, he knows, once ruled the Mediterranean world, and as far away as Mesopotamia and Britain and all Gaul. This was the Roman Empire. Here centered the most remarkable rule in the history of men, until the even more remarkable rule of Russia and World Communism today.

The Romans moved over the earth, building as they advanced, and one finds their roads still used in England, their bridges used in Spain, and their underground water system intact in Turkey. They were victorious in war, dominant in commerce, and supreme in their influence.

Wealthy as a nation and rich as men, with the highest standard of physical living ever known, they surrounded themselves with comforts and they lived in ease. As their wealth increased, they became more interested in their own enjoyments and their pleasures.

They built the biggest sports arena that had ever been seen, and they went there by the thousands to watch the games, the wrestling, the boxing, and the gladiators, growing soft themselves while they sat and watched the professionals. They built the biggest race tracks that the world had known, and they went to them each afternoon to gamble. They built the biggest baths that had ever been built, and they came and bathed in the warm water, and lolled on the couches, while the attendants anointed them and rubbed them with oils and unguents. They built the biggest banqueting halls, spending fortunes on them, and they drank and dined until they had to go to the vomit room, and then they came back to eat and drink again. Their women, too, shared their pleasures, and the marriage tie was relaxed and the old respect for wife and mother lessened.

The usual beginning disintegration of a people, the moral disintegration, was taking place. The Romans had become concerned with their comforts and their pleasures, and Rome was left without the devoted mind, and the dedicated character, and the soul of its people. Rome itself therefore was nothing, and it fell apart.

Today the ruins are here, but the giant sports arena is empty. The Forum is silent—only a few walkways, some broken shafts and towers spilled and lying on the ground. The baths are cracked and molding. The race track is an uncut field. This is the grandeur that was Rome. This is the empire that lost its moral character.

Paris is the most-talked-about city in the world. Almost everybody wants to go there, and there was a time when a person who saw Paris always wanted to go back.

It was gay then, and it was gentle. It was brilliant and it was warmhearted. A young man went there and the wine was red, and the girls were pretty, and he came away unashamed. An older man can look back now, even through the austerity of the years, and not be embarrassed. Here was a city where a young man watched the sun come up and wondered why it was in such a hurry. Here books were to be written, pictures painted, and songs created and sung. Here in Paris one admitted his dreams, even if he didn't make them come true. There was a lilt in the air, and the season always was spring.

Now one goes back, and he walks the streets of Paris, and he makes sure if it is the old Paris that he seeks, or the young man once more who was there. It is always easy for memories and longings to find disappointments, and the years are the greatest tricksters of all; but no matter the past, and with a careful discard of memories, any man who looks at Paris now must see that Paris is cheap and tawdry. Paris is blatant.

After a visit to Paris one can understand why Rome today is the gathering place of the discriminating. These people are getting away from the tinseled nights and the blaring carnival of Paris.

There has been, and there still is, so much more than the gaiety of Paris. There has always been the chant as well as the song. And today Sainte Chapelle still is there, the sun in the late afternoon still shines through the high windows in the miracle of color. The El Grecos are in the Louvre and a few of the Dutchmen are there, and one goes back to see. The bookstalls are open along the Seine on a sunny afternoon and the flowers are in the Bois. There is peace in Notre Dame and quiet streets now and then. The children still roll their hoops and the old men play at bowls. It isn't *all* gone, but don't walk those quiet streets too far; they end quickly.

The strip tease goes on day and night, and the bars and dance halls are a blaze of neon signs. The boulevards, where one walked in the afternoon or early evening, are a midway now, lined with shooting galleries, spinning wheels, popsickles, sugar candy, and

Teddy-bear prizes. The old quiet of the boulevard is staccatoed by the crack of the rifle, and the gentility is smeared by the barker's cry.

One cannot help asking what has happened to Paris. What has happened to France? More than the old grace and charm of France are gone. How strong is our ally now? How much can we depend on from France when the showdown comes? Two wars in one generation, both fought on the same soil, can drain the strength of a nation and sap its will.

22

In the middle of Russian territory, surrounded by a Communist state, the people of West Berlin, with assists from the United States, Britain, and France, have built a city that is brave and defiant, and they go their proud way, ignoring the walls that might topple over on them.

They have built up their industries and developed business. They have created a chamber of commerce, a board of trade, and a thriving stock market. The television tower in West Berlin is tall, and their schools are well attended. They have a "Free University" and a lending library. The people are living as normal a life as people could live, locked in as they are within an enemy state.

And all of it is new, for Berlin was practically flattened by Allied bombers. Even today there are vacant corners and a gap now and then in a block of houses, a store missing in a street of stores, but most of the city has been built back. A person goes along Kurfürstendamm, or any of the other main streets, and they have been completely rebuilt. Taxicabs, motor buses, motorcycles are shuttling past, well-dressed and well-fed people hurry along about their business, and the shops aren't quite Fifth Avenue but they are respectable places where one can get anything he wants, and of good quality. The supermarkets and drugstores are filled and stacked as high as those in the United States, and going into Woolworth's in West Berlin is like entering Ali Baba's cave.

Our hotel, the Windsor, was a delightful place, and the manager had us for dinner, the porter got tickets for us to the opera, the doorman knew somebody at the ballet, and the girl in the office got an afternoon off and took my wife shopping.

People everywhere in West Berlin treated us this same way, taking time to escort us toward our destination whenever we asked for directions, making room for us at their table, if the restaurant was crowded, and from some adjoining table leaning over to recommend the best dishes, if we were undecided. Whenever we stopped at any of the sidewalk cafés in the morning or rested at teatime in the afternoon, somebody was just about certain to come over and ask if we knew his cousin in Pittsburgh or her uncle in Kansas City; they all seem to have relatives in the United States, and a few of them have plans for coming here themselves.

It is a sturdy, fast-moving, and courageous city, and these people of West Berlin deserve all the credit they get. One might expect them to show courage, and to stand up and offer to fight, because their property, their lives, and their children are at stake; but this is no rear-guard action going on softly here in West Berlin, for these people speak on the radio and tell the Russians across town, and across East Germany, and on into Russia itself, just what they think of Russians and their communistic corruption of men and destruction of decency. They have the backing of American, British, and French troops, but they still have the courage themselves to speak their part, knowing what would happen to them if they were ever left in the city alone. What they have done in rebuilding their city takes energy, and what they are doing in standing up to the Russians takes guts.

After we had been in West Berlin for a while we decided that we wanted to go over and see the other part of the city, and this is no problem because the way between West Berlin and East Berlin is completely open. Anybody can travel back and forth between the two sectors as freely as he pleases, going by subway, bus, taxi, or he can walk, and no passport or papers are

required, only a superficial halt at the line and a word from the guard as he waves you on.

And here is a place where the Russians show that they, too, can blunder. For Russia is a fool to let anybody go from West Berlin into East Berlin, and see what is there.

We went over by taxi, hiring a man from a travel agency who was experienced at making the crossing, and we crossed at the Brandenburg Gate, the East Berlin guards smiling pleasantly and signaling us on. But we had driven less than three blocks when a policeman's whistle sounded behind us. I hardly heard it and paid no attention to it, but our driver jammed on his brakes and stopped instantly. He pulled over to the side of the street and got out, hurrying back toward the policeman who was far down the street and walking leisurely toward us. They stood for a while talking, and we could see the driver taking papers out of his pocket and cards from his billfold. Then together they walked on to the car and the policeman inspected it, saying nothing to my wife or to me and apparently paying no attention to us, though I saw him more than once shift his eye toward us.

He told our driver that he had crossed one wheel over the white line in the center of the wide street. Our driver made no answer, though there was no other automobile on the street, no bus, no bicycle, no pedestrian, there was nothing. The whole street was empty, and all was still and silent. Our driver stood back while the policeman went over the car, and once he looked at us deliberately, at both my wife and myself, and then the policeman fined the driver five marks—$1.20—and he paid it quickly.

We drove away at a slow pace, taking care to stay on the right-hand side of the street and away from the center line, although there was still no other automobile in sight and no person in sight except the policeman whom we could see standing there and watching us when we glanced out of the back window. When we were well out of hearing our driver told us how pleased he was to get off so lightly. He said that the last time they stopped him they had taken him to the police station, then had decided that they would not let him pay his fine in his own West Berlin money, nor would they change his West Berlin money into East Berlin money. They kept his car, while he had to walk back to the western sector of the city, change his money into East Berlin money, then come back to East Berlin and pay his fine.

We drove along the empty street, and the first persons we saw, after the policeman, were a group of small children and they had two teachers with them. No child ran or skipped, and none was talking and none smiled; they all just walked along like little sheep, and they held one another's hands.

We came to the main street, and I looked as far as I could see, and I counted three men and two women and six policemen. That was all. There was no other sign of life on the street. There was no automobile. No bicycle. Not even a dog or a cat was moving. A whole wide street and almost nobody on it. Even more than this stillness there was a silence so complete that I caught myself whispering to my wife in broad daylight as we walked on this open street, and I took her hand to be sure that even we were there. The few people we passed did not look at us, did not raise their eyes, and their feet were slow and reluctant.

The shops were almost empty, and in some of them there were only the few salesgirls who just stood there and looked at us when we came in. Some of the shelves were less than half full, and some were empty, and the shirts that I examined were of poor quality, yet costing $15.00—three days' work for a skilled laborer—and I could have bought a better shirt at home for $5.00, less than two hours' work for a skilled laborer. A woman's slip that could have been bought for $6.00 at home was priced at $35.00. There were people in the food stores and the butcher shops and they were buying. We learned later that the Russians see to it that the people have food and meat, and fuel in winter; but besides that, the Russians don't seem to care what the German people do for shoes or clothes or the other requirements of living.

I was told that the Russians figure that the people have to have food and heat or they can't work.

The main street is the only street in the whole of East Berlin that has any resemblance whatsoever to a modern city. Even this street is little more than a movie set, the front of the buildings making a big show, but there is little behind them. Behind an elaborate front there will be a shop only about the size of a two-car garage, and when one looks on through this shop and out at the back there is nothing there, only acres of flattened houses, broken stores and rubble, for the Russians have made no effort and no pretense of clearing up and rebuilding East Berlin. Where West Berlin is a city again, neat and busy, the Russians have let the waste lie in East Berlin with the mold and the weeds and let the Germans make out the best they can.

We drove around in some of these back areas and passed block after block where no one lives and there is only the trash and the desolation. We also drove into the area where people do live, the apartments small and jammed together. But even here we saw no one on the streets, no one moving at all, no woman on her way to market, no old men sunning themselves and talking, no child playing, no baby in a pen, and again no sight of a dog, a cat, or a pet of any kind. Just this stillness and the unlimited silence.

We drove past the corner of Friedrichstrasse and Unter den Linden where once there were big cafés, with tables and chairs spread far out on the wide sidewalks, and the waiters hurrying with the light beer and the dark beer. There, at this corner, back in student days, I had taught them the "Whiffenpoof Song" and Rudy Vallee's drinking song, and we had roared them out until late at night, and even at the other tables where no one knew the tunes, much less the words, they all lifted their steins and waved them as we did, and drank with us when the song was finished. But now not even a semblance of this came back as I stopped at the corner, for now there is only the rubble, and the waste, and the silence. It is this silence of East Berlin that one remembers.

I suggested that we go on, and we drove past the theater and the old opera house and the familiar church, and they are in ruins, dirty and sagging. We passed the hotel that once was so famous and so fashionable, and now it is smoke-stained and the windows flyspecked. There was no one on the streets, no one in sight, no one at all, and we were silent, too, as we drove on toward the Brandenburg Gate and West Berlin.

That night at six o'clock I went to the American library in West Berlin and I watched the people from the eastern sector come over across from their side and into the library. They were just off from work and had traveled on the subway from East Berlin and they jammed into the library, some of them running to get to the newspapers.

Some of them had brought sandwiches, and they sat at the tables eating and reading, never lifting their eyes from the paper as they read down one column and started at the top of the next. One could know which of the people in the library had come from the eastern part of the city by the clothes they wore, and the look on their faces, and by the way they didn't talk.

The preposterous and cruel situation in Berlin exists today because Josef Stalin had a longer plan, a shrewder mind, and more patience than Mr. Roosevelt or Mr. Churchill. While the three of them at Yalta were making and remaking nations, and parts of nations, they agreed to set up for Germany "a central Control Commission with headquarters in Berlin." After this they went on working together "in harmony, and taking such other measures as may be necessary for the future peace and safety of the world."

Mr. Roosevelt and Mr. Churchill, impetuous to settle the business and come to terms, to get it over with, and a little awed by this inscrutable man who sat across the table from them, anxious to placate him, agreed to his terms as he laid them out. In the whole sweep of war with battle lines stretching across a continent, in the air, and over and under all the seas, and with victory so near and so sweet, Mr. Roosevelt had no time to think of what might come after the fighting, and Mr. Churchill must have been tired.

The agreement on Berlin, even for a man who wanted to hurry home and hear the plaudits, or for one who wanted to go home and rest, is an example of amazing blindness which even yet cannot be understood. In the first place, they surrounded Berlin with Soviet territory, leaving the city 110 miles inside a Russian state. Then they gave Russia control of all roads and waterways into the city, and even accepted the air corridors that Mr. Stalin defined.

No small area, such as a city, has ever existed deep in foreign territory when it must be fed and supplied along a corridor which cannot be defended. Mr. Churchill's knowledge of history should have told him this, but he, too, agreed to Stalin's plan. It is still incredible, for no sensible man gives another man, even his most trusted friend, a fixed grip on his windpipe.

But they did it. And the time seems imminent when Russia intends to close her grip.

That night after I had come out of East Berlin, and after I had seen the people running for the newspapers, I thought about the obligation that our blunder in Berlin entails, and I thought back to the Geneva Conference of the summer of 1959 when our Secretary of State had spent weeks discussing, debating, and seeking some solution to the fate of Berlin and some disentaglement of the factors concerning Berlin.

Then Mr. Herter came home and he conferred with the President, and he conferred with his aides, and he made ready to give his report to the nation. The drums beat, the bugles sounded, and the television cameras rolled. Mr. Herter, rising to the height of his office and the pinnacle of our foreign policy, announced what he had learned at Geneva and what he had brought home to tell the nation. Russia wanted *all* of Berlin!

It is enough to break a man's heart. We, the American people, put our faith in this man, in the President who appointed him, and in the government to whom we entrust our lives, our freedom, the future of our nation, and the hopes of our children. And he comes back with the babble that Russia wants all of Berlin. It is as if we, and all the forces and interplay of forces in our government, were to send Mr. Einstein to the moon, to the planets, and throughout all space as our emissary to the universe, and he came back and told us that the sun rises in the east.

The moral courage and the political stamina to tell the American people the truth about what Russia really wants and intends to get, and where we stand today in our international relationships, and what is happening to us—to tell this, would cost votes and lose offices, but how a man could walk out erect and with his head high, if he said it.

23

London, the old mother of cities, seemed unchanged. The lions kept their timeless watch in Trafalgar Square and Nelson looked toward the sea. The Beefeaters guarded the Tower and the royal standard was flying. Big Ben tolled the hour, and all seemed safe. All secure.

But somehow, as we stayed on in London, and went here and there, and visited with friends, it seemed to me that London was not the same. One couldn't be sure about what it was, he couldn't put his finger on it; but there had been changes here, it seemed, of some kind.

The crowds still wandered the streets from Leicester Square to Piccadilly, and along the Haymarket and the Strand. The ancient taxis ambled on their way and the Bobbies strolled with their accustomed dignity. The Royal Guards, splashed with color and gleaming with metal, walked their posts and performed the high kick at each turn, slamming their feet. The men of fashion, the men of Mayfair, still wore bowler hats and carried umbrellas, and all the world stopped for tea. Surely this wonder back in a man's mind, this faint worry, was wasted. London was unchanged. England was forever.

A man walks the streets of London, and here history lies written before him. Here is *our* heritage, too. This is our past and here are the names of men who are a part of our nation. For all that divided us, and that still divides us, there is so much for us that is the same.

In our goings about London we went one day to the City and there was a crowd there, gathered in front of the Lord Mayor's house, and it was so large a crowd that it filled the area in front of the Royal Exchange and in front of the Bank of England, the people standing all along Threadneedle Street. Then we heard the drums and the fifes and we saw the marching men, their colors high, their swords bare as they marched in blazing splendor past the Lord Mayor, who stood in front of his house wearing the robes and furs of his office and taking the salute.

We asked what this meant, what was this parade. And we were told that this was a battalion of the Coldstream Guard, the soldiers who had stood for England, and fought for England, since King Charles, since three hundred years ago. But now the men of this battalion were marching past for their last time and were taking their final salute. They were being disbanded. Their colors were to be folded. And another fragment of the Empire, another bit of England, was to be put away.

The parade past, the men gone, their colors out of sight, we turned away, and I had not been mistaken. There was change here. England was going out of the business of ruling half the world. She no longer was chairman of the board and she had sense enough to know it. The Empire was gone, and England was a small island nation. Now what?

There would be no quick discarding of the past, no weakening of the law, no reduction of character. England would be forever. But there were adjustments and she would make them. One feels a little less of the old swagger perhaps, less of the lofty assurance, as England pulls up her socks and goes about the hardheaded business of getting her economy straightened out and fixing a new place for herself in the shifting power of the nations.

They still retain something of the grand manner, the Lord Mayor's furs gleamed that morning, and England holds to the strength and the mortice of tradition. They are sensible, though, as well as stubborn, and the changes that one senses in London today are the changes of a city, and a nation, working out a new kind of life that men can live by and still lose none of the old decency and honor of England.

This will be done, but it will not be easily done, for England is an island nation and is helpless under hydrogen bomb attack. The bravery of the Battle of Britain, and all the blood, sweat, and tears of all the Englishmen on the island might now be wasted, for one bomb could destroy London and England would be prostrate. Recognizing war as suicide, some Englishmen have become pacifists and appeasement is the beginning of their dealings with Russia. This is not true of the nation, but even the stanchest Englishmen, and there are no braver men, are sane, and they see the meaning of the hydrogen bomb and this island that is Britain.

We Americans would be wise if we also saw its meaning, and recognized England's position and her exposure, and took this into account as we consider our own position and judge our strength in Europe.

We hired an automobile and drove it ourselves, going out of London on a clear morning, the sun bright and the fields of England green as all summer.

This driving in England by an American is no casual accomplishment, for one sits on the wrong side of the automobile and drives on the wrong side of the street, and everything is left-handed. Taxis dart out from incorrect corners, trucks lunge out from where they have no business being, and every reflex is wrong, every grab for brake or button is wrong, and only the mercy of the law-abiding British public prevents destruction as a distraught American swerves out of the way at the last moment, unaided by the comments of his wife.

But we made it, going along the way first to Henley—and there the finish line of the Royal Regatta, and there we lifted our winning boat out of the water, and there, over at the pavilion, a small and rather nervous man, Edward, Prince of Wales, gave us our medals.

Up through Oxford, and a boy's rooms—the same bookshelf, the garden again with the flowers below the window, and the humility once more at being here.

Stratford. Kenilworth. Lichfield and the man who had lived here, Dr. Johnson, with all his common sense and his unwavering honor. On to the lakes, and here Wordsworth walked, and Coleridge, and De Quincey; here Lamb and Scott visited.

On to where Burns had lived, and it is an evil sin what they have done to Burns, and all that he was, and all that he wrote. They have turned every trace of him into a tourist show, a spectacle. Burns, of all men!

Glasgow and into the Highlands. Loch Lomond. Loch Katrine and Ellen's Isle. On through the greater Highlands, with the heather purple over the moors, and the soft fall of the mist, and a myriad of diamonds tangled in the heather.

Down to Edinburgh and the castle high on the rock. Late in the evening the soldiers march, their gay bonnets aslant, and one hears the skirl of the Scottish pipes and watches the swing of the British kilts, and he wishes that it might be true, that custom could live, and echo be real.

Then back to London again, and it was like coming home again. And walking away from that automobile was a comfort. We lived in a small hotel in London, the Milestone, out by Kensington Gardens, and we had thought of walking in the gardens that Sunday afternoon, but we decided instead to go to Hyde Park and listen to the orators.

In a corner of Hyde Park, a huge open space, there is perhaps the most unrestricted forum in the world, for here a man can stand and say *whatever* he believes. Every day the speaking goes on, but Sunday afternoon draws the largest number of orators and the biggest crowds.

There are only a few rostrums, and the speakers who get there first take them. Some speakers, wanting to wait until the crowds have fully assembled, and knowing that by then all the rostrums will be gone, bring their own boxes and they set them up wherever they please. Those who have neither rostrums nor boxes just stop wherever they are and start talking, or shouting, or singing, anything to attract attention and get some of the people to come and stand near them and listen. There are no rules, but the custom is that anybody can be heckled at any time, and the speakers are constantly interrupted by people in the crowd who disagree and want to answer back and argue. It is democracy in a minor key.

Each orator had his own little group that Sunday, and one was attacking the Labor party and another was going after the Tories. A man was shouting against atomic war and a woman was pleading for birth control. A speaker from the Catholic League was explaining the Church and a Jew was telling about Israel. A woman was preaching against horse racing and a man wanted to stop all fishing in the river Thames.

The biggest crowd was about a rostrum where a black man spoke. He was rather a large man, and his voice was not unpleasing. He spoke almost softly, commanding attention, and the people moved in close to him. Most of those who listened were colored men, some wearing the costume of Nigeria, some speaking in the flat tones of Jamaica, some I judged, from their dress and manner, to be from the French Congo and some, I was certain, were from the United States.

This man spoke so quietly that my wife and I moved nearer than we realized, and we were looking up at him as he told of black men in the world today. He spoke of these men in Africa, in Europe, in the United States. Then he spoke of Russia, and he said that Russia was the only friend that the black man has. This was fortunate for the black man, he said, because Russia is the most powerful nation in the world and her power is growing.

Black men could put their trust in Russia, he said, and their hate in the United States. Nobody threw stones at Negro children when they tried to go to school in Russia. Nobody kicked a Negro off a bus in Russia. There was no Little Rock in Russia.

He went on to say that the United States mistreats Negroes in the United States, and tries to keep them down everywhere, threatening in one country with guns, in another trying to buy with money, and always sending out missionaries to preach and get a hook in the black man's nose and lead him. But none of this would have any effect any longer, because the black men of the world were on the march, and they were safe now because now they had a powerful friend, Russia.

"You go back and tell the United States," he said, "that there is nothing that the United States can do about it. The black man is on the march! We will spot the United States all her money. We will spot the United States all her guns. And, just for good measure, we will throw in Jesus Christ. But not all of that together can stop us. Black man! You are on the march, step in step with Russia."

My wife and I walked away and on past Marble Arch. We took a taxi and went down to Soho for dinner. We mentioned what the man had said in Hyde Park, but we didn't talk about it. Tomorrow was our last day in England and we talked of the small inn where we had stayed in Broadway, of the deer in the park at Hampton Court, and the old British sailor and his American wife who have the antique shop at Windermere.

The next morning we packed early and then that afternoon we went out to John Keats's house and to the garden where he had heard the nightingale. We came back and walked along Regent Street and Piccadilly.

Then we decided to ride the bus one more time. We paid our sixpence fare and took a last look at Hyde Park Corner, at Knightsbridge, and the Albert Memorial. The next stop was Milestone, and this was our stop.

After dinner, and the waiters in the dining room had told us good-by, and the bar boy had brought us a glass of farewell port, we went back to our room and checked our belongings once more.

We were just fastening our suitcases when the car came, and it was time to go on out to the airport. We turned in our baggage, watched it being weighed, and waited for our flight to be called.

The stewardess was standing at the top of the stairs as we came into the plane, and she helped us get settled. She said that there was good weather out over the Atlantic, and that we would be landing in New York early in the morning.

24

Our stewardess was right about the weather, and the air was calm over the Atlantic, and our flight was steady. We slept most of the way but now and then I woke and looked out, and there was no moon and no stars. We came into New York a little ahead of schedule and the pilot made a smooth landing. We had been gone nine months.

We presented our passports, cleared customs, and caught a noon plane for Washington. And there in Washington I saw again, and it was good to see, the tall buildings jabbing at the sky, and the one white shaft, and then the great dome over the central building, and the flag was flying. One never leaves this, no matter where he goes or how far, he never leaves this.

I was excited about getting home again and was eager to land in Washington and begin my work there. There was so much to tell them and I believed that I could be of some help to the Department of State in my report, letting them know what I had seen and heard in all these countries where I had been working for them.

I had already heard from the Department of State and I knew their plans: "When you return to Washington, we should like to arrange a debriefing for you which would enable us to hear the experiences of your trip. What we have in mind is a general session in which you would give an informal talk summing up your experiences and impressions, to be followed by a question period. After this debriefing we would arrange personal interviews with people here for detailed discussions. If you can give us an advance notice of ten days to two weeks of your arrival date in Washington, we shall be most grateful."

I had given them the notice, and I knew that everything was all set for the general session and the interviews. I was grateful for another letter that I had received from the Department of State: "We should like to express our deep gratitude for your recent contribution to the Department's cultural exchange program. It is no exaggeration to say that you have been one of our most outstanding Specialists. To illustrate this, we should like to quote from several reports we have received about you." Then they quoted from reports sent in by USIS officials in the different countries I had worked in, and the reports were generous; but all that was behind me now, and I was interested only in the job here in Washington, for I knew that they would want to hear what a man with my experience in the past nine months had to tell. Certainly I wanted to tell them everything that I could, anything at all that would help the Department of State in their planning of our country's association with other countries.

I came into my hotel and called the Department of State and let them know that I was here, on time and ready. When did they want to see me? They told me to call back the next morning.

I did, and they said that if I had anything that I would like to do that day, I might as well go ahead and do it, and to call back the next morning.

I did, and they said for me to come on over and I could get my financial papers checked and my vouchers signed.

I did, and that day I talked with one woman for fifteen minutes about India, one man for perhaps ten minutes about Pakistan, and another man for about ten minutes about Iran. Their questions were the casual questions of small talk. Had I had a good time? Had I met their friends? How was the weather? Each of them received me because he had been instructed to receive me, and each of them was as courteous as possible; but I was interfering with their routine, and they kept eying the papers on their desks.

These three visits were my report, and this is the only report of any kind that I was asked for then, or have been asked for since, by the Department of State, after having represented them in Korea, the Philippines, India, Pakistan, Afghanistan, Iran, Lebanon, and Israel.

The letter about the general session, the debriefing, and so forth, was never mentioned.

I couldn't understand any of this, for I was accustomed to a different way of doing things. During the war we in intelligence wanted to talk to every man who came back from anywhere. He might not have much to tell, he might not be a smart man or an observing man, but we still wanted to talk to him, to ask him questions. We were bound to get *something*, maybe only the smallest detail, but it could play its part in helping us understand what we were up against, and help us figure out how to plan what must be done, and work out a way of doing it.

I couldn't understand this passing up a man who had been traveling around the world, going into all kinds of countries, and eight of them for the State Department itself. But after I had talked to other Specialists, I found out that this is the way it is done, and that nobody had been interested enough to talk to them either.

There is a good deal more that one doesn't understand about the State Department. The department's top administrative officer, Loy W. Henderson, appeared before a Senate Foreign Relations subcommittee and testified that there is no need for an academy to train our men and women for foreign service. The Army recognizes the need for its technical instruction and specialized training, so does the Navy, so does the Air Force, but the Deputy Undersecretary of State, speaking for the department, said that foreign service officers don't require such training.

The needs for this service can best be met, Mr. Henderson said, "by selection of qualified graduates from the colleges and universities in all parts of the United States." The department can carry on its program by "taking advantage of the wide range of educational training provided by these institutions of higher learning."

Doctors, lawyers, engineers, and all professional men and women have special training, but our foreign-service officers, going into competition with Russia's best, Russian men and women trained for decades, can just be picked up here and there from graduates of our colleges and universities which, so far as I know, make no pretense of training men for foreign service. It will probably be a surprise to these institutions to know that the State Department expects them to do it.

I have just come back from around the world, and from associating with a good many of these foreign-service officers, and a nicer crowd doesn't exist. They all are graduates and all have enjoyed the "wide range of educational training," from ornithology to freehand drawing, provided by our institutions of higher learning. A good many of them, a very high percentage of them, have even stayed on in schools and universities as teachers and professors, and later dropped out of teaching to join the foreign service; but even men with this background, some man who wrote his master of arts thesis on "The Lyrics of Lord Tennyson" and went on to teach social studies at a high school in Dallas, just hasn't received *all* the training that might be useful to a foreign-service officer in bucking the Russian experts in India, or Pakistan, or wherever else the Russians are playing propaganda rings around us.

A graduate of an American college or university can fill these jobs, according to State Department requirements, because just about any graduate is pretty good at a tea party and is fairly adept with a cocktail glass, and it's an old gag but the same tragedy that the Brahmins of the Potomac still look on their State Department jobs as considerably social. I drank a small ocean of tea around the world, and mopped up quite a few cocktails. I talked to professors, students, editors, and other intellectuals by the hundreds, but I never got near these people with whom Russia is dealing and with whom Russia is building the foundation of her new world. I never heard anybody among our officials mention getting near them, or trying to get near them.

Nobody on our side seems to have caught on that we Americans, and all mankind, are at one of those times in history when the whole social structure is being turned upside down and men are being reshuffled. They haven't heard that, once more, the Barons are at Runnymede, Cromwell is in London, and some farmers have fired across a bridge in Massachusetts. The passing of the city-state in Greece remade the world. The fall of Rome remade the world. The collapse of feudalism remade the world. The break-up of the British Empire and the end of European colonialism are now remaking the world. And we go right on wearing striped trousers, sipping cocktails, and sending nice young men into the ring with Joe Louis when he was in his prime.

25

The officials of the Department of State thanked me for stopping by for a visit to Washington, and that afternoon we caught a plane and flew on home to Georgia. Our neighbors had cut the grass and put flowers in the house.

I went back to work, but I still keep on thinking about what I heard, what I saw, and what I learned around the world. I learned two things for sure. Russia has hit on the shrewdest plan for taking over the world in the history of mankind, and so far she is being successful.

The other thing that I learned is that the United States is losing the respect of many of the people of the world, and with the loss of respect for us inevitably goes the loss of confidence in us. As I traveled and looked and listened, I couldn't help coming to believe that the old man in Korea was right and that Russia is taking the place of the United States in the minds and the loyalties of men, and that Russia is growing into the dominant nation of the world.

The Union of Soviet Socialist Republics, which is Russia, joined with other Communist countries, chiefly China, is dedicated and determined to take over the world, and rule the world, and destroy what they cannot rule.

The men who began this religion lived before Josef Stalin and others like them will live after Nikita Khrushchev, and anyone who thinks that he can change these men, or influence these men, is foolish, for each of them may be ambitious for himself but they all have the fervor of the martyr for World Communism. One might as well expect to change the Pope of Rome, or the Archbishop of Canterbury, as to vary these men one fraction in *their* faith, distorted and horrible as it is, or to shift them one degree in their steady course to their goal, which is to pull down nation by nation, continent by continent, until they arrive at the United States, and then, by whatever means are required, to destroy what must be destroyed of the United States and leave only that part standing, in structure and men, that they can use.

This is their plan, and it never changes. The threat may be aimed at Berlin today, the sword at India tomorrow, and always the plea of peace and friendship at Washington; but whatever they may say, whatever they may do, whether truth or lies, handclasp or murder, Russia and China have one goal. And they have no doubt that they will achieve it, that they will tear down the United States, and that they will rule the world.

What can we do about it?

We can first look at ourselves. Never mind those people out there in India, in Afghanistan, in Iran, and all the things that *they* do. Never mind what is wrong with them. What about *us*? What about Americans?

As individuals, we have no intention, each of us, of accepting his national responsibility. It is too much trouble to find out the truth about the standing of the United States in the world today and too unpleasant to admit our national dangers. So we follow the easy way of passing these responsibilities on to the politician.

And the politician, thinking of the easy way for himself, tells us not to worry, our missile strength is almost equal to Russia's. Lulled by such talk, and satisfied because we want to be, we sit in imagined security behind the Maginot Line of our missiles and bombs while Russia maneuvers a different kind of war and goes around us and takes the world.

The Republicans talk as Republicans, and Democrats talk as Democrats, each with his own measuring stick, accusing and defending as Republicans, as Democrats, and seeming to forget that which side is in office is not nearly so important as that the country is being looked after.

And here we are in the midst of an undeclared war for nations and continents, and for the souls of men, and on this side the AFL-CIO continues to look for fringe benefits. Over there the AMA figures on bigger profits. And everywhere the NAACP and the Segregationists want to know what color it is. The lobbyists tamper with the laws, the lawyers slick the taxes, and the politicians count the votes.

While this goes on, the United States swings back and forth on a high trapeze, holding on as best he can, and hoping that somebody remembers to put up the net.

And the peoples of the world watch!

When we talk of our democracy and our equality of men, these people say that it isn't true.

They also remind us that we have changed places with Russia in the spiritual and material approach to men. Russia, the godless nation, now preaches a religion that may destroy the souls of men but that wins their faith and their loyalty.

We have come to ignore the spirit of man, the small, silent craving, and we put our trust in the bluster of foreign aid, in money, in tractors, in sheep and cattle. Somewhere along the way we became so pleased with the way we live, and the things we have for ourselves, that we began to think that these things are the chief interest of other men. Somewhere we began to forget that Buddha had nothing material to offer mankind. And that Jesus had nothing to offer but the ideals of this world and the hope of another.

One remembers Rome and Athens, their decline and fall, and he cannot help but wonder if we are among those people that George Santayana had in mind when he wrote: "Those who refuse to learn from history are condemned to repeat it."

I live in Dunwoody, Georgia, a place so small that few persons ever heard of it except the people in Dunwoody itself—"Pop. 247"—and those other families who live nearby, along the roads that curve away beside the cornfields, the melon patches, and the peach orchards. Now and then there is an uncultivated stretch where the wild blackberries grow in summer, and the sumac bushes are scarlet under the green of the pines. Two black-top roads cross at Dunwoody under our pride and the proof of our progress, a new traffic light.

Mr. Spruill is our postmaster. Floyd Rakestraw runs the filling station. And Mrs. Sparks has a grocery store where the road forks.

A quarter of a mile on one side of us Jack and Mabel Barker are our neighbors. He collects Horatio Alger books as a hobby. Half a mile on the other side live Jake and Frances Reeves. They have chickens and they let us get our eggs from them.

This is our town.

Our house is built out of cypress and the floors are of old pine. It stands up above the Chattahoochee River—"Out of the hills of Habersham, down the valleys of Hall"—and there used to be a ferry here, Jett Ferry, a long time ago. People crossed over the river here and spent the night at an inn that once was on our property, but it burned, and then the next day they would drive by wagon or buggy the twenty-one miles on into Atlanta. From our house down the slope to the river are dogwoods and copper beech, redbuds and white oaks. We have songbirds and a covey of quail—nineteen birds—fed past my window yesterday afternoon.

This is my home.

My town and my home are only fragments of America, but they are all of America.

Here, too, are the wheat fields of Kansas, the sweat of the cowboy and the bleat of his scorched calf, the parade on Pennsylvania Avenue, and the umpire dusting the plate.

These are parts of our country, and the whole of it, and these things are us. These are the things that we stand to lose, for

Russia would destroy the filling station, and the grocery store, and our neighbors. These are the things that we want to keep. And it is not going to be easy.

Nothing for this generation of Americans will be easy. At a time that we are dazzled by our own good living we are confronted by a shrewd power that is determined to destroy us. Enjoying all our comforts, our extra money to spend, our little amusements, we will find it hard to admit the brutal reality of our national danger and to change our individual living to the clear-headed thinking, the discipline, and the stamina that are necessary, if we are to remain free men and the United States is to continue as a nation.

In this freedom, our first requirement is to understand that we *can* be overcome, either by the slow process of economic and spiritual engulfment, the process that is going on now, or suddenly by military destruction if Russia and China at any moment decide that we have allowed our defenses to weaken or that they themselves have passed us sufficiently in military strength to bring about this destruction. This is probably our most difficult requirement: to recognize that the United States can be overcome and that we, the American people, can be conquered.

With this knowledge, and with our admitting it to ourselves, it is then our responsibility to force our government, through individual and group pressure, forcing our President, whoever he may be, our Secretary of State, and our Department of State to end their pretense and their expedient silence, and to tell us the details of our national decline, our present lowered position in the world, and our immediate dangers, the obscure economic and spiritual dangers as well as the tornado of war. After they have talked, they then can tell us what is their plan, through forthrightness abroad and honesty untainted by politics at home, for saving this nation.

Once we know the truth of our position, and the facts of our dangers, if we American people then sit still as a nation, and continue self-centered as individuals, if we then do nothing to give the government the guidance that most governments require and the courage that they avoid, then the downfall of this nation is on our individual heads.